SERPENT DOMINION

Christopher Mitchell is the author of the epic fantasy series The Magelands. He studied in Edinburgh before living for several years in the Middle East and Greece, where he taught English. He returned to study classics and Greek tragedy and lives in Fife, Scotland with his wife and their four children.

BY CHRISTOPHER MITCHELL

THE MAGELANDS ORIGINS

Retreat of the Kell
The Trials of Daphne Holdfast
From the Ashes

THE MAGELANDS EPIC

The Queen's Executioner
The Severed City
Needs of the Empire
Sacrifice
Fragile Empire
Storm Mage
Soulwitch Rises
Renegade Gods

THE MAGELANDS ETERNAL SIEGE

The Mortal Blade
The Dragon's Blade
The Prince's Blade
Falls of Iron
Paths of Fire
Gates of Ruin
City of Salve
Red City

City Ascendant
Dragon Eyre Badblood
Dragon Eyre Ashfall
Dragon Eyre Blackrose
Dreams of Kell
God Restrainer
Holdfast Imperium
World's End

THE MAGELANDS DOMINION

Serpent Dominion
Demon Witch
Death Seer

Brigdomin Books Ltd
First Edition, June 2023
ISBN 978-1-915978-07-3

To Jane and the Shepherd's Hut

ACKNOWLEDGEMENTS

I would like to thank the following for all their support during the writing of the Magelands Dominion - my wife, Lisa Mitchell, who read every chapter as soon as it was drafted and kept me going in the right direction; my parents for their unstinting support; Marilyn Hopwood for reading the books in their early stages; James Aitken for his encouragement; and Grant and Gordon of the Film Club for their support.

Thanks also to my Advance Reader team, for all your help during the last few weeks before publication.

NOTE ON THE DOMINION CALENDAR

Due to a larger moon, Athumia's rotation is slower than that of the Earth, adding almost five minutes to each day; while the duration of Athumia's orbit around its Sun remains the same as the Earth's. This has brought the Lunar and Solar Calendars into alignment, allowing for Thirteen Months, each containing 28 days – creating a Solar Year of 364 days (with no Leap Day required). In response to this astronomical correspondence, High King Gahad devised the Dominion Calendar by shortening the existing months in the Divine Calendar to 28 days, and adding an extra month at the end of the year in his honour.

Each month (or 'inch') is named after one of the Twelve Ascendants (the old Gods); but over long millennia, the names have drifted from their originals.

In the Dominion Calendar, each year begins on the 1st day of Beldinch.

- Beldinch (January) – after Belinda, the Third Ascendant
- Summinch (February) – after Simon, the Tenth Ascendant
- Arginch (March) – after Arete, the Seventh Ascendant
- Nethinch (April) – after Nathaniel, the Fourth Ascendant
- Duninch (May) – after Edmond, the Second Ascendant
- Tradinch (June) – after Theodora, the First Ascendant
- Abrinch (July) – after Albrada, the Eleventh Ascendant
- Lexinch (August) – after Leksandr, the Sixth Ascendant
- Tuminch (September) – after Tamid, the Eighth Ascendant
- Luddinch (October) – after Lloyd, the Twelfth Ascendant
- Kolinch (November) – after Kolai, the Fifth Ascendant
- Essinch (December) – after Esher, the Ninth Ascendant
- Ghadinch (Extra Month) – after King Gahad, Praise be His Name

THE TWO EMPIRES OF ATHUMIA

The Two Empires of Athumia (in 1588, when *Serpent Dominion* takes place)

Two Empires dominate the continents of Athumia:

The Dragon Dominion – The Dominion originated in **Inopei** – a continent in the Eastern half of Athumia, with the arrival of the Dragon King. The calendar used in the Serpent Isle dates from the formation of the Dominion. The rule of the Dragons then spread south to encompass **Aucteran** and **Jalan**, and then the Dominion conquered the lands of the Bullan (**Klediomira Haga**). Upon completion of the conquests of Inopei, Aucteran and Jalan, the entire native population was exterminated by Dominion forces. There is no Dominion military presence on Klediomira Haga, as the Bullan are allied, rather than occupied. As tribute, the Bullan send soldiers each year to serve in the Dominion armed forces.

Much later (c.1300), when the Dominion began to cross the ocean to the Western half of Athumia, their forces also conquered **Elso** and **Irlan**. Dominion forces occupy Irlan, Elso and the **Serpent Isle**, ruling over the native inhabitants. It is the stated aim and belief of the rulers of the Dragon Dominion that all of Athumia should be united under their sovereign authority.

The Gunstian Empire – Centred around the city of **Great Gunst**, the Gunstian Empire covers the northern portion of the western continent of **Kinheria**. Their Empire also includes the tributary state of **Tannum**, a heavily-forested region. Shielded by mountains and the Tvali Desert to the south, and protected by oceans on its other three flanks, the Gunstian Empire is the only inhabited place left on Athumia not ruled by the Dragon Dominion. The Dominion have unsuccessfully invaded Gunst twice – in c.1050 and c.1350. Both invasions were defeated by the Gunstians, and the Dominion were forced to withdraw.

Social Hierarchy of Zamata (The Serpent Isle)

The Rulers	Dragons	Immortal Dragons	3	Igatz
		Mortal Dragons	2	
Aucterian Colonists	Upper	Aristocracy, Landowners, Bankers, Senior Officers etc	500	Mainly in Igatz
	Middle	Merchants, Smallholders, Junior Officers	4500	
	Lower	Farmers, Shopkeepers, Crafts	15000	
Foreign Soldiers	Military / Police	Bullan Soldiers	5000	Across Island
Northern Fleet		Dominion Navy (Aucterian)	5000	Handshore Naval Base
Native Police		Militia (Zamatan)	1000	Across Island
Native Zamatan Islanders	Upper	Farmers, Builders, Merchants, Militia Officers, Teachers	10000	Mainly in Kaugatz and Surrounding Villages
	Lower	Villagers, Crofters, Labourers, Servants	30000	
Descendants of former Colonists	Gunstians	Labourers etc	10000	Kaugatz
Sailors from Irlan	Irlanians	Sailors	3000	Igatz
Bottom of the Heap	Mixed Heritage	Zamatan/Aucterian	4400	Kaugatz
	Bullan Heritage	Zamatan/Bullan	600	

Dragon Royal Family

King Gahad & His Three Consorts

Snowdrift

♂ Tegru, 1541
♂ Naghad, 1497
♀ Macsin, 1456
♂ Malum, 1381
♀ Famula, 1319
♂ Saphben, 1266

Opal Min Tarsu

♂ Opelan, 493
♂ Rylan, 476
♀ Lykot, 401
♀ Natali, 352
♀ Marda, 331
♂ Tarsun, 278

Nightsheen

♀ Lykona, 1100
♀ Lenta, 1091
♂ Irvan, 1062
♀ Gilt, 1055
♀ Abda, 991
♂ Girvine, 928
♀ Shana, 899
♂ Konran, 834
♀ Tirna, 747

The numbers represent age in 1588

DRAMATIS PERSONAE

Zamatans

Lahnos Laimos, Horned Part-Bullan

Reyn, Part-Bullan with Horns and Tail

Friel Laimos, Colonel in Zamatan Militia

Leona, Friel's Assistant

Karl Laimos, Lahnos's Brother

Jola Laimos, Lahnos's Grandmother

Bauchlie, Zamatan Terrorist

Lupin, Part-Bullan Look-out

Aucterians

Cisca, Dragon Corps Lieutenant

Travers, Dominion Naval Lieutenant

Foley, Dragon Corps Officer

Polarn, Dragon Corps Officer

Sinda, Settler Aristocrat

Dragons

Tirna Min Gahad, Governor of the Serpent Isle

Meer Mon Adal, Governor's Aide

Rufus Mon Rafa, Governor's Mate

Kheran Mon Tirna, Governor's Son

Noxon Mon Konran, Emissary from Inopei

Gilda Min Gilt, Governor's Aide

Gahad the Mighty, King of the Dominion

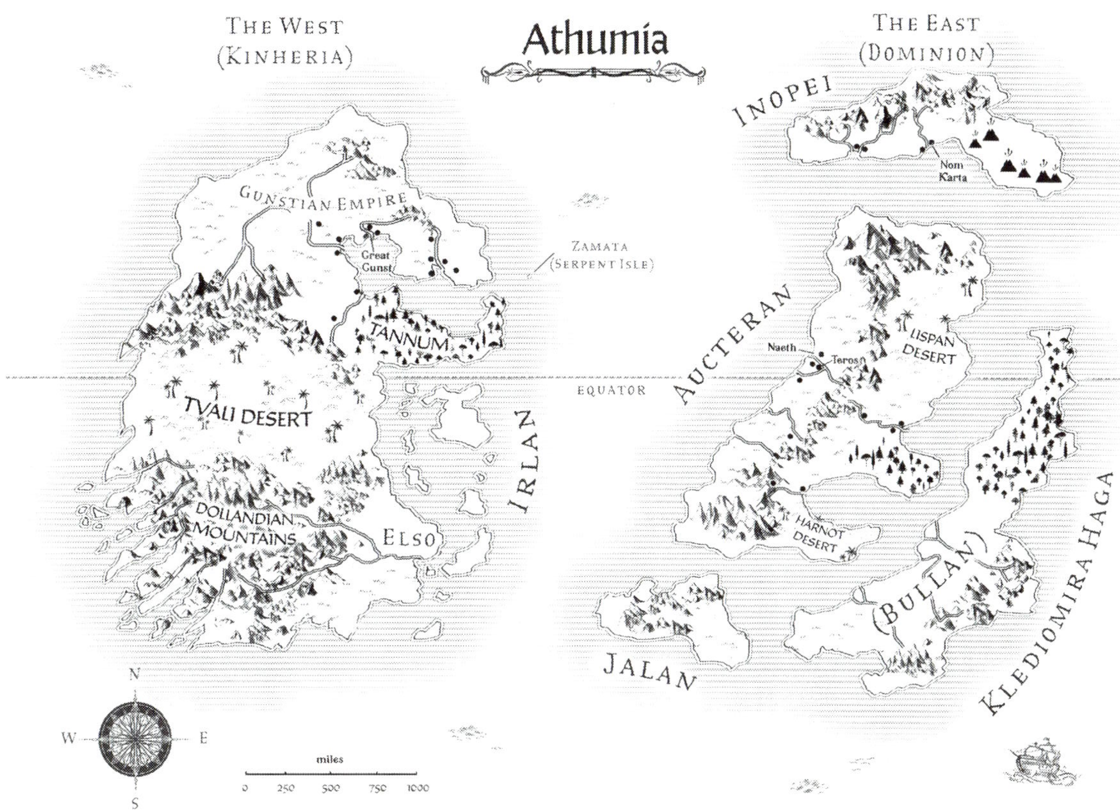
Athumia
The West
(Kinheria)
The East
(Dominion)
Gunstian Empire
Great Gunst
Zamata
(Serpent Isle)
Tannum
Tvali Desert
Dollandian Mountains
Elso
Irlan
Equator
Inopei
Nom Karta
Aucteran
Naeth
Teros
Lispan Desert
Harnot Desert
Jalan
(Bullan)
Klediomira Haga
N
W
E
S
miles
0
250
500
750
1000

Zamata – The Serpent Isle

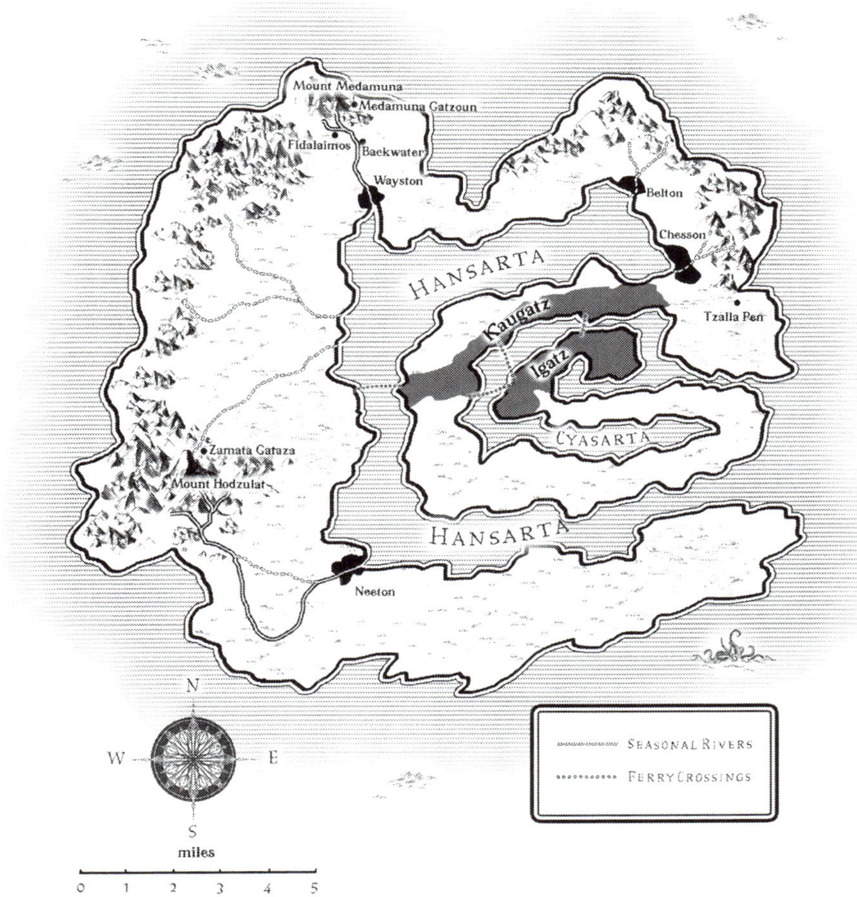

The Serpent Isle – Close-up of Kaugatz and Igatz

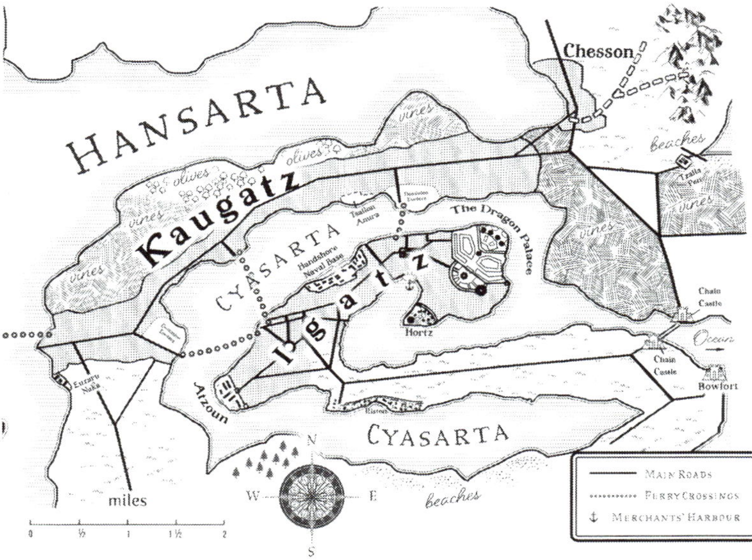

CHAPTER 1
THE UNDYING SERPENT

Igatz, Serpent Isle – 23rd Arginch 1588

Lahnos Laimos was not ashamed of his horns.

Reyn was; she couldn't help it. Hers had been filed off years before, ground down, right to the bone of her skull. They had grown again, but remained short, their tips blunt.

'You should take off your head scarf,' said Lahnos.

The young woman shook her head. 'Here – in the centre of Igatz? Are you out of your mind? Everyone is already staring at us because you...'

'I refuse to hide who I am?' he said.

They passed a group of well-dressed Aucterian merchants whose heads turned as one, their eyes narrowing at the sight of the three-inch horns growing from Lahnos's head.

'What's your problem?' Lahnos said. 'Have you got something you want to say to me?'

Reyn squeezed Lahnos's hand as she quickened her step, pulling him away from the group of frowning merchants. He thought about resisting, then allowed her to drag him along the wide pavement. He glanced up at the impressive buildings clustered around the tall entrance gates that led to the Dragon Palace. The wealth that had been spent beautifying one small part of the island was obscene – marble and gold, towers and spires – while many of the native islanders lived in abject poverty. Who was it for? Was it because the dragons who dwelt in the palace desired something aesthetically pleasing to gaze upon?

He was so absorbed in looking at the sights that he almost walked into a Zamatan militia patrol. They stared at him, as Reyn clung on to his arm; and he stared back.

'Do you want something?' Lahnos said.

One of the part-time soldiers nodded in the direction of the gutter that ran alongside the pavement.

'One of us will have to move aside, boy,' he said; 'and it won't be us.'

'Are you lost?' said another. 'Why don't you catch a ferry back to Kaugatz where you belong?'

'Have the Aucterian settlers ordered you to keep your fellow Zamatans out of Igatz?' said Lahnos. 'Well, have they?'

'You're not a true Zamatan, boy,' said the soldier. 'You're part-beast.'

Lahnos clenched his right fist, and Reyn began to pull him away.

'Go on, lad,' said another soldier. 'Into the gutter with you; unless you want to be taken into custody for disobeying an order of the town militia.'

'Lahnos, please,' said Reyn.

The soldiers eyed the young woman, their glances fixing on the scarf she was wearing to cover her hair.

'I wonder what she could be hiding under there, eh, lads?' said a soldier. 'And look at that skirt – it's a bit long for this weather. You got a tail, girl? Let's see it.'

'If you touch my girlfriend,' said Lahnos, 'I'll break your nose.'

The soldiers laughed.

'Where are you going?' said a corporal.

'The temple,' said Reyn.

The corporal nodded. 'Let them pass, lads,' he said. 'We ain't got time for this shit.'

Reyn pulled Lahnos's arm and they stepped down from the pavement. Lahnos stared at the militia soldiers as they walked along the dry rain-gutter.

'Collaborating bastards,' he muttered. 'You can't trust any Zamatan who works for the Aucterians; they've sold their souls to the Dominion.'

'Maybe we should go home,' Reyn whispered.

He shot her a glance. 'What? This was your idea.'

'No,' she said, 'it wasn't. I only mentioned that I wanted to see a dragon close up. Coming to Igatz was your idea. How did they know I had a tail? Can we go home?'

'Calm down,' he said, as they remounted the pavement. 'We're here now. The Temple of the Undying Serpent is fifty yards away. Don't you want to tell the others that we went to the top of the tower?'

Reyn said nothing. Instead, she was glancing at every group of Aucterians on the busy street as though they were a potential threat.

'Ignore them,' Lahnos said. 'We have every right to be here. This is our island, not theirs.'

They passed a café, where dozens of Aucterians were sitting under parasols drinking iced coffee. Several conversations stopped mid-sentence as they turned to stare at Lahnos. He smiled, nodding at them as if he were the king of Zamata. He slowed as he overheard someone whisper *freak*, his right fist clenching again, but Reyn dragged him onwards.

'If you get into a fight,' she said, 'then how will you take me to the top of the temple tower?'

He smiled at her. 'So, you *do* want to see the dragons?'

'I just want to get this over with,' she said.

They walked into the paved plaza in front of the great Serpent Temple. A few Zamatan peddlers were selling votive candles to the worshippers, and Lahnos glanced at them with disdain. He kept his mouth closed for once, aware that another group of town militia was eyeing him from under the shade of a palm tree. The huge doors of the temple were open, and Lahnos and Reyn stepped out of the burning midday heat and entered the cool shadows of the building's interior. The long aisle and pews were filling up with a mixture of

Zamatans and Aucterians, with a few sailors from Irlan also present, their heads bowed in prayer. A heady scent of incense drifted by, and the low drone of a choir could be heard coming from one of the temple's many side chapels. Reyn's gaze rose to the towering marble serpent-pillars that held up the great roof of the temple, and her mouth opened.

'What do you think?' Lahnos said.

'It's... it's beautiful,' she said.

A monk in long brown robes coughed, and then glanced at their linked hands. 'This is a place of worship,' he said in a low voice. 'You can hold hands outside.'

Reyn pulled her hand free of Lahnos's grasp.

The monk nodded, and kept his gaze averted from Lahnos's horns. 'Are you here to join the noonday service? If you are, then it is my duty to inform you that part-Bullan are required to stand at the back of the nave.'

'We're not here to take part in any service,' said Lahnos. 'We're just here to take a look around.'

'Then I would ask that you remain quiet once the prayers begin,' the monk said.

Lahnos said nothing, and the monk tilted his head slightly, and then walked away, his brown robes swishing off the marble floor.

Lahnos and Reyn glanced at each other, then they made their way past kneeling worshippers and rows of lit candles into the heart of the temple. Oil lamps that were hanging from long chains were giving off a dull glow, illuminating the worn and faded tapestries and paintings that adorned the temple walls. Lahnos saw a sign for the tower, and guided Reyn towards it. A monk by the foot of the stairs shook a wooden box at them, and Lahnos dropped in a couple of coins. The monk nodded, his eyes on the two horns coming from Lahnos's head, but he said nothing.

They came to the stone steps, and began to climb the spiral staircase. There were nearly four hundred steps to the top of the tower. Lahnos knew that – he had counted them on his only previous visit; and Reyn was out of breath when they reached the open viewing balcony. He watched her face as it lit up with joy, and was pleased that he had insisted upon making the journey.

'You can see the whole of Igatz from up here,' he said, as he leaned on the slender metal railings.

'It looks like an island,' she said. 'There's so much water.' She pointed. 'Is that Handshore?'

'Yes,' he said; 'and that's Kaugatz on the other side of the Cyasarta.' He placed a hand on her waist, and turned her to look in the other direction. 'And there's the Dragon Palace. This is the only place in the city where you can see inside the gardens.'

They gazed down at the wide, perfectly manicured lawns that sat in front of the enormous palace, its white marble shimmering in the bright sunlight. Fountains and artificial water-courses were glistening among the lines of cypress trees and irrigated grass, but no dragons were in sight. They watched for a while, and Lahnos sensed Reyn's disappointment start to grow.

'When do the dragons come out?' she said.

He shrugged. 'Who knows? Take your head scarf off.'

She shook her head. 'No.'

'You take it off when we're alone. We're alone now.'

'I don't want to.'

'Why not? You can't live in shame all your life, Reyn.'

'It's not shame I'm feeling; it's fear.'

'There's nothing to be afraid of.'

'Only you would say something like that, Lahnos. You display your horns as if you were proud of them.'

'I am proud of them. And, if I had a tail like yours, I would be proud of that, too.'

Reyn said nothing for a moment, then she pulled the scarf from her hair, revealing her two squat, flat-topped horns. Her eyes lowered, and her cheeks flushed.

He smiled at her. 'You are beautiful, Reyn.'

'I thought you didn't like my horns.'

Lahnos frowned. 'That's not what I said. I love your horns; and they're starting to grow back. I only meant that it was a pity that your mother made you file them down.'

'I need to tell you something,' she said, keeping her gaze lowered. 'I haven't been completely honest with you.'

Lahnos tensed a little. 'Go on.'

'The reason my horns aren't sharp...'

'I already know why, Reyn.'

'I tell people that my mother forced me to get rid of them when I was younger. It's not true.'

He narrowed his eyes. 'But someone must have done it.'

'I didn't run away from home because my mother made me file them down; I ran away because she was going to do it herself. I refused to let her.'

'But...'

'I was attacked,' she said. 'I was like you, once, and I wore my horns with pride. Ten men in Kaugatz did this to me. They were drunk; and they held me down and used a wood saw to cut them off. They were going to do the same to my tail, but I managed to run away, even though I was almost blinded by the blood running down my face. That's why I'm afraid, Lahnos. Please don't tell anyone else; I'm telling you because I trust you.'

'How old were you?'

'Fifteen.'

'Would you recognise any of the men that did it?'

She smiled. 'Did your thoughts go straight to revenge? It doesn't matter who did it; they all hate us – Zamatans, Aucterians, Gunstians... They will never accept us.'

Lahnos turned to stare at the gardens and the palace, his anger simmering. Reyn had been correct – his first thought had been a surging desire to kill the men who had hurt her; to take a wood saw to their stupid skulls. He noticed his hands were shaking with rage, and he took a long breath. Reyn was clever and beautiful, but she wasn't a fighter, and the image of her being overpowered by drunks made him feel sick.

'Are you angry with me?' she said.

'Of course not.'

'I'm sorry I lied to you. I don't trust people easily. It takes time.'

'We've been together for six months.'

'And you are the first person I have ever told.'

He wondered if he should tell her a secret of his own.

Her right hand darted upwards. 'Look!' she cried. 'A dragon!'

Lahnos squinted into the bright sunshine and saw a large shape in the sky, its wings outstretched as it soared over the blue waters of the Cyasarta towards the Dragon Palace.

'Which one is it?' said Reyn. 'Is it the Blessed Lady?'

'I can't see just yet,' he said. 'It doesn't look like the Governor.'

He waited a moment until the blue and red scales of the dragon became visible.

'That doesn't seem right,' he said.

'What's wrong?'

'None of the dragons on Zamata have those colourings. This one isn't a resident of the palace.'

'Are you sure?' she said. 'The Grand Convoy isn't due for another three months.'

He shrugged. 'I know. I'm only telling you what I'm seeing. No dragon living in the palace is red and blue; and I've seen them all. Either the convoy is early this year, or...'

'Or what?'

'I don't know. What would make the Dominion send a dragon out of season?'

A bell pealed from within the walls of the palace, and a green dragon rose into view, ascending above the white marble buildings. It circled once, soaring past the temple tower, then it banked and headed off to intercept the newcomer.

'That one is Meer Mon Adal,' Lahnos said.

Reyn lifted a hand to shield her eyes. 'Is he a god?'

'No. He's just an ordinary dragon. He protects the others.'

More bells began to peal around central Igatz, and Reyn refastened her scarf over her head, covering her brown hair as well as her horns. Down in the wide avenues surrounding the Temple of the Undying Serpent, crowds of Aucterians were glancing up at the noise from the bells, while militia soldiers were hurrying towards the palace. Lahnos kept his eyes on the two dragons, watching as they circled each other in the skies over the bay; then he felt Reyn tug his sleeve.

'We should go,' she said.

'But you haven't seen all of the dragons.'

'Something's happening,' she said; 'but we still have a good story to tell the others. Let's get a boat back to Kaugatz.'

Lahnos exhaled, then nodded. They turned from the view, and went back down the tower stairs. At the bottom, the monks monitoring the interior of the temple had gathered together, and several seemed agitated, while most of the worshippers were on their feet, listening to the incessant pealing of the town bells. Lahnos and Reyn strode across the smooth marble floor towards the entrance, and stepped back outside into the dazzling sunshine.

'Hey, you two,' said a soldier who was standing by the open doors.

Lahnos turned, ready to say something stupid, then he managed to close his mouth in time. The soldier facing them was no mere militiaman, but a Bullan warrior in full armour. Reyn gasped, and seemed to shrink.

'Over here,' the soldier said, his four-inch horns glistening in the sunlight.

Lahnos and Reyn walked towards him, then three other Bullan emerged from the shadows of the temple entrance to surround them.

'We've had a complaint,' said the Bullan soldier. 'Where's the knife?'

Lahnos raised his empty palms. 'What knife? I don't have a knife.'

One of the Bullan moved forwards and patted him down. 'He's clean, sir.'

'Where did you leave it, lad?' said the Bullan.

'I don't know what you're talking about. Do you think I would carry a knife into the temple?'

The Bullan officer frowned. 'You're coming with us.'

'Let my friend go,' said Lahnos. 'She has nothing to do with this.'

The four Bullan glanced at Reyn, their eyes roving over her head scarf.

'Who was the complaint about?' said Lahnos.

'A part-Bullan Zamatan civilian was reportedly intimidating some Aucterian merchants.'

Lahnos smiled. 'I'm the part-Bullan; let her go. Please.'

The Bullan officer in charge nodded. 'Get out of here, girl.'

Reyn's eyes widened. 'But...'

'Go,' said Lahnos. 'Don't worry about me. Get the ferry home and I'll meet you there.'

A mixture of relief and guilt flickered over Reyn's features, then she bolted, running through the temple plaza and disappearing down a side street. Two of the Bullan soldiers gripped Lahnos's arms and pulled them behind his back, then their officer led them off. Dozens of Aucterian civilians stared at the little procession as they marched across the plaza, and Lahnos glared at the smug expressions worn by several. Forbidden from entering the temple, the four Bullan had been waiting outside for him to emerge, all because he had possessed the audacity to walk through the streets of Igatz.

'Keep your legs moving,' said one of the soldiers.

'I know what to do,' Lahnos said. 'Do you think this is the first time I've been arrested?'

A soldier's hand clipped the back of Lahnos's head. 'That's enough of your cheek.'

A large Bullan guard post stood a few streets away from the entrance to the palace, and the four soldiers led Lahnos in through the front gates. The building looked like a fortress, with high forbidding walls, and barred windows. Lahnos was escorted into a wide reception area, where over a dozen Bullan warriors were standing. Lahnos had never been inside that particular guard post before, but he knew the routine.

He was led to a desk, where two Bullan were sitting.

One glanced up, his wide, animal-like nostrils flaring. 'Is this the troublemaker?'

'We arrested him leaving the Temple of the Undying Serpent, sir,' said the officer. 'We've searched him; he had no knife in his possession.'

'That's because there was no knife,' said Lahnos. 'Whoever made the report is lying.'

'Shut your mouth,' said the Bullan officer. 'Speak only when asked a direct question.'

If it had been a militia guard post, Lahnos would have been unable to resist the temptation to point out that he had broken no laws, but one did not provoke the Bullan, not if one wished to emerge unscathed.

'Name?' said the sitting officer, preparing a quill and paper.

'Lahnos.'

'Village?'

'Fidalaimos.'

'Age?'

'Nineteen.'

One of the other Bullan stirred. 'Fidalaimos? Are you Lahnos Laimos?'

'That's my name.'

'Any relation to Colonel Friel Laimos?'

'No.'

The Bullan stared at him, a slight smile tracing his lips.

'You are being charged with breach of the peace and carrying an offensive weapon, Lahnos of Fidalaimos,' said the sitting officer. 'How do you plead?'

Lahnos kept his features neutral. 'Not guilty.'

'I have a witness report,' said the officer, 'that claims you were threatening a group of Aucterian merchants with a knife. Do you deny it?'

'Yes.'

'Why are you in Igatz?'

'I was sightseeing. I wanted to visit the temple.'

The Bullan glanced at each other and, not for the first time, Lahnos wondered what they thought of people like him. He was a quarter Bullan, and his horns made that plainly evident to anyone who saw him. Did the Bullan despise him, or were they embarrassed that one of their own had coupled with a mere human? Or, maybe, was there a flicker of sympathy for him? The Aucterian colonists treated the Bullan soldiers almost as badly as they treated the native Zamatans, yet they never displayed the smallest sign that they felt slighted.

The two Bullan officers spoke in their own guttural tongue for a few moments, then the seated warrior nodded.

'Lahnos of Fidalaimos,' he said, 'this tribunal finds you guilty as charged. A hundred lashes of the whip, or twenty days in jail – which do you choose?'

Lahnos said nothing for a moment. A hundred lashes, especially if administered by a Bullan warrior, would probably cripple or kill him.

He swallowed. 'Twenty days.'

The officer nodded. 'Take him away.'

Two Bullan soldiers guided Lahnos away from the desk, and towards a doorway.

'You should know better, lad,' whispered one, as they walked. 'The Aucterians don't like Zamatans who walk about with...'

'With horns?'

'Yes. With horns.'

The other Bullan shook his head. 'You people shouldn't exist. I feel ashamed just looking at you. Was your mother a whore, or was it your grandmother?'

Lahnos clenched his fists, but managed to restrain his impulses. If he struck a Bullan, then it would be unlikely that he would be leaving the guard post alive. They reached the doorway, where a soldier on duty smirked, then said something in the Bullan language. One of the two escorts laughed.

'He asked if I was your daddy,' he said to Lahnos.

The other Bullan soldier frowned at his colleagues. 'Have you no shame? He might be your brother.'

A loud cry rang out behind them before the other Bullan could respond, and everyone in the hall froze, then turned. A member of the Zamatan militia was running in from the entrance, his eyes wide. The Bullan tensed, then an officer gripped hold of the militiaman's arm.

'Calm yourself, human,' the officer said. 'Do you have news? What did the arrival of the new dragon signify?'

The militiaman panted, then placed his hands on his knees. 'There's bad news,' he said.

'Are the Gunstians coming?' said the Bullan officer. 'Has their fleet been sighted?'

'It's worse,' said the militiaman.

'Worse than the Gunstians?'

'Bow your heads,' cried the militiaman, 'for His Majesty King Gahad the Mighty, the great dragon god, is dead.'

CHAPTER 2
BEARER OF BAD TIDINGS

Cyasarta, Serpent Isle – 23rd Arginch 1588

Lieutenant Cisca of Naeth wished she was back in Inopei. Even her home continent of Aucteran would do; anywhere, in fact, but the Serpent Isle. The impossible had happened – King Gahad was dead, and the last place she wanted to be was on a ship arriving at some remote island outpost barely two hundred and fifty miles from the hostile Gunstian coastline.

A warm wind blew over the wooden flight deck of the huge dragon carrier, as Cisca gazed out at the nearby town of Igatz. Their escort of four frigates had gone on ahead, leaving the gargantuan carrier to crawl through the Cyasarta inlet and into the calm waters of the greatest natural harbour in the entire world. Great chains had blocked the entrance to the inlet, and the operation to lower them had dragged on interminably. Cisca sent a silent prayer to the dragon gods that her stay upon the Serpent Isle would be brief. Besides carrying the news of King Gahad's death to the colony, their mission was to bring back the governor of the island – Lady Tirna Min Gahad, the eighth daughter of the dead dragon king, so that she could attend the emergency meeting that had been called to discuss the future of the Dominion. Cisca's heart clouded with anxiety. Without King Gahad, what future did the Dominion have?

A great rattling sound of grinding metal tore across her senses as the four anchors were dropped into the bay two hundred yards from the shore of Igatz. The sails had already been taken down, and the giant carrier eased to a stop, the anchor chains straining. A ship's whistle sounded, and sailors bounded across the deck, doing whatever it was that sailors did at times like those. Cisca's father had been a sailor in the Dominion Navy, but she had seen what twenty years of service upon the oceans had done to him, and had opted instead to join the Dragon Corps, a diplomatic service under the aegis of the Dominion Army. Her father hadn't minded – she was an officer, and that was all that mattered.

She scanned the skies, but saw no sign of Lord Noxon Mon Konran. The red and blue dragon had taken off from the carrier over an hour before, choosing to fly to Igatz rather than wait for the ship to anchor; and there had been no sign of him since. Cisca knew she shouldn't feel relieved, but she did. Lord Noxon had been nothing but rude and unpleasant during the forty-six-day voyage from Inopei, and as the lowest-ranking Dragon Corps officer of the five assigned to administer to his needs, Cisca had often borne the brunt of his ill temper. Perhaps, if she were lucky, she wouldn't have to see him again until it was time to depart.

'Lieutenant Cisca,' came a sharp voice from behind her.

She turned and saluted, her back straightening as her senior officer approached across the wide flight deck.

'At ease, Lieutenant,' said the Dragon Corps major. 'Why aren't you preparing your things for the trip ashore?'

'Sir?' said Cisca. 'I was under the impression that I was to remain on board the carrier to await the return of Lord Noxon.'

The major sighed. 'No. You are supposed to be below, getting ready to board the ship's tender. Do you imagine that Lord Noxon shall require no assistance while in Igatz?'

'I…'

'Step to it,' said the major. 'An officer from the garrison stationed on the island is waiting for you by the ship's tender, which leaves in ten minutes. If you are not on it, there shall be serious consequences.'

'Yes, sir. Sorry, sir.'

Cisca raced off, dodging between groups of sailors who muttered unkind words about lazy army dragon-minders as she passed. She reached the narrow stairs leading to the next deck, and hurried down them, almost tripping before she reached the bottom. She turned left and headed towards her cabin, but the route was full of sailors moving crates and barrels. She tried to push past, but the minutes were ebbing away, and she gave up. She needed to be on the tender, with or without her possessions, or the major would make the return voyage even more unpleasant than the outward leg had been. She found another flight of stairs and sped down them, reaching the deck from where the tender could be accessed. She ran along the narrow passageway, then straight into the back of a long queue that had formed. A mixture of sailors and officers with large bags over their shoulders were waiting by a gangway, which led down onto the smaller vessel. A naval lieutenant at the head of the queue caught her eye, and gestured for her to approach.

'Lieutenant Cisca?' he said.

She nodded, too out of breath to answer.

'You have priority,' he said. 'Come forward.'

Cisca eased past the others in the queue, while trying to ignore the harsh glances and muttered curses that were sent her way.

The naval officer eyed her. 'My name is Lieutenant Travers, and I was sent from Igatz to meet you. Where are your things?'

'I didn't have time to collect them,' she said. 'I was only informed that I would be going ashore a few moments ago.'

He shook his head at her. 'You could be in Igatz for several days. Never mind. Follow me.'

The naval lieutenant strode through the hatch and on to the gangway, and Cisca went after him. The tender was secured fore and aft by ropes to the side of the huge carrier, and Cisca tried not to glance down at the deep water on either side of the slim gangway. She stepped on to the deck of the smaller ship, and the naval officer gestured at the others in the queue, signalling that they could also embark.

'Thank you,' said Cisca.

'Best move out of the way,' said the officer; 'unless you want to get knocked overboard. Come with me. Is this your first time on the Serpent Isle?'

'Yes,' she said, as they strode towards the bow of the ship.

'Right. Here are a few simple instructions – stay in Igatz. Do not venture into Kaugatz alone under any circumstances. Understood? Have you worked with Bullan before?'

'Not closely, no.'

'Then stay away from them, if at all possible. They might serve the Dominion, but they hate our guts.'

'There are Bullan stationed on the Serpent Isle? Why?'

'There are five thousand Bullan on the island. Why is another story. Also, watch out for the resident Gunstians. They usually stay clear of Igatz, but one or two sometimes cross over from other parts of the island, usually in an attempt to convert us to their religion.'

'Did you say Gunstians?'

He smiled. 'I did. This island used to belong to them, and several thousand descendants of their colonists still live here. Needless to say, they hate us even more than the Bullan do, and only marginally less than the native Zamatans. Stay away from them, too.'

Cisca's eyes widened. 'But I thought...'

'You thought what? That the local islanders love us?'

'Well, not exactly; but don't the Zamatans worship the dragon gods, just as we do?'

They reached the railings by the fore deck, and the officer turned. 'Forget everything you might have learned about the Serpent Isle in Aucteran, Lieutenant Cisca. The situation here is tense, and complicated. Half of the island will mourn the passing of His Majesty King Gahad; the other half will celebrate.' He reached out a hand.

She glanced at it, then they shook hands. 'How long have you been based upon the island?'

'I've been here for three years,' he said. 'I am your liaison officer, assigned to ensure you don't get lost. I have one rule – inform me before you decide to leave the palace grounds.'

'I very much doubt I shall be leaving the palace while I am here. I work for Lord Noxon Mon Konran, the messenger dragon sent to bear the news from Inopei. I imagine that I will be busy attending to his requests.'

Travers smiled again, in a way that annoyed her. 'Lord Noxon Mon Konran will have a dozen of the palace staff running about after him. Your presence ashore is merely a formality. There are five Dragon Corps officers on board the carrier assigned to him, are there not?'

'There are.'

'And are you the lowest ranked?'

Her face flushed. 'I am.'

'Then I'm sorry to tell you this, but the other four have rather stitched you up, as it were. Protocol requires at least one officer to remain ashore with Lord Noxon, while the others all have invitations to stay in the beach mansions in Riston, south of Igatz.'

Her features fell.

'Not to worry, though,' Travers said. 'While your superior officers are sunning themselves and swimming in the waters of the Cyasarta, you will be able to sample the delights of Igatz, under adequate supervision, of course.'

Cisca stared out at the bay as the tender began to move away from the carrier. How dare the other officers of the Dragon Corps behave so frivolously when King Gahad was no more? Didn't they understand the gravity of the situation?

'Based on Inopei, were you?' said Travers.

She nodded. 'In Nom Karta, the capital. I was there when King Gahad visited, the day before he was killed. That's how I ended up on the carrier – I volunteered to help spread the news to the overseas colonies.'

'You were there, eh? What do you know about His Majesty's death?'

'About as much as any human, I guess,' she said. 'I had been in Nom

Karta for a year and a half, serving a variety of junior members of the Royal Family. I didn't actually see King Gahad the day before he died – I was busy arranging potential dragon suitors for one of His Majesty's granddaughters. But, I heard the rumours. I was told that he had been visiting his palace by the volcanic mines, and that he had apprehended a strange witch with odd powers – a witch that he wanted to bring back to the capital. Then, he returned to his volcano, and was slain by that witch. I don't understand how, but the entire palace built on to the side of the volcano was destroyed. The dragons are calling her a demon, and they are hunting her. It doesn't make sense, though – how could a human have powers of any kind?'

Travers chewed his lip. 'Are you aware of the Thirteen Gifts of Theodora?'

'Well, yes, but only from history books. Any humans with those powers were wiped out a thousand years ago.'

'That's partly true. They were wiped out in the Eastern continents, along with every native who used to dwell in Inopei and Aucteran.'

Cisca frowned. 'It is not very polite to bring up such matters, Lieutenant Travers. Wait; are you saying that the natives of the West still retain some of those ancient powers?'

'That is exactly what I am saying, Lieutenant Cisca.'

'Do you have proof of this?'

'Of course not. Everyone on the Serpent Isle knows it, though. The chances are that some of the native Zamatans are Gifted.'

She narrowed her eyes and smiled. 'Impossible.'

'Really? You are aware that the Dominion has invaded the Gunstian Empire twice over the last few hundred years, I assume?'

'Naturally.'

'So, tell me, Cisca, how do you imagine the Gunstians were able to defeat the world's mightiest armed forces – not once, but twice? Their Empire is the only part of this world that has remained out of the Dominion's control – how? How could mere humans overcome the power of the dragons? The answer is simple – the natives of the West retain some of Theodora's Gifts.'

'Is this a trick you play on all new arrivals to the island, Travers? You fill their heads with nonsense, lies and rumours?'

Travers turned away, as if offended by her dismissal of his claims. 'Believe what you wish,' he said. 'If the rumours you shared with me are true, and a human witch with strange powers is on the loose, then don't be too surprised if the rulers of the Dominion soon decide that Gunst was behind the death of His Majesty. Then you can draw your own conclusions.'

Cisca stood in silence for a while, watching as the tender approached the shoreline of Igatz. A huge building of white marble dominated the headland to their right, while towers and steeples punctuated the skyline beyond. The town seemed wealthy, and many small boats were plying the calm waters of the Cyasarta. A small jetty was protruding into the waves from the base of the large white building, and the tender turned a little to starboard to aim for it.

'Is that the Dragon Palace?' she said.

Travers eyed her. 'And will you believe me if I say it is?'

'Yes, because if you are lying, then I would discover the truth quite quickly on my own.'

'Do you know how many dragons dwell within its walls?'

'Five, I believe,' she said. 'Governor Tirna Min Gahad, her mate, their infant dragon, and two others.'

He nodded.

'Lady Tirna is being recalled to Inopei,' she said.

'Is that so?'

'Yes. All twenty-one children of King Gahad are required to attend a meeting in Nom Karta, to discuss...'

Cisca's voice trailed off as a piercing scream split through the air. All over the bay, flocks of sea birds took to the skies, and every face on the tender turned towards the palace. From behind its high walls, a great white and purple dragon rose into view, her enormous wings extended. The scream echoed out again, coming from the dragon's mouth, and Cisca put her hands to her ears. The dragon beat her wings, then soared off over the tender, the wash of air causing the small ship to sway from side to side.

'There goes the Blessed Lady,' said Travers. 'We can assume that Governor Tirna has just heard the tragic news about her father.'

'Her grief mirrors that of her siblings in Nom Karta,' said Cisca, as she watched the white and purple dragon fly towards the north. 'It was terrifying to be in the presence of so many mourning dragons. What shall we do without King Gahad to guide us?'

Travers opened his mouth, then seemed to think better of it, and turned back to face the palace.

The tender docked at the small jetty, and sailors tied its ropes to several iron cleats. A gangway was set in place, and Lieutenant Travers led Cisca to the front of the queue, and then helped her up onto the jetty. A gate at the end of the jetty led into the interior of the palace grounds and standing guard by the entrance were two Bullan warriors wearing Dominion armour. Cisca felt her nerves jangle as she glanced at them. They were tall and broad, with thick muscular arms, but it was their horns and wide, flaring nostrils that got her attention. Then she caught a glimpse of their tails, and her stomach started to turn.

'Stop staring at them,' Travers whispered. 'Please don't tell me this is this first time you've ever seen Bullan?'

'Of course I've seen them before,' she said. 'They protect the dragons in Nom Karta. It's just... I have never been so close to any until now. They were posted on the outer defences of the city, and we were forbidden from going there.'

Travers hushed her as they approached the gate.

'Good afternoon,' he said to the Bullan. 'This is Lieutenant Cisca of the Dragon Corps, assigned to the service of Lord Noxon Mon Konran. She is to be accorded all rights and privileges within the palace compound during her stay. Please ensure that she is afforded all courtesy.'

One of the Bullan grunted, then they moved aside to let Travers and Cisca enter the palace grounds. They came into a huge open garden, with trees lining the wide paths and streams flowing past vast lawns.

Upon one of the lawns, three adult dragons were weeping and lamenting, while a small child dragon sat in silence close by. On a neighbouring lawn, Lord Noxon was speaking to a hushed crowd of human courtiers, his blue and red scales making him readily recognisable.

'I should report to Lord Noxon,' Cisca said, 'to let him know that I am at his service.'

Travers nodded, then he followed Cisca as she made her way towards the blue and red dragon. Cisca strode across the trimmed grass of the lawn, then waited for the dragon to catch her eye. He glanced at her several times, but pretended not to recognise her. Perhaps it wasn't a pretence, she thought; perhaps he held humans in such low esteem that he had already forgotten who she was. At length, after a long address to the palace staff, he narrowed his eyes at her.

'Why are you staring at me?' he said, his low voice booming out.

Her face flushed. 'I am Lieutenant Cisca, and I...'

'I know who you are!' the dragon bellowed. 'Do you think me a fool? Of all the useless servants upon that accursed ship, you were surely the worst. Well? What do you want? Speak.'

'I have been assigned, my gracious lord,' she said, 'to assist you in your stay upon the Serpent Isle.'

'They sent *you*?' he said, then he started to laugh. He glanced at the palace staff as he did so, and several of them joined in with the laughter.

Cisca said nothing. She had been trained for these situations, and she would retain her dignity, at least in public.

'The best service you could do for me, wretch,' Lord Noxon said, his laughter ending as abruptly as it had started, 'is if you stay out of my way. Grave matters beyond your ken are to be discussed before our departure, and I will be displeased if you get in my way. You are dismissed.'

'Yes, my lord,' Cisca said, bowing. She retreated away, stepping backwards over the lawn, her gaze lowered.

Travers was waiting for her on the gravel path.

'Say nothing,' she said.

He nodded, and then led her away from the dragons and towards the palace. She waited until they had rounded a line of trees, then she came to a halt and placed a hand to her face. Don't cry, she told herself. You are an officer in the Dominion armed forces, and you shall not cry.

'Can I speak now?' said Travers.

'Are you going to mock me? Are you going to tell me that you were right?'

'No,' he said. 'I was going to offer to procure you some spare clothes. After all, I doubt you wish to wear the same outfit for every day of your stay. There are clean uniforms in the laundry building, and the woman in charge owes me a few favours.'

'Thank you,' she said.

'Can I ask – whatever possessed you to join the Dragon Corps? There must be easier ways to serve the Dominion.'

Cisca took a breath. 'Let's just say that my initial conception of dragons was not the same as the reality.'

He smiled. 'I have a feeling you might come to think of the Serpent Isle in the same way. Look on the bright side: at least you won't have to run around after his lordship all day. He dismissed you from his presence, and that means you are free to enjoy yourself.'

'And how would one do that?' she said.

'The island will be entering a period of official mourning,' he said, 'but that doesn't mean the bars will all be closed.'

He set off towards the palace buildings. Cisca took one look over her shoulder at the dragons, then followed him.

CHAPTER 3
FATHER FIGURE

Igatz, Serpent Isle – 23rd Arginch 1588

Leona glanced out of the carriage window at the position of the sun, and suppressed her frustration. For over two hours, she had been waiting on the colonel, her employer, while he paid a visit to one of his many mistresses within the town of Igatz. Some of those he called upon were in their early twenties, others older; some were beautiful, others not so much; but all were either rich or held influential positions within Igatz society.

A bell pealed somewhere in Igatz. Leona had heard the sound several times over the preceding hour, but she wasn't sure what was causing it. A faint fear that the island was under Gunstian attack had flitted through her thoughts, but she had dismissed it. If the Gunstians were coming, then the colonel would have known about it. She sat back in the carriage and tried to relax. The vehicle was parked a street away from the house that the colonel was visiting, and was within sight of the walls of the massive Dominion fortress of Atzoun on the south-western peninsula of Igatz, as far from the Dragon Palace as it was possible to get without leaving the town. The nearby streets oozed with opulence, with large stone townhouses and elegant mansions owned by wealthy Aucterian merchants and town administrators. The younger Leona had hated the colonists, but after working for the colonel for two years, she had got used to them. She still despised many but had realised that, like the Zamatans, they were just people, with good and bad spread among them. Her idle thoughts turned back to her errant employer. While his morals, or lack of them, repelled her, she found him fascinating; so fascinating, in fact, that she had been happy to appear demure in his presence, so that she could observe, and learn all that she could from him. The colonel was very handsome, although not quite as handsome as he thought he was, and his self-confidence knew no bounds. She had been attracted to him when they had first met, but her feelings towards him had changed, and at some point in their relationship she had begun to think of him as a father figure. She groaned inwardly at the thought of the colonel as her father. He was the right age, but he hardly set a good example.

Her eyes fastened on to the sight of a figure running towards the carriage, and she smiled. The colonel was carrying his dress jacket in one hand as he sprinted across the street. He gave a quick nod to his driver, then opened the side door and leapt in as the carriage got under way. He closed the door, exhaled, then laughed.

'Did her husband come home, sir?' Leona said.

'What?' said the colonel. 'No. Her husband happens to be stationed in Handshore Naval Base today, but thanks for asking.' He pulled on his jacket, and smoothed down the lapels.

'Your cufflinks, sir?' she said.

He patted down his pockets and retrieved a pair of silver cufflinks from one. He placed them on to a palm and stretched out his arms towards Leona.

'So,' the colonel said, as Leona began attaching the first cufflink to his shirt sleeve, 'when did they begin?'

'Sir?'

'The bells, Leona.'

'About an hour ago, sir.'

'Oh. That long. How unfortunate.'

'Were you so... distracted, sir, that you didn't hear them when they started?'

'Indeed I was. Lady Catlin is an extremely distracting young woman. The entire island could have sunk into the waves and I doubt I would have been any the wiser. It was only after I began to get dressed that I heard anything. I don't suppose you know the cause?'

Leona finished with the cufflinks and sat back. 'No, sir.'

'Well, there are several options,' he said, 'most of which can be immediately ruled out. Let's see if all of my training has been put to good use. Name me some possible reasons.'

'My first thought, sir,' she said, 'which I dismissed, was that the island was under attack by the Imperial Gunstian Fleet.'

He smiled. 'And why did you dismiss that possibility?'

'Because, sir, if the Gunstians were going to invade, then you would have known.'

'Maybe I did know, but chose not to tell you.' He raised a finger for silence, then tapped on to the small window that sat between the carriage and his driver. 'My office, good man. Make haste.' He turned back to Leona. 'Go on.'

'My second thought,' she said, 'was that something bad has happened to one of the dragons in the palace.'

'Interesting theory,' he said, 'but wrong.'

'Why, sir?'

'Never mind that. Any other thoughts?'

'A fire?'

He squinted at her. 'Then where is the smoke? The sky is perfectly clear, Leona. One more guess.'

'Perhaps the Grand Convoy has arrived early this year, sir?'

'Ah, now we're getting somewhere; although I would doubt it's the entire convoy. The tides and winds are predictable, and any ocean crossing this early in the year would have had to have originated in Inopei, not Aucteran. And the Grand Convoy, as I'm sure you know, sets sail from Naeth in Aucteran. You did know that, didn't you?'

'Yes, sir.'

'Then we are left with the conclusion that some other fleet, or ship, has arrived unannounced from Inopei. Did you notice any dragons in the sky?'

'No, sir. The carriage window was facing the fortress walls of Atzoun.'

'Good point. I suppose that we shall have to wait until we reach my office. I imagine that there will be someone there waiting to give me the news.' He moved his head to the left. 'Do I have any lipstick on me? I was in a hurry when I left Lady Catlin's townhouse.'

She glanced at his neck, and saw a small red smear. 'You have a little, sir.'

He took out a handkerchief and passed it to her. She dabbed it against her tongue, then wiped the offending blemish from his neck.

'You had better keep that,' he said. 'Imagine the fuss if I happened to pull that out of my pocket at another lady's residence.' He smiled. 'Don't look at me like that, Leona.'

'Like what, sir?'

'Like you are a disapproving aunt. Business is business; you know that.'

'And was Lady Catlin just *business*, sir?'

'You know I'm not going to answer that directly. Your Gift makes it unwise to reveal too much.'

Leona gazed out of the window at the passing streets, annoyed that he had brought up her Gift. Whenever he did so, her old suspicion returned that he only valued her for that one thing. It also annoyed her that he felt able to discuss it openly; the Gifts of Theodora were among the most taboo subjects on the island, spoken about only in hushed whispers, if at all.

'We may have to postpone the rest of the day's activities,' he said, seemingly oblivious to her discomfort; 'depending, of course, on the meaning of the bells. What do I have on for this afternoon?'

She shook her head and sighed. 'You have a meeting with your former wife's lawyers, but I know that you already knew that.'

'Did you now? What a pity to have to miss that. I was looking forward to it.'

She felt a tingle in the back of her head that told her he was lying. He smiled at her, and she knew that he had done it deliberately. He never lied to her without knowing the effect it would have upon her.

'Tell me,' he said; 'your twentieth birthday is coming up soon. What would you like?'

A little more honesty, she thought. 'I'll think about it.'

'You are my most valued advisor, Leona,' he said, then he paused, and smiled again. 'Did you tingle?'

'No, sir.'

'Then you know it must be true. As my most valued employee, you deserve something special this year, for twenty marks the true beginning of adulthood, in my opinion. What about a new outfit? Jewellery? Books? I know you hanker after a good read. What if I let you loose in one of Igatz's better bookshops for twenty minutes? One minute for each year. Whatever bundle you're gripping on to by the end shall be yours.'

She narrowed her eyes at the thought. 'Maybe.'

A bell pealed again, and the colonel glanced out of the carriage window, a minute trace of anxiety flickering across his eyes. He tapped his hand once off his knee, a sure sign that he was desperate to know what was going on. She read him well, Leona thought, but she had had plenty of practice.

Their carriage approached the large militia headquarters along the cobbled streets, and drew in close to the building that housed the legal team, where the colonel had his office. The driver stepped down from the front of the carriage and opened the side door.

'Many thanks,' said the colonel, as he descended to the ground. 'Keep the carriage close by, in case I need it again today.'

'Yes, sir,' said the driver.

The colonel turned, and offered a hand to assist Leona. She took it, and gathered her skirts in with her other hand so they wouldn't snag on the carriage steps. They entered the building, and saw one of the young

Aucterian lawyers who worked for the colonel waiting by the front door of the office, clutching a folder of papers in his right hand. As far as Leona knew, the colonel was the only Zamatan on the island who had colonists working for him.

'Sir,' the young Aucterian said, 'I was looking for your advice on something.'

The colonel raised an eyebrow as he pulled a set of keys from a pocket. 'I thought you were waiting here to tell me what the bells signified.'

'The, uh, bells, sir?'

'Are you telling me that you haven't noticed the incessant pealing of the town bells for the last hour?'

The colonel unlocked the door and entered his office, followed by Leona and the young lawyer.

'This case I am working on, sir...' the lawyer went on.

The colonel took off his jacket and handed it to Leona. 'And which case is that?'

'The one where the Bullan arrested a member of the militia for suspected theft, sir,' said the lawyer. 'Do I have your permission to take it on?'

The colonel sat behind his desk. 'The Bullan don't usually get these things wrong. Do you believe the member of the militia to be innocent?'

'Yes, sir; I do.'

Leona felt the tingle in the back of her head, and touched the lobe of her left ear with a finger.

'I see,' said the colonel. 'Let me look into this case a little further, and I'll come to a decision. For now, go outside, and find out why the damn bells keep ringing.'

The young lawyer saluted, then hurried from the room. Leona closed the door, and hung the colonel's jacket on to a wall hook.

'He was definitely lying, sir,' she said. 'He does not believe the militiaman to be innocent.'

The colonel nodded as he scanned through a pile of letters on his desk. 'He's probably taking a bribe from the family of the accused man.'

'That's what I suspect,' she said. 'What are you going to do about it, sir?'

He shrugged. 'Nothing. Store it up for later, I suppose.'

There was a knock at the door, and the young Aucterian lawyer came back into the room. He stared at the colonel, his eyes wide, and his bottom lip quivering.

The colonel frowned. 'Well? What did you discover?'

'I... the...' the young lawyer mumbled. 'Sir, the...'

'Come on; out with it,' said the colonel.

The young man burst into tears. 'King Gahad is dead!'

Leona's mouth fell open, then she glanced at the colonel. For the first time since she had met him, he looked bewildered and at a loss for words. He stared at the young lawyer, whose sobbing was the only sound being made.

'Is this true?' the colonel said.

He had kept his eyes on the lawyer, but Leona knew the question was for her. She had felt no tingle in her head, but she knew that there was a difference between truth and belief. The lawyer hadn't lied, but he could be mistaken.

'The Governor's staff have announced it officially,' the lawyer sobbed. 'A dragon carrier has arrived in Igatz bearing the news – His Majesty King Gahad was murdered in Inopei two months ago.'

'But he's an immortal dragon,' said the colonel. 'How does one murder an immortal dragon?'

'They're saying it was the work of a demon witch, sir,' said the lawyer. 'She used ancient powers to destroy him. What shall we do? The Dominion... The island... I...'

'Get some fresh air,' said the colonel. 'In fact, take the rest of the day off, and tell the others in the legal team to do the same. I shall not force you all to work on a day like today. Go.'

'Thank you, sir,' the lawyer sobbed, then he retreated from the office.

Leona fell into a chair.

'How could this news possibly be true?' said the colonel.

'It might not be, sir,' Leona said. 'He believed it to be true, but what if the enemies of the Dominion are spreading rumours to push us off balance?'

'Did you detect any lies?'

'No, sir.'

'Then the news must have come from the Governor's staff, and they would have issued it only if they had known it to be true and verified. It seems you were right about a ship arriving out of season. If King Gahad was murdered two months ago, then that ship must have set out from Inopei not long after His Majesty's death. A demon witch – did you hear? It sounds like a Gunstian attack to me. Only a highly-skilled and Gifted Gunstian agent could conceivably have carried out such an audacious assassination attempt. What's more, if I have managed to reach this conclusion in under a minute, then we can be sure that our dragon overlords in Inopei are entertaining similar thoughts.'

'Unless Gahad's own family killed him,' said Leona, 'and they are placing the blame on to Gunst.'

The colonel raised an eyebrow. 'Please don't repeat such accusations in public; I implore you, Leona. I am more open-minded than most, but if any Aucterian heard you say such words you would be liable to be arrested for treason.'

'But you suspect it, too?'

'What I suspect shall remain buried within my own mind – and I recommend that you do the same. Pour me a glass of something strong.'

Leona stood, and went to the large drinks cabinet. She had only ever seen the colonel drink in his office after winning a case in court, and she wondered how nervous he was beneath his calm exterior. She extracted a wine decanter, and half-filled a glass.

She passed him the glass and he frowned at it.

'A half glass of wine? Is that the best you can do? I asked for something strong.'

'Should you be drinking at work, sir?'

'Work? I don't think we'll be getting much work done today. The supposedly ever-living supreme and almighty deity of the world has been murdered by a witch, and now his twenty-one children are about to start a fight over who gets to rule the Dominion.'

'Who will be the new king, sir?'

'Two dragons in particular will be pressing their claims to the throne, I imagine,' said the colonel. 'Lord Tegru is the eldest son of Gahad, but Lord Naghad is the stronger of the two – he is the strongest of all the children.' He shook his head. 'I have to say – if Gahad's assassination was the work of the Gunstians, then I feel a little twinge of respect for them. One death, and the entire world order collapses.' He sipped from the glass, then downed the rest in one. 'I shall need to schedule a few off-the-book meetings. Clear my diary; and tell anyone who asks that I have been overwhelmed by grief. Unlike the others, I shall need you to keep working, Leona. I imagine that the truth will be at a premium over the coming days.'

'Yes, sir.'

'What is your opinion on this?' he said.

'My opinions are possibly treasonous, sir.'

'Try to think dispassionately. Push your feelings to one side and analyse the situation critically.'

She nodded. 'Well, sir,' she said; 'if the Gunstians are behind King Gahad's death, then the island is in grave danger. It seems inconceivable that they would create such chaos and not take advantage of it by re-conquering Zamata. However, if the Gunstians had nothing to do with it, then they will be as surprised by this news as we are – and they will also be unprepared.'

'I concur,' he said. 'Therefore, our priority is to arrange a little discussion with my Gunstian contacts, and find out what they know. It is entirely possible that the Gunstian government would have kept this a secret from their agents on the island, however; they know that several of them have been compromised.'

She smiled. 'Compromised by you, sir?'

'Indeed, although I am not the only agent on Zamata who is being paid by both sides.'

Leona shuddered. Why did he trust her with such knowledge? She would never betray him, but how did he know that? His trust sometimes felt like a burden weighing down upon her young shoulders.

The door to the office opened again, and another Aucterian lawyer entered.

'I thought I told you all to take the rest of the day off?' said the colonel.

'Sorry, sir,' said the lawyer. 'I was about to leave, when a non-commissioned officer from the Bullan regiment arrived here asking to speak with you. Should I send him in?'

'Thank you; yes,' said the colonel.

Leona narrowed her eyes. She loathed the Bullan – not merely because of how they looked, although their appearance frightened her, but due to their reputation among the islanders for brutality and violence. They were ostensibly on Zamata to maintain law and order, but everyone knew they were only there to protect the Aucterian colonists from the native inhabitants of the island.

A broad-shouldered Bullan soldier entered the office, and Leona almost flinched.

The colonel smiled. 'How can I help you, Sergeant Jagha Locatu?'

Leona blinked. How did the colonel know the soldier's name? All Bullan looked identical to her, their savage features indistinguishable.

The Bullan soldier nodded. 'Colonel Friel Laimos, I am here to inform you that your nephew has been arrested and sentenced to twenty days in the cells for breach of the peace. I thought you would want to know.'

The colonel's eyes tightened. 'Breach of the peace?'

'And for carrying an offensive weapon, though the boy was unarmed at the time of his arrest.'

'What weapon was he supposed to be carrying?'

'A knife,' said the soldier. 'In my opinion, Colonel Laimos, there is no substance to either of the charges; but the complaint was made by some high-standing Aucterian merchants, and the law is clear.'

'I see. I assume we are talking about Lahnos, and not one of my other nephews?'

The soldier nodded.

'Where is he being held?'

'In the Temple District, Colonel Laimos. He was visiting the Tower of the Undying Serpent.'

'Was he alone?'

'He had a young woman with him, but she was not mentioned in the complaint, so she was released.'

'One more question,' said Friel Laimos; 'was my nephew walking around the Temple District with his head uncovered?'

'He was.'

'Thank you, sergeant,' said the colonel. 'I shall not forget the courtesy you have shown me in coming here today. Has the garrison been put on alert due to the news from Inopei?'

'We have; and I am due back in my barracks.'

'Then I shall not detain you any longer.'

The Bullan soldier nodded, then left the office.

Leona exhaled. 'I didn't detect any lies, sir.'

'No, you wouldn't,' said Colonel Laimos. 'The Bullan are many things, but they are seldom dishonest. Sergeant Jagha Locatu is a good man.' He smiled. 'I can see from the expression on your face that you find that hard to believe.'

'The Bullan have raped, tortured and murdered many Zamatans, sir. They...'

The colonel raised a finger. 'All true. The Zamatans also do these things on occasion, as do the Gunstians and, indeed, the noble Aucterian colonists. Would you condemn every race and people for the vile actions of a minority? There is good and bad in all – this is something I have tried hard to teach you.'

Leona lowered her gaze, scarcely believing that the colonel would defend the barbarism of the Bullan. Her thoughts went to another detail.

'Can I ask, sir,' she said; 'what was the significance of your question regarding your nephew covering his head?'

Friel gazed at her, as though pondering whether or not to reveal something. Leona frowned. He had been willing to speak openly about the Gifted, and about the fact that he was being secretly paid by both the Gunstian and Dominion governments at the same time. What could be so bad about his nephew that he would hesitate to tell her?

'I don't like to judge people,' he said, 'but be warned – I will judge your response to what I am about to tell you. You are aware that I have many family members living in the little village of Fidalaimos, on the slopes of Mount Medamuna?'

'Yes, sir; I am aware of that.'

'One of those family members ran away from home four years ago. He now lives in Kaugatz, and is blissfully unaware of the fact that I have agents keeping an eye on him. Watching over him, as it were. He has a tendency to speak his mind, and that is one of the things that gets him into trouble.' He paused. 'The other thing that marks Lahnos out is his horns.'

Leona kept her features neutral, despite her inner revulsion. Horns? She felt nauseous.

Colonel Friel Laimos gazed into her eyes. 'I sense you are struggling to retain your composure, my dear Leona.'

'I'm just surprised, sir,' she said, a little too quickly.

'Why? There are approximately six hundred Zamatans on the island who display at least one physical attribute of the part-Bullan. Their numbers will never be fully known, as so many choose to hide the fact. In Kaugatz alone, I estimate there to be three hundred part-Bullan, all clustered in the same small area of slum housing. That is where Lahnos lives; among his people, as it were.'

'Was Lahnos's father… a Bullan, sir?'

'No. His mother's father was Bullan. And, before you ask, I do not know the circumstances by which his mother was conceived. My nephew has four siblings, but none of them have horns or tails, despite sharing the same ancestry. Lahnos was just unlucky, although he does not see it that way. He wears his horns with pride.'

Leona said nothing, not trusting herself to speak.

'You shall accompany me to the Bullan guard post in the Temple

District tomorrow morning,' the colonel said, 'and we shall see if we can secure my nephew's early release. I trust you will keep any unsavoury opinions to yourself?'

'I shall try, sir. My main feeling is one of pity. His grandmother was probably raped by a Bullan, and...'

'We don't know that,' said Colonel Laimos. 'She may have been a prostitute or, just maybe, they were in love. It happens. I cannot be the only Zamatan with the ability to see beyond outward appearances. Therefore, I would ask you to show my nephew no pity about his situation. He wouldn't thank you for it.'

'And we shall collect him from prison in the morning, sir?'

'Yes. Pack some things for a few days.'

'Sir?'

'This isn't Lahnos's first brush with the law,' said Friel. 'I think it would be wise to remove him from the centre of the island for a while. With King Gahad's death, I have a feeling that things are about to get interesting in Kaugatz, and I would rather that Lahnos is not around if events turn ugly.' He smiled. 'Perhaps it is time to pay my old village a visit.'

CHAPTER 4
BACK TO THE FARM

Igatz, Serpent Isle – 24th Arginch 1588

The Gunstian's fist hammered into Lahnos Laimos's chin as they rolled together on the filthy cell floor. Lahnos's head jerked back, but he kept his hands tightly gripped round his opponent's throat, choking the life from him.

'Horned beast!' the Gunstian gasped. 'Demon!'

'Is anyone going to separate them?' said a sitting Zamatan prisoner from the opposite end of the cell.

'Why?' said another. 'Let them kick the crap out of each other. If we're lucky, we'll have one fewer Gunstian, or one fewer part-Bullan on the island.'

The Gunstian's eyes started to close as Lahnos increased the pressure on his throat. His arms went limp, and Lahnos pushed him to the side, then battered his right fist into the man's nose, spraying blood onto the cell floor. Lahnos got to his feet, and smiled at the other prisoners.

'Anyone else want to make a comment about my parentage?'

The other prisoners looked away. The Gunstian groaned from the floor, and lifted his hands to his bloody nose. Lahnos eyed him, then took a seat, making sure he had a good view of the cell's occupants. He folded his arms over his chest, and leaned back against the wall. His chin hurt, but he refused to show any weakness in front of the others. He still had nineteen nights in the cells to endure, and he wanted to be able to walk out on his own two legs when his time had been served.

'Hey,' said one of the Zamatan prisoners.

Lahnos glanced at him.

'Have you ever gored anyone with one of those horns?'

Lahnos shrugged.

'I reckon they're more of a liability in a fight,' said another. 'Someone could grab hold of them from behind.'

'Do you know why they're still sharp?' said Lahnos.

No one spoke.

'I'll tell you,' Lahnos went on; 'it's because no one has ever got close enough to me with a file or a saw. Several have tried. All have failed.'

The cell fell into silence, with the only sound coming from the bells of the Temple District.

'When are they going to stop ringing those damn bells?' muttered one of the prisoners. 'We get it – the dragon is dead.'

'Show some respect,' said another. 'King Gahad ruled this world for... well, I don't know exactly, but it was a long time.'

'That foul demon didn't rule the whole world,' said the Gunstian, as he pulled himself onto the stone bench that ran along the wall. 'He never conquered the sacred lands of Gunst.'

'Shut up,' said a Zamatan. 'No one wants to hear your crap.'

'The truth hurts, does it?' the Gunstian said, smiling through the blood covering his lower face. 'Right now, the demon-king Gahad is burning in the fires of eternal torment, paying the price for his sins.'

One of the Zamatan glanced at Lahnos. 'Punch him again, horn-boy.'

Lahnos didn't respond.

The Gunstian spat a gobbet of blood onto the floor. 'That horned abomination will also suffer after his death. The fiery pits will consume him. He is a sign! A sign that the sinners of this island will soon meet their end, when the righteous of Gunst shall trample over those who worship the false serpent gods. His fate is sealed, but it is not too late for the Zamatans to repent. Cease your wickedness and return to the true faith! Open your hearts to...'

'Shut your mouth!' cried a Zamatan. He pointed a finger into the Gunstian's face. 'If you don't, then you won't be getting up from what we do to you. The boy let you off lightly – we won't.'

The Gunstian smiled, but said nothing. Lahnos eyed him for a moment, then glanced at the small barred window next to the ceiling. A patch of blue sky was visible, and he thought he saw a dragon flying past in the distance, but it might just have been a sea bird. He wondered how he felt about the dragon-king's death. Gahad had meant nothing to him, and he loathed the Dominion occupation of the island, but were the Gunstians any better? The last time the Gunstians had been in control of Zamata, they had orchestrated a frenzy of religious oppression, looting the monasteries and casting down countless numbers of the sacred serpent pillars that had once been common in the countryside. They had burned serpent-worshippers in the centre of Igatz, and terrorised entire towns and villages. That had all been a century before, but the collective memory of the islanders did not forget such things; nor did it forgive. Compared to the Gunstians, the rule of the Dominion seemed almost benign, if one was prepared to overlook the crass injustices perpetrated against the native Zamatans.

Two Bullan soldiers appeared at the barred gate of the cell. One glanced at the bloody face of the Gunstian prisoner, but if he felt any emotion about it, he didn't show it.

'Lahnos of Fidalaimos,' said the other soldier; 'stand and approach the door.'

Lahnos frowned, then pulled himself to his feet. 'Am I being transferred?

The soldiers ignored his words, then one of them unlocked the door.

'Come with us,' one said.

The other prisoners said nothing as Lahnos walked out of the cell, though a couple gave him sympathetic nods. Lahnos took a breath. Had the soldiers seen what he had done to the Gunstian? Was he being removed for a punishment beating? He kept his expression blank as the Bullan relocked the door, then one gripped his arm and they led him off down the passageway. They passed several other full cells, and Lahnos's horns earned a few hostile glances, then they ascended a flight of stairs. Lahnos was led to a doorway, and one of the soldiers opened it. Inside were two Bullan officers, and two Zamatans. One was a girl his age, who was gazing at the floor, while the other was a middle-aged man that Lahnos recognised.

'Here he is, Colonel,' said one of the Bullan officers.

'Thank you,' said Friel Laimos. 'Would I be right in saying that his release is conditional upon him remaining out of Igatz and Kaugatz for the next year?'

'That is what we agreed, Colonel,' said the Bullan officer. 'Are you prepared to act as his guarantor in this regard?'

'I am,' said Friel.

'Then you may take him from the guard post. Please ensure that he has left the central districts of the island before sunset this day.'

The four Bullan left the chamber, and Friel gazed at his nephew.

'Why did you do that?' said Lahnos, his anger rising. 'I don't need your help.'

'No?' said Friel. 'You wanted to spend the next nineteen days in jail?'

'Better that than a year exiled from Kaugatz. You had no right to make a deal on my behalf.'

'I had every right, nephew. Legally speaking, I am your guardian.'

Lahnos laughed. 'My guardian? Tell me, uncle, how have you been guarding me these past few years? Be honest, I am nothing but a nuisance to you, and you want rid of me. Do I embarrass you?'

'You're starting to,' said Friel. 'Come on; there's a carriage waiting outside for us.'

'Are you going to dump me beyond the town limits?'

'No. I am taking you back to Fidalaimos.'

'Eat shit, uncle. I am never going back there. My home is in Kaugatz.'

'You mean that charming slum apartment – the one you share with a dozen other part-Bullan, including your girlfriend? What was her name – Reyn, was it?'

Lahnos clenched his fists. 'Have you been spying on me?'

Friel laughed. 'I spy on the entire island, nephew. Did you honestly think I was unaware of your lifestyle? Your name has cropped up in several crime reports these last few years, and I have intervened discreetly from time to time. Did you never wonder why your sentences seemed a little on the lenient side? Or why your apartment has never been raided by the town militia? You associate with known thieves, arsonists and prostitutes, and it is only a matter of time before you are found guilty of something that I will not be able to save you from.'

Lahnos stared at his uncle. 'I haven't seen you in four years.'

'I know, but I have seen you. Here is your choice. Come with me, and I will set you up in Fidalaimos. House, job, money – I can even arrange for Reyn to be sent out to join you, if that is something you would want. Or, I walk out of that door, and leave you here. The Bullan will ask me what has happened, and I will be forced to tell them the truth – that you refused to honour the deal that I have brokered on your behalf. The punishment for breaching a sentencing deal for Zamatans is one year in jail. Either way, you will not be spending the next year in Kaugatz. Is that understood?'

'You bastard.'

Friel shrugged. 'And I thought I was being generous.'

Lahnos chewed his lip. 'Shit; I have no choice, do I? I'll come with you. I want Reyn, but if any of the villagers in Fidalaimos even look at her the wrong way, then you know what will happen.'

'Do you always think with your fists, nephew? When are you going to start using your brain? You are nineteen years old – a year might seem like a long time, but believe me – it's not. One year from now, this island might look very different.'

Lahnos frowned. 'What's that supposed to mean?'

'Let's get into the carriage, and I'll tell you more,' Friel said. He gestured towards the door, and Lahnos saw the young woman again, whom he had almost forgotten was standing there.

'Who's the girl?' he said.

'This is Leona,' said Friel, 'and you will treat her with respect. She works for me as an advisor and secretary, and I rely upon her. Anything you say to me can be said in her presence.'

Lahnos glanced at Leona, but she kept her eyes lowered. He shrugged, and opened the door. They filed out, and a few Bullan watched them as they crossed the large reception hall where Lahnos had been brought the previous day. They stepped outside into the bright spring sunshine, and Friel gestured to a waiting carriage. A driver in militia uniform opened the side door, and Lahnos climbed in. Friel then helped Leona into the carriage, then he joined them and the driver closed the door.

'The journey shall take a few hours,' Friel said.

'I know,' said Lahnos.

Friel smiled. 'I was speaking to Leona. She has never been to Fidalaimos before.' He turned back to his assistant. 'We shall be taking two ferries – one to cross the Cyasarta, and then another across the Hansarta, and then we shall take the road north towards Wayston. Fidalaimos lies a couple of miles beyond that.'

Leona nodded.

'Doesn't she speak?' said Lahnos.

'Let's all be honest here,' said Friel. 'Honesty is good, yes?'

Lahnos shrugged.

'Leona hasn't knowingly met a human with horns before, and I think she is feeling a little uncomfortable.'

Leona glanced up, her eyes widening.

'Was that too honest?' said Friel. 'I thought it best to get it out into the open before we went any further.'

The carriage began to move, the two ponies pulling it through the wide streets of the Temple District of Igatz.

'Do I make you feel queasy, Leona?' said Lahnos.

She stared at him. 'Yes. No. A little bit. Sorry.'

Lahnos laughed. 'Back in the cells, a Gunstian called me an abomination, and told me that my mother was burning in an eternal fire for being a whore. I can live with a little bit queasy.'

Friel nodded. 'It is too much to hope that you ignored said Gunstian?'

'I strangled him into submission and then broke his nose.'

'Why?' said Friel.

'Isn't it obvious? My life changed when these horns grew. There were only two paths open to me – either I could file them off and pretend they didn't exist, and then live my entire life in fear of being discovered as part-Bullan; or I could accept who I was, and learn how to defend myself. I have to fight back, each and every time I am insulted. If I don't, then I will be ground into the dirt.' He glanced back at Leona. 'What would you have done if, at age fifteen, you woke up one morning to find horns growing out of your head?'

'I don't know,' she said.

'Look at me when you speak to me. Don't gaze at the carriage floor.'

Leona lifted her eyes and swallowed. 'How did you react? I mean, on that first morning?'

'I tried to hide them. I tried to pretend that they would go away if I ignored them. My brother was the first to notice.' Lahnos glanced out of the window at the elegant streets of Igatz, as an old bitterness awoke inside his chest. 'He stared at me like I was a monster. Then my grandmother got involved. She wanted to hide me away until she could file them off. It was at that exact moment, when she sat me down and described the kind of life she wanted me to lead that I knew I was going to run away.'

'What did your parents say?'

'My parents are dead.'

'Hence I am his legal guardian,' said Friel. 'Now, Lahnos, I want you to remember what I said about Leona in the guard post. I trust her completely, so do not take offence at what I am about to say.' He turned to the young woman. 'Lahnos's mother, my sister-in-law Netta, was murdered by a mob of Aucterian townsfolk because she was Gifted.'

Rage swept over Lahnos. 'That's none of her damn business! Why did you tell her that?'

'Because I wished her to know,' said Friel. 'Netta was suspected of killing an Aucterian farmer's crops, and the mob appeared in Fidalaimos that night. They dragged her from her home and beat her to death.'

Lahnos put his hands to his face and wept. For years, he had pushed the past from his mind, only for his irresponsible uncle to tell a complete stranger.

'Lahnos was seven years old at the time,' Friel said.

'That's terrible,' said Leona. 'I'm so sorry, Lahnos.'

'In order to seek justice, or perhaps revenge,' Friel went on, 'my elder brother Falken, Lahnos's father, travelled to Wayston, and was never seen again.'

'The bastards killed him, too,' said Lahnos.

'Possibly, though that has never been proved. Two Aucterian farmers were eventually arrested for the murder of Netta. The militia did nothing – it was left to a local detachment of Bullan soldiers to make the arrests. Both men are still in prison.'

'Are they?' said Lahnos.

'Yes. I doubt it will ease your pain, but I have occasionally used my influence to ensure that both have been refused early release. I will see to it that they serve their full sentences.'

'They deserve death.'

'If they had been Zamatan,' said Leona, 'they would have hanged.'

'I know,' said Friel. 'The laws of this island are unfair, and anyone who denies this basic fact is either a fool or a liar.' He lowered his voice. 'The question is – now that King Gahad is no more, what are we going to do about it?'

Lahnos looked at his uncle with contempt. 'You are a collaborator. You are a colonel in the militia – one of those filthy Zamatans who help the Dominion rule this island.'

'Yes,' said Friel; 'that is one of my guises. My position in the militia allows me to keep abreast of political developments, and to make contacts among various groups of interest. Answer me this, nephew – who would you rather be in control of Zamata? The Gunstian Empire, or the Dragon Dominion?'

'Neither,' Lahnos spat. 'The Gunstians would force us all to worship their god, and the Dominion is only interested in the island as a strategic base for their navy. Damn them both.'

Friel smiled. 'Good answer.'

Leona began to look agitated.

'Speak your mind,' said Friel. 'Don't sit there and squirm.'

Leona's eyes narrowed. 'I don't know if I should say what I'm thinking, sir.'

Friel sighed. 'Have I not been honest with you? Have I not bared some of my family secrets before you? Speak your mind.'

Leona took a breath. 'Can we trust Lahnos, sir?'

'I don't know,' said Friel.

'Then should you be speaking about treason in front of him?'

'I realise that I am taking a risk,' he said. 'However, momentous events are upon us. The death of King Gahad will bring disruption and chaos, but it will also bring opportunities. Lahnos is intelligent and, despite his rough ways, I know that he cares deeply about this island. I would doubt, for example, that he would go running to the Aucterians to denounce me as a traitor. In times of revolution, one must reach out and take a chance.'

'Revolution?' said Lahnos.

'Will you do your part, if the day comes?' his uncle said.

'And how am I supposed to do my part if you're taking me to Fidalaimos?'

Friel smiled. 'The fact that I wish to remove you from immediate danger does not imply that I see no role for you in the future. Well? Can I rely on you?'

'I don't know. I mean, I want the island to be free, but we're trapped between the two mightiest powers on Athumia. And would a revolution make any difference to people like me or Reyn? The Zamatans would still despise us. You talk about trust, but Reyn is the only person I trust.'

Friel nodded. 'Let us travel in silence for a while,' he said. 'I wish to think, and I advise you both to do the same.'

The colonel closed his eyes and leaned back against the carriage seat. Lahnos and Leona glanced at each other for a brief moment, then both looked away. Lahnos gazed out of the window. They were passing the enormous Naval Base of Handshore, where the great Northern Fleet of the Dominion was stationed. Long rows of shipyards and dry docks sat next to endless squat buildings, while the vast harbour held dozens of warships and supply vessels. Further out into the waters of the Cyasarta were more ships, all anchored in the calm bay. Were it not for its excellent harbours and strategic location, no one would care about the tiny island of Zamata. The idiot Aucterians insisted upon calling it the Serpent Isle, but no Zamatan ever named it that. What would happen if the huge fleet ever left the island? It seemed clear to Lahnos that the Gunstians would arrive if the Dominion forces evacuated, and that would make the lives of the Zamatans even worse. The Gunstians viewed the part-Bullan as vile demons, and all would be burned at the stake.

The main road branched, and the carriage took the wide street that ran for a mile towards the ferry port that sat halfway between Handshore and Atzoun – the same ferry port where Lahnos and Reyn had arrived in Igatz the previous morning.

His thoughts went to his mother. Lahnos's memories of his parents were vague and fleeting, but he remembered her smile. Of his father, his primary recollections came from the desperate period following his mother's death, when the village had been plunged into fear and shock. His father had been angry. No. His father had been more than angry; he had been transformed into the living embodiment of an all-consuming but impotent rage. His five children had been scared of him; too scared to say anything in his presence, and a guilty part of the seven-year-old Lahnos had felt relief when his father had left the house one day never to return. That relief, however, had soon turned to sorrow, as the five children were taken in by their grandmother, and the aunts and uncles who lived in the village. The siblings had all still lived in Fidalaimos, but in separate houses, and nothing had ever been the same. Lahnos had gone to his grandmother's home, a rough cottage on the edge of the village, where he had helped her each day with the housework, and with the chores required on the small farm run by the Laimos family. The only missing uncle had been Friel, who had already broken away from the village to make a new life for himself in the centre of the island.

The carriage slowed as it reached the ferry terminal. They joined a queue of other carriages and wagons, and waited for the next boat to arrive. When it docked, the driver pulled on the reins, and the ponies hauled the carriage up a ramp and onto the wide deck of the vessel. Sailors came by, securing each vehicle in place with ropes, and the boat got underway, the wind filling the sails.

Lahnos noticed Leona gazing out of the same window at the view of the Cyasarta.

'Are you from Kaugatz?' he said.

She nodded.

'Were you born there?'

'Yes.'

'How did you end up with my uncle?'

'I'd rather not say.'

Lahnos shook his head. 'Fine. You seem to know everything about me, but you won't divulge your own secrets. You don't trust me, do you?'

'I believe trust has to be earned.'

'And I haven't earned it?'

'No.'

Lahnos turned away from her. Friel stirred as the ferryboat reached the terminal in Kaugatz. It was a different port from the one Lahnos and Reyn had departed from, and led into one of the two Aucterian enclaves within Kaugatz.

Friel tapped on the driver's window. 'Pull over by the fort when we get off the vessel, my good man.'

'Yes, sir,' said the driver.

'Why are we pulling over?' said Lahnos.

Friel smiled. 'Trust me.'

The boat docked, and the foot passengers disembarked, followed by the wheeled vehicles. Friel's driver guided the carriage down the ramp and onto dry land, then parked fifty yards away, by the side of a small Dominion fortress manned by Bullan soldiers. They waited a few moments, then a postern gate in the side of the fortress opened, and two soldiers emerged, a frightened-looking young woman wearing a headscarf walking between them. Friel opened the carriage door, and signalled to them.

'Here she is, Colonel Laimos,' said one of the soldiers.

'Thank you, Corporal Ngaji Dorsa,' said Friel.

Lahnos gasped as he stared at the young woman.

'Lahnos?' she said.

'Reyn?'

'Come on, miss,' grunted the Bullan corporal. 'Get into the carriage.'

Lahnos leaned out with a hand and pulled Reyn up. She sat down next to him as the door closed, and he held her close, and they kissed. Lahnos grinned at her.

'I heard you got twenty days,' Reyn said, as the carriage began to move off again. 'And then, this morning, Bullan soldiers arrived at our apartment and took me away. The others in the building thought we were being raided, and everyone was panicking. I was terrified when the soldiers called out my name.' She glanced at Friel and Leona, and her eyes narrowed at the sight of the colonel's uniform. 'Who are these people, Lahnos? What's happening?'

'Good morning, miss,' said Friel. 'I am Colonel Laimos, Lahnos's uncle, and this is my assistant, Miss Leona.'

Reyn narrowed her eyes. 'You have an uncle in the island militia, Lahnos?'

'Yes,' he said. 'Sorry I didn't tell you, but I was too embarrassed to admit it.'

Friel chuckled.

'And,' Lahnos went on, 'he made a deal with the Bullan to get me out of jail early, but it came at a cost. I'm being exiled from Kaugatz and

Igatz for a year. Wait, Reyn – before you say anything, just listen to me for a minute. I have to go back to my old village, and I want you to come with me. If you'd rather stay in Kaugatz, then I'll be disappointed – more than disappointed – but I'll understand. It's not fair to drag you out into the countryside if you don't want to come. And, I had no idea that my uncle had arranged for you to be here when we got off the ferry.'

Reyn said nothing, her gaze flitting between Lahnos and Friel.

'If you would prefer, miss,' said Friel, 'I can halt the carriage and let you out before we reach the next ferry terminal.'

'Where would we live?' she said.

'I have a number of properties in and around Fidalaimos,' said Friel. 'I could find you one in an out-of-the-way location.'

'Why would we want to remain out-of-the-way?' said Lahnos.

Friel smiled. 'Not every person who is part-Bullan wishes to parade that fact, nephew. I am merely offering Reyn a range of options.'

Reyn's eyes darkened. 'How does he know that I'm...? Did you tell him about me, Lahnos?'

'I told him nothing,' said Lahnos. 'My uncle has been spying on us.'

'I have been looking out for you,' said Friel. 'There is a difference. Should I have pretended that you didn't exist? What kind of uncle would that make me? At the same time, I stayed out of your lives, and didn't interfere with the choices you made. Unfortunately, Miss Reyn, my nephew is now known to both the Bullan soldiery and the island militia. If I hadn't acted this morning, then there is a good chance he would have been imprisoned for a far longer period than twenty days.'

'If, for some reason, I don't like it in Fidalaimos,' Reyn said, 'am I free to leave?'

'Of course!' said Friel. 'You are not a hostage or a prisoner. Lahnos is also free to leave any time he wishes, so long as he does not enter Kaugatz or Igatz. Personally, though, I hope you will both stay in the village.'

Reyn glanced out of the window then nodded. 'I'll try it.'

'Thanks,' said Lahnos.

Reyn turned to Leona. 'Is she part-Bullan, too?'

Leona's eyes narrowed.

'Clearly not,' said Reyn. 'Does she speak?'

Lahnos laughed. 'Not much.'

They boarded another ferry at the western tip of Kaugatz and sailed across the clear waters of the Hansarta, where the carriage took the main road north. The closer they got to Wayston, the more Lahnos began to feel a knot of dread and anxiety form in the pit of his stomach. They passed the wide, open fields of wheat, and travelled through several small villages and townships, as the huge black bulk of Mount Medamuna loomed in front of them. The main road turned east in the centre of Wayston, and the carriage diverted up a small track that led north, where it began to climb the slopes of the mountain. They passed the small Aucterian settlement of Backwater, where the murderers of Lahnos's mother had lived, but no one in the carriage mentioned the fact. Friel slept for most of the way, or at least pretended to, and Lahnos felt uncomfortable talking too much in front of Leona, so he sat in silence, holding on to Reyn's hand. The track became rutted and uneven for the last mile's ascent, with vineyards, and groves of olives and citrus fruits on either side.

'Nothing's changed,' said Lahnos. 'This is exactly how I remember it all.'

Friel opened his eyes, then tapped on the driver's window. 'Take the next left, if you would.'

The driver nodded, and steered the ponies on to another rough track.

'We aren't going to the village?' said Lahnos.

'Not yet,' said his uncle. 'For tonight, we shall stay in a little cottage of mine. I think your grandmother and siblings will require some warning before you make your appearance in Fidalaimos.'

The carriage ascended a slope through a forested glade, and stopped in front of a large stone mansion set into the southern flank of the mountain. It was wide and palatial, with verandas and large shuttered windows. Orange and lemon trees flanked the house and its garden, and their branches were thick with scented blossom.

'You call this a cottage?' said Reyn.

Friel smiled. 'Indeed.'

'Does grandmother know about this?' said Lahnos.

'None of the family know that I own this particular abode,' said Friel. 'I keep it maintained, but I confess that I haven't stayed here in quite some time. Not since I was married, in fact.'

'Where's your wife?' said Reyn.

'She walked out on me some time ago,' said Friel. 'For some reason, she disapproved of me keeping mistresses.'

Reyn snorted.

Friel laughed. 'I recall her making a similar sound when I tried to explain myself.'

The driver dismounted and opened the side door. Friel stepped down on to the dry, dusty ground, then he assisted Leona to descend. Lahnos gazed out at the mansion, then joined them. He held out a hand for Reyn, and she took it.

'What a view,' said Leona, staring to the south-east. 'You can see the whole island from up here.'

The others turned, and they all stood in silence as they took in the sight of Zamata spread out before them. Farms and fields were laid out across the land to the south, which was dominated by the great mountain of Hodzulat, a peak almost as high as that of Mount Medamuna. The waters of the Hansarta and Cyasarta inlets were shimmering in the afternoon sunshine, and Lahnos could make out the gleaming white marble bulk of the dragon palace in Igatz.

'Look,' said Reyn; 'the Temple of the Undying Serpent. I can see its tower from here.' She glanced up at Lahnos. 'Yesterday, we were up there, and now we are here.'

'I'm glad you approve of the view,' said Friel. 'Now, let's get you settled in.'

CHAPTER 5
NEGLECT

Igatz, Serpent Isle – 25th Arginch 1588

'Tomorrow,' said Lieutenant Travers, as he and Cisca walked along one of the avenues of the palace gardens, 'I will take you shopping for more suitable clothes. You must be burning up in that dress uniform.'

Cisca smiled. 'Considering that my luggage is still on board the dragon carrier, I'm grateful that you managed to find me anything to wear.'

'Any news of your departure?'

'None so far. The summons from Inopei was very clear, though. The rest of the Royal Family expects the others to return to the capital as soon as they can.'

They stopped in the shade of a cypress tree, and Cisca gazed out over the waters of the bay. The huge dragon carrier had remained anchored a few hundred yards from shore, and supply boats were shuttling back and forth, re-stocking the ship for its return voyage across the ocean.

'I confess that I am not looking forward to the trip back,' she said.

He smiled. 'While I would do almost anything to get back on a ship. What's the point of being in the navy if I'm based on land all the time?'

'It isn't the ship that worries me; it's being back under Lord Noxon's authority.'

'I'm not envious of that aspect,' he said. 'I don't mind the dragons being in charge, but I prefer them as distant rulers, worshipped from afar.'

They turned, and came face to face with two dragons. One was a huge adult male with green scales, while the other had white and silver scales, and was a child dragon, small enough to sit beneath the branches of the tree.

'You can worship me from here, human,' said the green dragon. 'It makes no difference to me.'

'My Lord Meer Mon Adal,' said Travers, bowing low; 'I merely meant that the awe I feel in close proximity to your greatness can sometimes be overwhelming.'

The green dragon laughed. 'And what about you, woman?'

'Me, my lord?' said Cisca, her stomach muscles tightening.

'Yes, you,' said the dragon. 'Do you have a complaint you wish to make about Lord Noxon? You are one of his officer-assistants, are you not? Are you unhappy in his service?'

'No, my lord,' said Cisca, keeping her eyes lowered. 'It is a great honour to serve his lordship.'

'Lord Noxon is rude,' said the child dragon. 'I don't like him, either.'

'Hush, little Kheran,' said Meer. 'Dragons never insult their own kind in front of humans. What would your noble mother say if she heard you speak like that? The Blessed Governor has enough to worry about without her son spreading gossip.'

The young dragon glanced away, though Cisca couldn't tell if it was in shame or defiance.

'What is your name, woman?' Meer went on, his green scales shining in the bright sunlight.

'Lieutenant Cisca, my lord,' she said.

'Perhaps I shall see what Lord Noxon has to say about your comments,' said Meer. 'I am sure he would be interested to know that one of his lowly assistants holds him in contempt.'

'My lord, I... Please, I did not wish to cause offence.'

Meer laughed again. 'Look at her tremble, little Kheran. This can be your lesson for today: that every human, no matter how they appear on the outside, is weak and feeble on the inside. This is why we rule, and they serve. Are you listening, little Kheran?'

'Yes, Lord Meer,' said the young dragon.

'Good,' said Meer. 'Off with you, humans. I am sure there must be some work that needs doing.'

Travers and Cisca bowed low, then hurried away down a gravel path.

'I don't know how you do it,' said Travers, as soon as they were out of earshot of the dragons. 'For someone in the Dragon Corps, you seem to have a real talent for annoying them.'

'Perhaps I should ask for a transfer when I get back to Inopei,' she said. 'If Lord Meer tells Lord Noxon what I said, then he could make my life unbearable in the capital.'

Travers laughed.

'It's not funny,' she said.

'Sorry.'

A shadow flickered overhead, and Cisca glanced up to see the white body and purple wings of the island's Governor, the Blessed Lady Tirna, as she flew above the palace. She had disappeared for several hours after learning the news about her father's death, and had barely left the confines of the palace since. Cisca watched as the dragon soared out over the waters of the bay, before circling a few times above the huge dragon carrier.

'I wonder what she's doing?' said Cisca.

'Presumably, she's discovering how comfortable her voyage to Inopei is likely to be,' said Travers. 'Those carriers can hold up to four dragons, yes?'

'That's right; five at a squeeze.'

'There are six dragons currently on the Serpent Isle,' Travers went on, 'which means that not all of them will be departing.'

'Of course they won't all be departing,' said Cisca. 'The Dominion would never leave the island unprotected.'

Travers gave her a wry smile. 'No? I had wondered if perhaps the orders from Inopei had included an instruction to evacuate the Serpent Isle.'

'Are you mad?' she said. 'Why would the Dominion even consider such a course of action?'

'The expense of it all, for one thing,' said Travers. 'How much do you think it costs to keep the entire Northern Fleet based here? The Serpent Isle is a tremendous drain on Dominion resources, and what does it receive in return for its investment? A lump of rock in the middle of the ocean inhabited by surly natives.'

'The island is a strategic asset. It's far too valuable to give up.'

'It is only valuable for two reasons. The first is if we intend to invade Gunst again – then the island would be required as a staging post. The second is to prevent a Gunstian invasion of the East.' He raised an eyebrow. 'Does such a prospect sound even remotely likely? The Gunstians have only a handful of small vessels that can cross the ocean, and any that made it as far as Aucteran would be obliterated by our defences.'

'King Gahad made a personal pledge to always protect the Serpent Isle.'

'Yes, but our beloved monarch is dead. Who knows what his twenty-one children will decide to do; assuming of course that they are capable of coming to a joint decision. As far as I can see, the present situation is the least satisfactory from a Dominion point of view. We should either get the third invasion of Gunst over with, or we should pack up and leave.'

'You say the most outrageous things,' she said. 'The purpose of the Dominion is to bring peace and prosperity to the entire world, and Gunst is the only part of Athumia that remains hostile to our rule. Why would we give up?'

'Then you think a new invasion of Gunst is the more likely outcome?'

'I'm not saying that.'

'That's what the evidence points to. If the dragons end up blaming

Gunst for King Gahad's death, then that will be a signal that they are preparing a new invasion. A righteous war of revenge to conquer Gunst and annihilate the last of Theodora's Gifted.'

Cisca shook her head as they reached the side of the main palace building. 'You sound a little unhinged at times, Travers. Perhaps you have spent too long on this island.'

He smiled. 'Perhaps you are right.'

'I shall go to my room,' she said, 'to freshen up, and to avoid bumping into Lord Noxon.'

'Remember – don't leave the palace grounds without me.'

'I wouldn't dream of it.'

She turned and entered the cool interior of the palace. Most passageways were designed for dragons, with high vaulted ceilings, and tall stained glass windows to allow in some of the daylight. The palaces within the Dominion capital on Inopei were among the largest buildings in the world – with room to house over two hundred dragons – and, despite having dwelt in Nom Karta for two years, Cisca had only become familiar with a small number of the palaces there. Compared to them, the dragon palace in Igatz seemed tiny. She turned into a human-sized service corridor, and ascended a flight of narrow stairs to reach her quarters. Her room was cramped and windowless, which seemed a tragedy considering the beautiful views on offer overlooking the Cyasarta. She unlocked her door and entered, then she lit a small oil lamp to provide a modicum of illumination. She went over her confrontation with Lord Meer as she stripped off the dress uniform. The blouse was sticking to her back with perspiration, and she grimaced as she peeled it from her skin. She had brought a few loose dresses and more comfortable uniforms with her on the voyage, but they were all in her cabin on the dragon carrier, and the only clean thing she had left to wear was another dress uniform that Travers had borrowed from the palace laundry.

She sat on the bed, as misery threatened to overwhelm her. She felt homesick, but not for Nom Karta. The capital of the Dominion was a dragon city, and she had never considered it to be her home. No, it was

Naeth she missed – the familiar streets and houses of the great harbour city on the coast of Aucteran; the smells, the sights, and the constant noise. Her neighbourhood had been a poor one, and the apartment block where she had lived had been shared by a dozen other families, where everyone knew each other. They had all been so proud of her when she had been accepted as an officer in the Dragon Corps. An officer! Such a thing was scarcely to be conceived. Many in her neighbourhood had become soldiers or sailors, but Cisca had been the first officer that anyone could remember. Her parents had worked themselves into poverty to pay for her education, and yet all she wanted to do was go home. How could she ever tell them about her doubts; that she might have made the biggest mistake of her life? The Dragon Corps was full of the children of aristocrats and landowners – the sons and daughters of the rich – and they had perceived her lowly background from the moment she had opened her mouth on her first day of officer training. And now, her career was Lord Meer's to decide. If he told Lord Noxon what she had said, then her future prospects looked bleak.

Someone tapped on her door.

She pulled on a dressing gown and stood, then opened the door an inch.

'Yes?' she said.

A palace courtier bowed. 'All officers are required to attend the audience chamber immediately, ma'am,' he said. 'Her Blessed Lady, Governor Tirna Min Gahad wishes to make an address.'

'I'll be as quick as I can,' Cisca said.

The courtier bowed again, then hurried away. Cisca closed the door, sighed, then began pulling on the clean dress uniform.

Ten minutes later, Cisca was approaching the vast audience chamber in the heart of the palace. It was circular, with a domed marble ceiling that had been pierced with a dozen skylights to let in the sunshine. In the centre of the smooth polished floor was a raised platform, where Lady Tirna was standing, her purple wings folded against the scales of her white body. Five other dragons were arrayed to her right, including Kheran, the young son of the Governor, along with Lords Meer and Noxon. To the Governor's left, dozens of humans in uniform were standing with their heads bowed, while a hundred Bullan soldiers stood guard by the four large entrances to the chamber. Cisca joined a small group of junior naval officers as they made their way into the hall, then she found a place to stand at the rear of the waiting humans.

'Subjects of the Dominion,' Lady Tirna said, her clear voice filling the chamber, 'the grievous news that reached us two days ago has torn my heart asunder and, while I desire nothing more than to mourn the loss of my great and beloved father, I must also attend to my duties as a member of the Royal Family. Listen now to my pronouncements. I shall be departing the Serpent Isle upon this evening's tide.'

The dragon paused for a moment as an audible gasp came from the humans present in the hall. Cisca's eyes widened. That evening? She would be back on board the dragon carrier that evening?

'Speed is essential,' Tirna went on; 'for the fate of Athumia hangs in the balance. It is a forty-four-day voyage to Nom Karta, where the other members of my illustrious family await my presence, and every moment spent here upon the Serpent Isle only prolongs the uncertainty that plagues our beloved Dominion. Accompanying me on the voyage will be my nephew Lord Noxon Mon Konran, my brother's son; and Lady Gilda Min Gilt, the daughter of my sister. As grandchildren of the mighty King Gahad, their presence in Inopei shall also be required. The other dragons shall remain here to defend the island and to maintain its good governance.'

Cisca swallowed. If Lord Noxon was returning, then so would she. A tight knot of worry formed, as she imagined forty-four days of Noxon scowling at her.

'My esteemed mate, Lord Rufus Mon Rafa,' Tirna went on, 'shall assume command of the Serpent Isle in my absence, and Lord Meer Mon Adal will assist him. Together, they shall care for my infant son, and await my return – for return I shall, once the future of the Dominion has been assured. Look for me when autumn comes, when the winds shall bear me back across the vast ocean from Inopei.' She turned to her left. 'Humans, you are dismissed, so that you can prepare what is needed for this evening's voyage. Go. Some of you I shall see on the dragon carrier, while others I shall see again upon my return.'

The humans bowed low, then exited the great hall. Travers caught sight of Cisca as she walked through one of the four arched entrances, then he shrugged and strode away. Cisca frowned, and hurried after him.

'Is that all I get?' she said. 'A shrug? Were you not intending to say goodbye?'

'You're leaving in a few hours,' he said, 'and I find goodbyes to be awkward and pointless.'

'Oh. I thought...'

'You thought what, Lieutenant Cisca?'

'Never mind. Goodbye.'

She turned and walked away, before her anger prompted her to say something stupid. Travers had shadowed her for every moment she had spent in Igatz, and he wasn't even going to say goodbye? His companionship had been the only positive thing that had happened to her during her time on the island, but it had clearly meant nothing to him. She emerged from the interior of the building into the blazing sunshine of the gardens. To her left was the path that led to the small jetty. She glanced at the beautiful gardens, then decided not to wait any longer. She would catch the next tender going to the dragon carrier, and shake the dust of the Serpent Isle from her boots. A dragon soared overhead, and she looked up to see Governor Tirna's niece, Lady Gilda Min Gilt, flying towards the carrier. Lord Noxon would no doubt soon be making the same short journey, and Cisca knew she needed to be back on board to attend to his needs. She walked along the path and joined a queue of other officers waiting by the stone jetty. A tender was making its way towards shore, and Cisca kept her eyes lowered, too annoyed to speak to any of her colleagues. With Travers having shadowed her every move, she had barely spoken to any of the other officers during her short stay, and she knew she should have made more of an effort.

The tender docked with the jetty, and a group of sailors began unloading a few crates and trunks from the open deck, as the officers waited to embark. The sailors piled up the cargo by the end of the jetty, then signalled for the officers to go on board. The queue began to move, and Cisca strode along with the others. She glanced at the pile of crates and trunks as she was about to step onto the gangway, and her eyes widened. Sitting among the pile was her own luggage from the dragon carrier, transported from the ship at last.

She rolled her eyes, and stepped out of the queue.

'Excuse me,' she said to a sailor, pointing at her trunk. 'My luggage is here. It needs to be sent back to the carrier.'

The sailor nodded, then consulted a document in his hands. 'Name?'

'Lieutenant Cisca of the Dragon Corps.'

The sailor's finger went down the list inscribed on to the document.

'No, ma'am,' he said. 'Your luggage was ordered to be brought ashore.'

'There must be some mistake,' she said. 'My luggage was supposed to arrive yesterday, but Lady Tirna Min Gahad has just announced that we are leaving on this evening's tide.'

A faint smile traced its way over the sailor's lips. 'There's been no mistake, ma'am.' He showed her the document. 'It says here that you're staying on the island.'

'What?'

She peered at the document, and saw her name and rank written about halfway down. To the right of her name was written one word – staying.

'I can arrange a couple of lads to help carry your things to the palace, ma'am,' the sailor said.

Cisca stared at him, too stunned to speak.

'Ma'am?'

'No. Leave it here for now. There must have been an administrative mix-up. Yes; a mix-up. I'm supposed to be on that boat.'

'There will be another tender along in an hour, ma'am. That should be long enough to sort it out. Now, if you don't mind, I am rather busy.'

'Of course,' she said. 'Thank you.'

She turned and walked back along the jetty, ignoring the glances from the other officers. The Bullan soldiers at the entrance to the palace gardens nodded at her as she made her way along the path, but her mind was too preoccupied for her to make a response. She needed to be on that damn ship. Otherwise... She slowed her pace a little. What if it hadn't been a mix-up? A surge of relief made its way through her at the thought. No mix-up meant that she wouldn't have to endure a long voyage under the glare of Lord Noxon and her superior officers; but it also meant that she would be stuck on the island for months to come.

She entered the palace and slowed her pace, conscious that her haste had caused her to start perspiring again. Courtiers, officer and servants were bustling through the palace hallways, all busy with the preparations for the Governor's departure. Cisca made her way towards the area of the palace set aside for Lord Noxon, but was stopped at a set of massive doors by two Bullan soldiers.

'Only authorised personnel can enter Lord Noxon's quarters, ma'am,' said one.

'I am authorised,' she said. 'I work for Lord Noxon. My name is Lieutenant Cisca.'

The soldiers looked sceptical, then one nodded.

'Wait here, ma'am,' he said, then he pushed open the doors, strode through, and re-closed them firmly behind him.

'If you work for Lord Noxon,' said the other soldier, 'why haven't we seen you here before?'

'Because he told me to stay away,' she said.

The other soldier emerged from the dragon's apartments, and shut the doors again behind him.

'Well?' said Cisca, feeling a little intimidated by the Bullan, but determined not to show it.

The soldier handed her a note.

'What's this?' she said.

'Why don't you read it, ma'am?' said the soldier.

She took the note and unfolded it. It was her severance papers, dismissing her from Lord Noxon's service for gross neglect of her duties. It had been signed by her superior officer in the Dragon Corps, and at the bottom was a command to report to Lord Rufus, the acting Governor, for further instructions.

'But... but...' she said, her mind spinning.

One of the Bullan grunted. 'The major who gave me that said you haven't once offered your services to Lord Noxon since you got here, ma'am. He said, and I'm quoting, that you were "spectacularly useless".'

'But Lord Noxon told me to stay away.'

The soldier shrugged.

'Do you know where Lord Rufus is?'

'His Blessed Lordship is still in the main audience chamber, ma'am.'

She lowered her eyes. 'Thank you.'

She trudged away, aware that the two Bullan were probably laughing at her humiliation. Gross neglect? Her military record would take years to recover from the damage, and any hopes of promotion out of her lowly status could be safely forgotten about. She made her way back to the great circular audience chamber, oblivious to all who passed her in the wide hallways. What would her parents say?

Lord Rufus Mon Rafa, a huge dragon with burnt-orange scales, was standing upon the central platform in the audience chamber, already taking the Governor's place before Lady Tirna had even departed the island. To his right stood Lord Meer, while little Kheran was standing awkwardly to his left. In front of the three dragons were over a hundred humans, all lining up to present their requests or reports to the new Governor of the Serpent Isle. Cisca joined the queue, and waited.

The minutes passed, and over an hour had gone by before Cisca took her place at the front of the queue.

'Kneel before the august Lord Rufus Mon Rafa, woman,' said Meer.

Cisca did as she was bid, keeping her eyes lowered.

'I know this one, my lord,' Meer said to Rufus. 'She has been dismissed from Lord Noxon's service for incompetence and impertinence.'

'Then why is she here?' said Rufus. 'What am I supposed to do with her?'

'We have been asked to find a role for her in the palace, my lord,' Meer said.

'I don't have time for this nonsense,' Rufus said. 'I have an island to run. Assign her to the kitchens, or to the laundry service.'

Kheran glanced up. 'I will take her. Can I have her, father?'

Rufus turned his long neck to glance down at his son. 'And why would you want her, son? Did you not hear Lord Meer? This woman is incompetent.'

'I feel sorry for her, father.'

Rufus and Meer shared a glance, then the acting Governor turned back to Kheran.

'Very well, son,' he said. 'You may have her.' He looked down at Cisca. 'You there – report to my son's quarters at dawn tomorrow. If you fail in your duties again, I will pick you up and drop you into the ocean. Dismissed.'

'Yes, my lord. Thank you, my lord.'

Cisca stood, then backed away, her gaze lowered, and the next petitioner took her place at the front of the queue. Cisca raised her eyes a little, and saw the child dragon smiling at her. She tried to smile back, but the effort seemed beyond her. She wanted to weep. Her career was in ruins, and now she was going to have to act as a babysitter to a child who felt nothing but pity for her. And, if he tired of her, she would have to face the wrath of his father.

She turned as she left the audience chamber, and strode in the direction of the gardens. What did child dragons like to do to pass the time, she wondered. She rounded a corner, and frowned. Lieutenant Travers was chatting to a couple of other naval officers, with his back to her. She considered ignoring him, but the idea of catching him off-balance was too tempting.

She strode up behind him, and coughed gently.

Travers broke off his conversation and turned. He raised an eyebrow. 'You still here? See, I told you goodbyes were awkward.'

'It turns out that you're not getting rid of me that easily,' she said. 'I will not be leaving with this evening's tide.'

Travers narrowed his eyes, then smiled. He glanced at his erstwhile companions. 'I'll catch up with you all later,' he said.

The naval officers took the hint, nodded, and then they walked off, leaving Travers alone in the hallway with Cisca.

'What happened?' he said.

'I was dismissed by Lord Noxon for gross neglect, and now I have been assigned to assist Lord Kheran.'

He smiled. 'You're stuck on the island?'

'It's not funny.'

Travers started to laugh. 'That,' he said, 'is a matter of opinion.'

CHAPTER 6
THE GIFT OF TRUTH

Fidalaimos, Serpent Isle – 26th Arginch 1588

'We had nothing to do with it,' said the hooded man, his Gunstian accent grating on Leona's ears. 'I swear it.'

Colonel Laimos nodded, then he took a sip from his tankard. A serving girl with a loaded tray passed by, and he waited until she had moved away from the tavern booth.

'Perhaps,' Friel said, 'your superiors decided to keep you ignorant of their actions.'

The hooded Gunstian shrugged. 'Perhaps. But, if that were the case, then we would still have heard something – not from them, but from our contacts in the Imperial Gunstian Fleet.'

'How so?' said Friel.

The hooded man leaned in closer. 'If Gunst had been responsible for the death of the demon-king Gahad, then the fleet would be standing by, ready to re-conquer this island. However, I happen to know for a fact that the fleet is a thousand miles away, hunting Irlanian pirates along the southern coastline of Tannum. Why would they be there, Colonel Laimos, if we had killed Gahad?' He drained his tankard. 'Whoever did the deed has my respect, but it wasn't us.'

'My intelligence states that whoever did it was Gifted.'

'That seems logical,' said the Gunstian. 'Could any normal human have slain the mightiest demon on Athumia? It's possible that it was a rogue Gunstian agent, acting without official orders, or maybe the Dominion didn't manage to slaughter every Gifted in the East after all.'

'No, they were quite thorough.'

'Beasts,' muttered the Gunstian. 'Regardless, I am expecting Gunst to get the blame. We are a convenient scapegoat for all of the Dominion's problems. Now, I have some news for you, Laimos.'

'Yes?'

'The demon-governor has gone.'

Friel blinked, then nodded. 'When?'

'Tirna Min Gahad departed the island last night, taking two other winged demons with her. They boarded their dragon-ship and have sailed away.'

'Already? That was quick.'

'The Dominion is in turmoil. They're panicking. This is our chance, Laimos. A boat shall be arriving soon, with weapons and money. The fleet might be a thousand miles away, but we are not completely unprepared. Certain contingency plans have been formulated, in case of unforeseen circumstances. I need you to be at the coastline north of Mount Medamuna, at the usual cove, to greet the boat, and to hide its cargo.'

'When will it arrive?'

'A few nights from now. I will let you know nearer the time. Do you plan on staying in Fidalaimos for a while?'

'No.'

'You might want to consider changing your plans.'

'I have another trusted contact here who can meet the ship,' Friel said. 'I need to return to Igatz.'

'Another trusted contact?' said the Gunstian. 'Who?'

Friel chuckled. 'Come now; you don't expect me to answer that, do you? Send word to me when you know the boat's arrival time and date, and my contact will be there.'

The Gunstian said nothing, his hood covering his features, then he slid a bag of gold across the table.

'You are an expensive asset, Colonel Laimos,' he said. 'You had better be worth every penny.'

Friel swept the bag beneath the folds of his overcoat and stood. He glanced at Leona. She got to her feet, and they walked out of the shadows of the tavern, and into the bright sunlight of a spring morning. Their carriage was parked next to a row of little stone cottages a hundred yards along the village street, but Friel turned, and they took another lane.

'I feel like walking today,' he said. 'Did you detect any lies?'

'No, sir,' Leona said. 'He believes everything he said to be true.'

Friel raised an eyebrow. 'Everything? That makes a pleasant change. He usually throws in a few little lies to keep me on my toes. Perhaps the death of Gahad has truly surprised them.'

'But if they didn't know, sir, then how could they have a boat ready to come here with weapons and money?'

'The eastern coastline of the Gunstian Empire lies two hundred and fifty miles from Zamata, Leona. That's a three-day voyage, and I happen to know that the Gunstian agents based upon the island have several boats hidden among the caves north of Medamuna. If one of them set sail as soon as they heard the news about Gahad, then that boat will already be berthed in one of the military bases along the Gunstian coast, being loaded with supplies.' He frowned. 'That means it would get back here in three or four days from now.'

Leona gazed at the road as they walked along the street. 'Can I ask another question, sir?'

'You don't need to ask permission.'

'Sorry, sir. What will the Gunstians want us to do with a boatload of weapons?'

'They will expect us to arm the local islanders, Leona; starting with the Gunstians who dwell here, and then any Zamatan who wishes to overthrow the rule of the Dominion.'

'And what will they expect in return?'

He smiled. 'Now we get to the heart of the matter. I won't answer that question just yet. I want to take you to meet someone.'

'Who, sir?'

'My trusted contact, Leona – who else?'

'Oh. I, uh, thought, sir...'

'Yes? What did you think?'

'I thought you were referring to Lahnos when you said that, sir.'

Friel laughed. 'Lahnos? My nephew? No, Leona. Lahnos has potential, and I have a role in mind for him, but he has not yet reached the status of trusted contact. Do you think Lahnos would be able to resist telling the Gunstian sailors what he thought of them? And what would the sailors make of his horns?'

'I was reading a book on Colonial Law last night, sir.'

'That was an abrupt change-of-subject. Did you glean anything of interest from its pages?'

'Yes. I learned that there is no such thing as an early release from prison contingent upon the accused being exiled from a particular region of the island.'

'It appears that you have caught me out. Well done; I wondered if you would.'

'Why did I not sense you lying when you spoke to your nephew?'

'I was careful with my words, Leona. I did not actually speak any lies. I led Lahnos to believe something and he accepted it without asking any plain and straightforward questions. I did, of course, have to bribe the Bullan soldiers on duty, but as they were more than keen to see Lahnos sent away, they were happy to play along with my little ruse.'

'But why? Why would you want Lahnos removed from Kaugatz?'

'Because I need him for something, and if he had remained in Kaugatz, then it is indeed likely that he would have got himself into trouble again before too long.'

'What do you need him for, sir?'

'There are certain questions that I shall refrain from answering, Leona, and that is one of them.'

She halted on the road, as she realised they had walked beyond the boundaries of the small village. On either side of the track, orange groves spread out into the distance, and their scent filled the air.

'Where are we going?' she said.

'Once,' Friel said, 'there were seven great serpent monasteries upon Zamata.'

'Did you bring me out here to give me a history lesson, sir?'

'One of the greatest of those monasteries, and the largest, was situated a mere mile from where the village of Fidalaimos now stands.'

'Gatzoun Medamuna, the monastery to which you are referring, sir, was destroyed by Gunstian raiders over nine hundred years ago.'

'Indeed it was, and its ruins are extensive. I often played there in my youth, and got to know them quite well. It is a fine place to hide something, or someone. Look at me, Leona – I am about to tell you a secret. When you hear it, you will only be the fourth person on Athumia who knows it. Telling you makes me vulnerable to blackmail, and you could, if you wished, destroy me with this knowledge.'

'I already know enough to destroy you, sir. I know you take secret payments from both the Gunstians and the Dominion, and I have often seen you bribe soldiers and officials.'

'Yes, but this secret is more personal. Have you heard of a Zamatan rebel and criminal by the name of Bauchlie?'

'Yes, sir. He is wanted for murder, arson, sabotage and various other crimes, along with treason. I also know that he is believed to be dead.' She narrowed her eyes. 'Is this your trusted contact? Have you been hiding a notorious rebel terrorist in the ruins of the monastery?'

Friel smiled. 'No. I have been hiding my son.'

Leona's mouth opened, but no sound came out.

'I can tell what you're thinking,' Friel said. 'Surely I must be too young to have fathered Bauchlie?'

'That wasn't what I was thinking, sir, but yes; you are too young. I thought Bauchlie was in his late twenties.'

'He is. His mother and I were only sixteen when he was born. We never married, and we kept my role a secret. It was his mother's idea; at the time I would have been happy for everyone to have known, but she didn't agree. Bauchlie was raised by her, but I never missed a monthly payment to help them. I did what I could, or should I say I did as much as she would allow me to do.'

'But Bauchlie is a murderer, sir.'

Friel said nothing for a moment, his eyes darkening.

'Sir?'

'Is it murder, if the death occurs in warfare?'

'We are not at war, sir.'

'Perhaps we are. I would define the rule of Zamata by the Dominion as an armed occupation. Bauchlie would agree. I play my part, and he plays his.'

'Do you condone what he has done? Wait, if he is your trusted contact, does that mean he takes your orders? Did you order him to carry out those murders and assassinations?'

'Would you be upset if I said yes?'

'I thought I knew you.'

'You do know me, Leona. Apart from Bauchlie and his mother, you know me better than anyone alive. Bringing you here to Fidalaimos was my way of showing you even more of who I am. I need you, Leona, and not just for the Gift of Truth that you possess. You anchor me.'

Leona said nothing.

'Perhaps you should go back to my cottage for now,' Friel said. 'I can deal with Bauchlie on my own. Take the carriage. Rest. But say nothing to Lahnos or anyone else about what you have learned today.'

Leona stared at him as he turned and continued up the track. She stood there until he had disappeared round a gentle curve, hidden by the orange groves. Her thoughts went to some of the murders carried out by his son. A naval officer and his wife – cut down on the streets of Igatz with crossbow bolts. Three young Aucterian sailors, ambushed on their way home after a night in a tavern. An aristocratic lady who had just purchased an enormous tract of land on Zamata, murdered in her own bed, her throat slit. Then there was the fire that had burned down a Dominion arms depot on the outskirts of Kaugatz, killing four men trapped inside. She felt sick, and used. Now that she knew the truth, she was an accomplice. With a few words, Colonel Laimos had turned her into a criminal. Her duty was to report what he had told her to the local Bullan guard post in Wayston, but she knew she would never do so. Did the Colonel also know? What if he suspected that she might betray him? Maybe he would have his son murder her, too, if he thought she might turn him in to the authorities.

She turned, and walked back towards the village, her heart sore.

The journey back to what Friel called his 'cottage' was uneventful. A few villagers had glanced at her as she had made her way to the carriage, having seen her in the company of the locally-famous Colonel Laimos, but none had spoken to her. She was glad about that, as her tongue seemed frozen to the inside of her mouth.

The carriage dropped her off at the front gates of Friel's secluded mansion, and she entered through the main door, to the sound of laughter coming from a large room to her left. She walked into the room, and saw Lahnos and Reyn wrestling on one of the large couches. Reyn was wearing no shawl, and her stubby horns were visible amid her tousled brown hair; while her tail had come loose from her short skirt, and was swishing about behind her.

The laughter ceased as both looked up at Leona.

'Having a good stare, are you?' said Reyn.

'I didn't mean to interrupt. I'm sorry.'

Leona began to walk from the room, then she heard Reyn mutter *slut* under her breath. Leona halted, then turned.

'What did you call me?'

Reyn smiled. 'Nothing.'

Leona felt the tingle in the back of her head at Reyn's obvious lie.

'You called me a slut,' she said.

'Did I?' said Reyn.

'Why?' said Leona. 'Have I done something to offend you? I thought I had been polite. Why do you hate me?' Her eyes tightened, as her anger fought with a deep sense of injustice.

Lahnos glanced from Reyn to Leona. 'We don't hate you.'

'She does,' said Leona. 'Why else would she have called me that?'

Reyn shrugged. 'I'm only stating the obvious. Friel Laimos is old enough to be your father; aren't you ashamed? Are you the reason his wife left him?'

'No. I am not having an affair with the colonel. I work for him, but I am not sleeping with him. I have never slept with him, and he has never tried to sleep with me.'

Reyn snorted.

'I believe her,' said Lahnos.

'Are you taking her side?' said Reyn.

'No. I'm on your side, Reyn – always. But, I think you might have made a mistake.'

'Come on,' snapped Reyn. 'Really? Look at her, Lahnos. Why else would a middle-aged man drag her about everywhere he goes? They're joined at the hip.'

'I completely agree,' said Lahnos; 'but I still believe her.'

'Thank you,' said Leona.

'All right then,' said Reyn. 'Say she's telling the truth – then why does your uncle take her everywhere he goes?'

'She's not with him now.'

'Yeah, but look at her face. They must have had a fight. She's upset about something.'

'I'm not surprised she's upset, Reyn – you called her a slut.'

'She was already upset before I said that.'

'I think you should apologise to her.'

'I will, if she gives me one good reason – other than the obvious – why someone rich and powerful like Friel Laimos wants her by his side all the time.' She glanced at Leona. 'Well? I'm waiting.'

Leona glared at the young woman. 'It's a secret.'

Reyn laughed. 'She doesn't trust us.'

'She told me that trust has to be earned,' said Lahnos. 'Personally, I think we earned it when she found out about my parents, and from the fact that you are letting her see your horns and tail. Maybe Leona thinks that trust only goes one way.'

Leona narrowed her eyes. She knew that the colonel would be upset if she told them the truth, but she was still furious with him. She made a quick calculation in her head, then she strode across the wooden floor of the room and took a seat opposite Lahnos and Reyn.

'You're right,' she said. 'I know more about you than you do about me. But, before I tell you, you should know that the colonel will not be happy at what I am about to reveal to you. He doesn't want people to know what I do for him.'

'Tell him we forced it out of you,' said Lahnos. 'I can handle my uncle's anger.'

Leona took a breath. 'I have the Gift of Truth.'

Lahnos and Reyn stared at her.

'I am ready to hear your apology now,' Leona went on.

'Prove it,' said Reyn.

Leona shrugged. 'Fine. Tell me something, and I will tell you if it is a lie or the truth.'

Lahnos grinned. 'All right. Reyn was once arrested for slapping a militia soldier across the face.'

Leona smiled. 'True.'

'Hey!' said Reyn. 'I can also play this game. Lahnos once fell into the Cyasarta because he was so drunk he couldn't walk.'

Leona felt a tingle in her head. 'That was a lie.'

Reyn laughed. 'Yes, it was the Hansarta.'

'And that's true,' said Leona.

Lahnos nudged Reyn. 'We'd better be careful what we say around this one.'

'Shit,' said Reyn. 'No wonder Colonel Laimos keeps her close.' She glanced at Leona. 'I'm sorry. I shouldn't have called you what I did. I was wrong.'

'Thank you,' said Leona. 'If possible, try not to let on to the colonel that you know. You were right before – we did have a... disagreement. He sent me back here, but I can't tell you why. I'm not just burdened with being his truth-detector; I am also burdened with many of his secrets. What I told you was a secret about me, but I will never betray the colonel's trust. I hope you understand.'

'I had guessed that you were in his confidence yesterday in the carriage,' Lahnos said. 'Now it makes more sense.'

Leona nodded. 'What's it like having a tail, Reyn?'

'It depends,' she said. 'When I'm walking through the streets of Kaugatz, my tail is a constant source of embarrassment; something I must keep hidden at all costs. But, when I can be in a place where I don't have to hide it, like here, then I love it.'

'I love it, too,' said Lahnos. 'I love everything about you.'

'Even when I was being a bitch to Leona?'

'You made it right,' he said.

'You are not the first person to assume something sordid about my relationship with the colonel,' said Leona, 'and you won't be the last.'

'Let's walk into the village,' said Lahnos. 'I'm sick of being cooped up in this house. My uncle told me he would take me to see my grandmother, but he doesn't seem to be in any hurry.'

'Is that wise?' said Leona.

'If we do it,' said Reyn, 'I'm covering my head.'

'We should take the carriage,' said Leona, 'in case we need to leave in a hurry.'

Lahnos smiled as he glanced at the two young women. 'Be prepared,' he said. 'I intend to walk down the main street of the village with my magnificent horns on display. There may be violence.'

Leona swallowed.

Reyn arranged the shawl over her head and changed into a longer skirt, then they took the carriage into the village. The colonel's driver had looked a little wary, but had obeyed Leona's orders. He halted by one end of the main road through the village, and Leona asked that he remain close by.

'If you see us running,' said Reyn, as they stepped down to the ground, 'get ready to go.'

The driver glanced at Lahnos's horns, and frowned.

Lahnos stretched his arms, then rolled his shoulders. The sun was out, but there was a slight chill in the mountain air, and Leona shivered.

'Walk by either side of me,' said Lahnos to Reyn and Leona. 'If there's trouble, then run to the carriage.'

'Do we have to do this?' said Leona. 'It's not too late to go back to the cottage.'

Lahnos smiled. 'I lived in this village for fifteen years,' he said. 'I am not afraid.'

'But...'

'Sometimes Lahnos just has to do these things,' said Reyn.

'Let's go,' he said.

He strode off down the road, and the two women hurried after him. They passed the first house, and a face appeared at a narrow window. Leona took a breath, and tried to calm her nerves. What did she have to worry about? She didn't have horns or a tail. Next to her, Reyn's eyes were wide, but Lahnos was holding his head high, a defiant smile across his lips. A small group of villagers were chatting by the entrance to a butcher's shop, and they turned as Lahnos approached. They fell silent, their mouths falling open.

'Good afternoon,' said Lahnos. 'What a beautiful day.'

One of the older women put a hand to her mouth and gagged, while another started laughing nervously. On the other side of the street, two men emerged from the tavern where Leona and Friel had met the Gunstian agent, and both glared at Lahnos.

'Get out of our village, freak,' one shouted.

'This is my village,' said Lahnos, 'but you're welcome to try to make me leave.'

'Is that Lahnos Laimos?' cried an old man. 'Someone fetch his grandmother.'

Lahnos grinned at the old man. 'That's right; I am Lahnos Laimos.'

One of the men who had left the tavern picked up a stone, and threw it at Lahnos. It glanced off his arm, and struck Reyn on the back. Lahnos came to a halt, turned, and clenched his fists.

'Did you just hit my girl with a stone, you coward?' he said.

'It was meant for you, beast!' cried the man.

Lahnos raced across the street and charged into the two men. One jumped back a step in surprise, and Lahnos punched the other in the face. Lahnos's fists moved quickly, and he struck the man again, doubling him over. Lahnos brought his knee up, and it cracked off the man's chin, and he toppled to the ground. The other man shrank backwards, and Lahnos laughed at him. A crowd was starting to grow in the village, and their anger was palpable. In the middle of the street, Leona edged closer to Reyn, as the rage-filled faces of the villagers surrounded them.

Lahnos pushed his way back to the two young women, and a rotten orange spattered across his back.

'You don't frighten me,' he cried. 'None of you frighten me. If any of you have the guts to face me, then do it. Or would you rather just throw things like cowards?'

'Shame!' someone cried.

'Shame?' said Lahnos. 'I am not the one who should be ashamed. I have nothing to be ashamed of. This is my village!'

Leona noticed several men approaching from their right armed with makeshift weapons – axes, wooden poles, and kitchen knives, and the crowd parted to let them through.

'You'd best be leaving, boy,' said one, 'or blood will be spilled.'

'It'll be your blood,' spat Lahnos, his fists raised.

'Everyone, stop – please!' cried Leona, but her voice was lost amid the anger in the street.

'What are you waiting for?' Lahnos shouted at the armed men. 'Come on!'

One of the men lunged forward with a long wooden pole, and Lahnos gripped the end of the weapon in his left hand. He pulled the pole towards him, then drove his right fist into the man's face, breaking his nose. The man screamed, and Lahnos ripped the pole from his grasp.

'Who's next?' he cried, as he hefted the pole in both hands.

An old woman barged her way into the centre of the crowd, and stepped between Lahnos and the men with weapons.

'Go home, all of you,' she said, her voice calm but firm. 'There will be no more fighting in my village.'

The crowd hesitated.

'Now,' the old woman cried. 'I will take care of this.'

The crowd began to edge away, then it dispersed, the villagers glaring at Lahnos as they cleared the street. A few helped the two men who had fallen get to their feet, and led them away.

'That's right,' said Lahnos. 'Keep walking.'

The old woman turned to face him. Her eyes flitted over Reyn and Leona, then went back to Lahnos.

'Trying to impress the girls, are you?' she said.

'Just reminding the village of who I am, grandmother.' He smiled. 'Did you miss me?'

The old woman said nothing for a moment, then she slapped him across the face.

CHAPTER 7
MEMORIES

Fidalaimos, Serpent Isle – 27th Arginch 1588

Lahnos opened his eyes and smiled. The small room where he had slept was exactly the same as he remembered it. Even his old broken toy dragon was sitting on a table where he had left it four years before. He swung his legs out of bed, and pulled on some clothes. Light was coming in through the worn window shutters, and Lahnos could hear the sounds of the farm where the rest of his family worked. Apart from Uncle Friel, of course. He wondered if his uncle had heard about the disturbance in the village the previous day. His grandmother hadn't mentioned Friel's name since Lahnos had arrived at her squat cottage on the edge of the settlement, but he wouldn't be surprised if Friel knew. He seemed to know everything. Lahnos smiled as he thought about the two men he had punched in the street. His knuckles were still sore, but that was nothing compared to the pain and shame the two men would be feeling.

His smile slipped, and he realised that he missed Reyn being around. He had become used to waking up by her side each morning, but his grandmother had refused to allow her to stay in the cottage, and she had gone back to Friel's place with Leona. It was probably for the best, he thought. No one had discovered Reyn's horns or tail, and she would want to keep it that way. He didn't mind that she lacked his sense of pride about being different – she had gone through a tougher time than he had – but he still hoped that one day they would be able to walk through Igatz hand-in-hand without her caring what anyone thought.

He picked up the wooden dragon. Its left wing had fallen off, and several of its talons were missing. He had been trying to fix the toy on the morning he had discovered that horns were starting to grow out of his head. He remembered it perfectly. He had been holding the toy in his right hand, and had then scratched his head with his left. He wondered how his mother would have reacted if she had been alive at the time. His grandmother had been certain about what course of action to take, but would his mother have agreed? He liked to believe that his mother would have accepted him for who he was, that she would have been proud of him, no matter what; but he would never know for sure.

He put down the toy and stood, keeping his head lowered so that his horns wouldn't hit the low ceiling. He took a breath, and opened the door. It led out directly into the cottage's main room, which was split into a living area with a hearth, and a small kitchen. He scanned the room for his grandmother, then saw his older brother sitting by the dining table.

'Karl,' he said.

His brother raised his eyes, his gaze going straight to the horns on Lahnos's head.

'How have you been?' said Lahnos.

'What do you want?' his brother said, a deep frown clouding his features.

'Some breakfast would be good,' Lahnos said. 'Was that what you meant?'

'You know what I meant.'

'Explain it to me.'

'Why are you here?' Karl said. 'Why did you come back to Fidalaimos? What do you want?'

'Uncle Friel brought me here. It wasn't my choice. My home is in Kaugatz.'

Karl hesitated. 'Uncle Friel brought you to the village?'

'That's right,' said Lahnos. He walked over to the table and sat down opposite his brother. 'How are the others?'

'Do you care?'

'Yes.'

'You ran away four years ago,' Karl said; 'and you haven't made any attempt to get in contact with me or our sisters, or our grandmother.'

'You know why I ran away. I remember telling you my reasons on the morning before I left. If I had stayed, then grandmother would have tried to file my horns off. And you would have helped her do it, Karl. Don't try to deny it.'

'I wasn't going to deny it. You should have let us file those damn things off. They're disgusting. You could have lived a normal life without them, but no. You had to play the martyr, and go running off to some slum in Kaugatz where you could live with the other freaks who look like you.'

Lahnos laughed. 'And you wonder why I haven't been in contact? If you're so disgusted by my horns you could always try to file them off now, brother. Why don't you try?'

'Because you've turned into a violent thug. I know what you did in the village yesterday.'

'The last time we fought, I was fourteen, and you were seventeen. You beat me. You burst my lip and gave me a black eye. And look at you now, Karl. You're shaking with anger. You want to hit me but you know that, this time, I would beat the shit out of you. If I was weaker than you, would you try to take my horns from me? Did you bring a file or a saw with you, in case you managed to catch me sleeping?'

Karl's left eye twitched. 'You have shamed this family.'

'You didn't answer my question. If you were stronger than me, would you take my horns by force?'

Karl said nothing.

'How honourable of you, brother,' said Lahnos. 'How brave.'

Karl kept his gaze lowered. 'We want you to leave Fidalaimos. That's what I came here to say.'

'Who's "we"?'

'Auntie Fenna, Uncle Frickel, and our three little sisters. None of us want you here.'

Lahnos hid the pain in his heart. It was no more or less than he had been expecting, but his brother's words had hurt worse than any punch in the face.

'Will you go?' said Karl. 'Will you leave us in peace?'

'You would need to speak to Uncle Friel about that.'

'What if I gave you money to go? We don't have much, but we'll give it to you if you walk out of Fidalaimos today, and never come back.'

'You're not listening to me, Karl. Uncle Friel brought me here, and it's up to him where I go next.'

Karl looked confused. 'Why? What has Uncle Friel got to do with this? I heard a rumour that he was in the village yesterday, but I haven't seen him. Do you work for him?'

'He's my legal guardian, at least until I turn twenty-one. He brought me here from Kaugatz. I should probably go looking for him.'

'Don't. Please. Don't walk through the village again.'

'Make up your damn mind, brother. You just offered me money to walk out of Fidalaimos.'

'I didn't mean it literally. We could put you in a carriage so that no one will see you. If you walk down the main street again, you will be lynched.'

'I thought you would approve of that.'

Karl tightened his eyes. 'I don't want you to be beaten to death, Lahnos. The men you hit yesterday are screaming for revenge, and they have friends who would be more than willing to... I don't have to tell you this; you know what I'm talking about.'

'You're talking about what they did to mother.'

Karl nodded. 'It was the damn Aucterians who killed her, but it will be our own people, the villagers of Fidalaimos, who will kill you if they get their hands on you. Where is Uncle Friel? I need to speak to him. And you must stay indoors while I'm gone. Do you understand?'

Lahnos shook his head. 'No.'

'No? What do you mean?'

'If you leave this house, then so shall I. We're brothers. Let's walk down the street together. Let's show these bastards that we're not afraid of them.'

Karl stared at him. 'You are out of your mind.'

'No. I just refuse to live in fear.'

The front door of the cottage opened, and their grandmother walked in. She glanced at Karl, and her frown deepened.

'What are you doing here?' she said. 'You should be at work.'

'He wants me to leave the village,' said Lahnos. 'The whole family wants me to go.'

'I told you not to interfere, Karl,' said the old woman. 'Go.'

Lahnos's brother muttered something, then he got to his feet and strode from the cottage. His grandmother closed the front door behind him, then walked over to the table.

'Have you had anything to eat?' she said.

Lahnos shook his head.

The old woman went into the kitchen half of the room. She rummaged around for a few things, then brought over a plate of bread and a bowl of olives, and placed them onto the table in front of her grandson.

'Thanks,' he said.

The old woman sat. 'Can we have a civilised discussion, Lahnos?'

He popped a few olives into his mouth. 'I don't see why not.'

'You are still a boy, Lahnos,' she said. She smiled. 'I can see by the expression on your face that you disagree. Very well, you are a young man. You were such an innocent little boy, naïve and trusting, too trusting at times. I miss that little boy.'

Lahnos chewed a mouthful of bread.

'And then, one day,' she went on, 'everything changed.' She pointed at his horns. 'Those things changed you. The horns turned you into a beast, but not in the way that you might imagine. I am not talking about your appearance; I am talking about what dwells inside your heart. You are filled with anger, and you are always looking for a fight. Is that how you want to live the rest of your life? You are strong now, and quick with your fists – will that always be the case? If you do not change your ways, my beautiful boy, you are destined for a life of violence and misery.' She watched him as he ate in silence. 'I failed you, Lahnos. After your parents were gone, I took you in. I wanted to protect you. I wanted to guide you...'

'You wanted to cut my horns off.'

She nodded. 'Yes. I still believe that this is the right course of action. With those horns, you will never get a job, and with no job, how will you ever find a wife and start your own family? Will you live on the streets? Will you die a lonely, violent death, Lahnos? My heart breaks at the thought. Your Uncle Friel would sometimes send me little notes, telling me that you were still alive. I could guess the rest by what he left out.'

'My horns aren't the problem,' he said. 'If people could look beyond appearances, then my life would be easy.'

She laughed. 'Of course, but is such a thing likely? People shouldn't judge others by how they look, but they do. It might be cruel and unfair, but it is the way of the world. You can't change that, Lahnos. When a beautiful young woman walks down the street, is she unaware that the men are looking at her with lust in their hearts, and that the women are judging her? It's human nature, and it cares nought for your feelings. Swallow your pride. Endure a few moments of pain, and then you shall be free.'

'I am already free.'

'No, Lahnos. Your horns have trapped you. Everyone who looks at you sees nothing but what is growing out of your head. No one looks beyond – all they see are your horns. You have allowed them to define who you are.'

Lahnos sighed. 'Can we end this conversation now? My horns are staying, and I will resist anyone who tries to take them from me. Even you, grandmother.' He stood.

'Where are you going?' she said.

'To find Uncle Friel.'

'No. You stay here, and I shall look for Friel.'

Lahnos glanced at the front door.

'Did you hear me, Lahnos? Do not step outside.'

'Karl told me that the villagers would kill me if I walked down the street again.'

'I cannot control their anger,' his grandmother said. 'Not after what you did yesterday. The only reason that they haven't broken into the house and dragged you out is that I promised I would speak to you, and that I would resolve the situation. If you let me take your horns, then I will go outside and show them to the rest of the village. That will calm them down. They will go home after that.'

Lahnos shook his head. 'No. I would rather be killed by a mob than allow you to do that.'

His grandmother got to her feet, and moved to block his way to the front door.

'To leave this house,' she said, 'you will have to push me aside. I will try to stop you, Lahnos. Are you prepared to strike me?'

'I don't want to hurt you, grandmother.'

'You have already hurt me, in more ways than you can possibly imagine.'

He eyed the door, wondering if a mob had assembled outside in the street. If it was true, then he would go down fighting.

'Get out of my way,' he said.

'No.'

He took a step towards the door. 'I do not fear death.'

'Do you love only yourself?' she said. 'Are you truly so selfish? If you are murdered this day, then what about those you will leave behind? Not just me – what about the young women you were with yesterday? I saw the way one of them was looking at you, the one with the headscarf and the long skirt. Do you imagine I do not understand what that signifies? Would you leave that girl to face the world alone?'

Lahnos stared at her. 'Reyn would hate me if I let you take my horns.'

'Reyn? She loves you, doesn't she? If you won't stay inside for me, then do it for her. I have already seen one member of my family murdered by a senseless mob – do not force me to watch another.'

'What will be, will be,' he said.

He placed a hand onto his grandmother's shoulder, and pushed her to the side. She lashed out at him, her fists striking his arm and chest, as tears streamed down her cheeks. He raised an arm to shield himself from her blows, and his elbow cracked off her chin. The old woman cried out, then slipped and fell to the floor of the cottage.

'Grandmother!' he said, crouching. 'I didn't mean it.'

She clutched her chest as her mouth opened. Her eyes seemed to be bulging from their sockets, and she made a strange choking, gasping sound.

'Grandmother!' he yelled. 'What's happening? I'm sorry.'

She gripped his hand. 'Don't... leave... the house.'

Her head fell to the side, and she fell silent. For a few seconds, Lahnos remained frozen, his eyes staring in disbelief at the motionless body of his grandmother. She wasn't breathing, but her fingers were still curled round his hand in a tight grip.

His vision blurred, but not from tears. Everything went black, and Lahnos felt as though he was floating within a silent, lightless void. An image appeared of a young girl and boy playing together on the grass. Someone else was present, and Lahnos realised that he was looking out from that person's eyes at the playing children.

'It's my turn!' the girl shouted, snatching a wooden toy from the other person's hands. Lahnos looked down, and saw the empty hands, but they belonged to someone else. Lahnos felt himself panic, then the image changed, and he was watching a wedding. The bride and groom were beaming from under the arched trellis. Spring flowers adorned the bride's hair, and were littered in thick piles on the ground, covering her sandals. A crowd of villagers cheered, and threw more flowers at the couple. Lahnos stared at the faces of the bride and groom, and realised that he was looking at his own mother and father. They seemed different from how he remembered – younger, and happier. They gazed at each other, and kissed.

'Mother!' Lahnos cried, but his voice was lost in the void, as the image faded.

A new image appeared, of the village at night. Men with lamps and swords were stalking through the streets, while the villagers were hiding within their stone cottages.

Six men approached the person from whose eyes Lahnos was looking out.

'Where is she?' one of the men said, his Aucterian accent ringing through the night air. 'Where is the Gifted witch?'

'She's not here,' the person said. 'She's gone.'

'Liar,' said the man. 'We know you are her mother-in-law. Step aside.'

'No. You are not welcome here. Go home.'

A fist lashed out and struck the person, and Lahnos's vision went blurry for a moment. The next thing he knew, he was watching a struggling woman be dragged out of the cottage. Two men were pulling her arms, while others were forming a circle on the street.

'Stay indoors,' called out one of the men, his eyes roving around the shuttered houses of the village. 'If anyone stops us, they will be next.'

Lahnos gazed out from the open door of the cottage.

'Please!' the woman cried. 'I have five children!'

The person watching from the cottage entrance turned away as the fists and boots came down upon the woman in the street. Hands went to the person's ears, and the woman screamed.

The image faded. Lahnos sobbed. What had he just witnessed? How could this be happening? Had he died? Was he lying dead on the floor of his grandmother's cottage, and had entered a pain-filled afterlife? Were the Gunstians right? Maybe he was in the fiery pit they always talked about, destined for an eternity of suffering.

'Mother,' he gasped.

His vision cleared again, and he saw his father's face. It was the one he recognised – scarred with bitterness and rage, his eyes burning with a desire for vengeance.

'You don't have to do this, son,' said the person.

Lahnos gasped. Was he in his grandmother's mind? Was he seeing what she had seen?

'I must,' said his father. 'There is no choice.'

'But the colonists in Backwater will kill you,' she said.

'I am not going to Backwater, mother. I am going to Igatz. I am going to hammer on the gates of the Dragon Palace until someone listens to me.'

'But the children, Falken; what about the children? They have already lost their mother; do you intend to leave them fatherless also?'

Lahnos's father broke down in tears. 'I have no choice, mother. I cannot live like this. The pain I carry is too much to bear.' He wiped his eyes. 'I will go to Igatz, and I will get justice for Netta. I will be back. I swear it.'

The old woman watched as her eldest son walked out of the cottage, then the vision changed again, and Lahnos saw Friel sitting at the kitchen table of the cottage, his features shrouded in the thick shadows cast by a small oil lamp.

'I'm sorry, mother,' he said. 'I can't find any trace of him.'

'Then he might still be alive.'

'It's possible,' said Friel. 'But, it is just as likely that the Aucterians threw him into the Hansarta. Why did you let him leave?'

'Do you think I wanted him to go? I begged him to stay. Will you keep looking?'

Friel nodded. 'Of course. I want to follow up on a rumour that a few Zamatans were kidnapped into slavery and sent to the Dominion. If I find anything out, I will let you know.'

'Slavery?' said the old woman.

'Yes. A prison ship departed Igatz a few days ago, packed full of convicted Zamatans. They're on their way to Aucteran, for a life of bonded labour. If I had wanted rid of someone, but I didn't want to leave a body that might be found, then that's where I would have put them. But please don't get your hopes up. Even if Falken was on that ship, there might be no records that I can track down.' He stood. 'I'll send more money for the children as soon as I get back to Igatz. Goodbye, mother.'

The vision faded, and refocused on the village street. The old woman was looking through a market stall piled high with spring vegetables, and the sun was warming the back of her neck.

'Granny Jola!' cried a voice, and the old woman turned.

'What's the matter?' she said to the old man. 'I haven't seen you run like that in years.'

'There's trouble in the main street,' the man said.

'What kind of trouble?'

The old man swallowed. 'It's your grandson Lahnos. He's back.'

The image swirled away, and was replaced by a darkness that was complete. Lahnos felt as though he were floating again.

'Am I dead?'

No, said a woman's voice inside his head. *You are not dead, Lahnos.*

'What is happening to me? Is my grandmother dead?'

She is, Lahnos. She had a heart attack when she fell.

'I killed her.'

It was an accident. You didn't mean for it to happen.

'All those things I saw – were they true?'

They are.

'Who are you? Are you my grandmother?'

It is time to wake up, Lahnos.

'I don't know how. My mind has broken.'

I will fix it for you. I have been watching over you, Lahnos; and I will continue to watch over you. Be brave, and look after Reyn. She needs you. I will help you to be brave. Now – awaken.

A wave of energy burst through Lahnos's mind, and his eyes snapped open. He gazed up from the floor of the cottage, and saw Uncle Friel gazing back down at him.

'Are you all right, Lahnos?' his uncle said. 'Can you speak?'

Lahnos sat up. His eyes turned, and he saw the body of his grandmother lying next to him. A sheet had been placed over her, but her right hand was still clutching his. He pulled it free, and stared at his fingers.

'I didn't mean it,' he said.

Friel nodded. 'What happened?'

'She fell. We argued, and she fell. Then...'

Friel sat down on the floor next to him, and wiped the tears from his face.

'She was a very old woman, Lahnos,' he said. 'It's not your fault. My mother's mind was strong, but she had been carrying a burden of pain and grief too heavy for anyone to bear.' He took his mother's hand. 'She is at peace now. What about you? You were unconscious when I walked into the cottage.'

Lahnos stared into his uncle's face. 'Do you want to cut off my horns?'

Friel blinked. 'What? No. Of course not, Lahnos. What you do with your horns is your own business.'

'Can I... can I trust you, uncle?'

'Yes. Remember the journey from Igatz. I proved that I trusted you, Lahnos, by the words I spoke. You can trust me in return.'

Lahnos narrowed his eyes. 'You know, don't you? You know what happened to me. I don't understand how you know, but you do.'

'Yes, Lahnos; I know. I'm just waiting to hear you say it.'

'How can I even begin to explain?' he said. 'It was as though I could see grandmother's memories, as if I were looking out from her eyes. I saw mother, and father, and I even saw you. I watched my mother die, uncle. How could that be possible?'

'I think you already suspect the truth, Lahnos. You are Gifted.'

'No.'

'Yes. Thirteen Gifts were given to the people of this world by Theodora. The Gift of Truth is the First Gift, but there are twelve others. You are aware of the Gift of Truth, are you not?'

Lahnos said nothing.

'Leona told me last night,' Friel said. 'She confessed that she had revealed her secret to you and Reyn. I was annoyed at first, but then I thought – why shouldn't you know? You are family. But, you must keep Leona's Gift a secret, just as I shall keep your Gift a secret.'

Lahnos put his head in his hands. 'I don't want to be Gifted. The horns are enough. Now there are two reasons for a mob to lynch me.'

'The mob outside has gone home, and I have a carriage waiting to take us to my little cottage. Leona and Reyn are there. I like Reyn; you have found someone very special, and I hope you hold on to her. Can you stand?'

'Why has the mob gone home?'

'Because I promised them I would remove you from the village. You should have waited for me before marching down the main street, Lahnos. I had a careful plan for re-introducing you to Fidalaimos all worked out. Still, never mind. What's done is done, and now I shall have to bury my mother.'

'I'm sorry.'

'I know.'

'How did you know I had a Gift?'

'Perhaps I shall tell you later.'

'What Gift is it?'

'You have the Gift of Death-Reading; the ability to see the memories of someone who has just died. It is rare, but I knew of two others on Zamata who had the same Gift. They both worked for the Dominion. The Gunstians, too, are always hunting for people with this Gift.'

'Why?'

Friel stood and extended his hand. Lahnos took it, and got to his feet.

'Come on,' Friel said. 'Reyn is anxious to see you. Let's not keep her waiting.'

CHAPTER 8
IN THE SERVICE OF LORD KHERAN

Igatz, Serpent Isle – 1st Nethinch 1588

Cisca pulled back the branches of the tree. 'Found you!' she cried.

The child dragon roared with laughter, then turned to run away. As he moved, his right wing swung out, catching Cisca across her chest, and sending her flying backwards through the air. She landed on the manicured lawn, stunned and winded. Oblivious to her distress, Lord Kheran Mon Tirna kept running, then he turned his long neck, and his eyes widened. He trotted over to where Cisca lay, and prodded her with his nose.

'Are you alive?'

'Yes.'

'Good. Get up; I want to keep playing.'

She groaned. 'Could I please have a moment to recover, my lord?'

'Did I hurt you again?'

'Only a little, my lord. I will be fine soon.'

She gazed up at the blue sky, as her chest throbbed with a dull pain. For four days, she had been catering to the whims of the dragon child – running, hiding, chasing, reading him stories and listening to him chatter about his illustrious family. He had never once meant to hurt her, yet her body was covered in bruises; and he seemed to have little conception of how strong he was, or how fragile humans were in comparison.

She sat up, and exhaled.

'Are you ready now?' Kheran said. 'Shall I hide?'

Cisca forced a smile on to her lips. 'Of course, my lord.'

'Little Kheran!' cried a booming voice over the palace gardens.

The dragon child's expression changed, and his eyes narrowed. Cisca pulled herself to her feet and stood to attention as Lord Meer Mon Adal emerged round a thick line of tall cypress trees.

'There you are,' Lord Meer said. 'It is time for your morning lesson, little Kheran.'

'But I was playing,' said the child dragon.

'I can see that,' Meer said, 'but the time for playing is over for now. You can play with your human pet after your lesson.' He glanced at Cisca. 'And you, woman – you should have noticed the time. You are aware of when Lord Kheran begins his lessons, are you not? You should have brought him back to the palace. Now he is late, because of you.'

'My humble apologies, Lord Meer,' said Cisca, her eyes lowered.

'I will see you after lunch, Cisca,' said Kheran.

'I will be at your service, my lord,' she said, bowing.

Lord Meer led the child dragon away, and Cisca grimaced. She touched her ribs, and almost yelped in pain. She began to limp over the grass, heading towards her new quarters within the palace. Her change of residence had been one of the better things that had happened to her over the previous few days. Serving as Lord Kheran's latest favourite human had seen her moved to a plush and spacious apartment with a wide balcony that overlooked the waters of the Cyasarta. Her bed, too, was bigger, and she was looking forward to lying down in it for a few hours.

'Good morning, Lieutenant.'

She turned, and frowned at Travers. 'What do you want? Are you here to laugh at me again?'

The naval officer smiled as he walked towards her over the gravel path. 'I was coming to see if you required any assistance in getting to your quarters. That's a nasty limp you have.'

'I'm fine.'

He shrugged. 'I was only being friendly.'

She halted, and stared at him. 'You aren't my friend, Travers. You made that quite clear when you thought I was returning to Inopei with the dragon carrier.'

'Don't you think you might be over-reacting? I spent two days by your side, and was just getting to know you when, suddenly, you're leaving, presumably never to return. I was moving on. These things happen, Cisca. People come and go from the Serpent Isle all the time. I was protecting myself. And now that you are staying, you have rebuffed my every attempt to make it up to you. You will be in this palace for months. I will be in this palace for months. Does it make sense to ignore each other?'

'What do you want from me, Travers?' she said. 'Before, you had to shadow me – it was your job. But I no longer have to ask your permission if I wish to leave the grounds of the palace. I am under the sole authority of Lord Kheran. Why are you still following me around?'

Travers smiled, but said nothing.

Cisca shook her head at him, and carried on limping towards the palace.

'I hear you have a new apartment,' he called after her; 'with a balcony.'

'Yes,' she said. 'Are you jealous?'

'A little. Can I see it?'

She laughed. 'Are you trying to invite yourself into my quarters?'

'Yes. Is it working?'

Cisca said nothing.

'I have ointment for your bruises,' he said. 'I could apply some for you.'

She shuddered at the thought of his hands rubbing ointment into her bare skin. It had been a long time since any man's hands had touched her.

'You are much too forward,' she said.

'You didn't answer my question.'

'You can come to my apartment, but there will be no ointment.'

He smiled and strode forward to catch her up, and they entered the cool confines of the marble palace.

'Don't you have work to do?' she said.

'Not at the moment,' he said.

'And what is it that you do? I mean when you are not shadowing newly-arrived members of the Dragon Corps?'

'Governor Tirna insisted upon having a detachment of naval officers in the palace on hand for any emergency,' he said. 'There are six of us. On any given day, one of us remains in the central audience chamber from dawn till dusk, and then another from dusk till dawn; in case we are needed.'

'You work one day out of every three?'

'I wouldn't call it work. When I am on duty, I sit at the back of the hall and drink coffee until my head is about to burst. In my three years of service on the island, I have been called upon to do something for the Governor a total of four times. Is it any wonder that I volunteered to look after you when you arrived?'

They came to a set of elegant marble stairs, and she gasped in pain as she lifted her leg onto the first step. He reached out with a hand, but she ignored him, and struggled onwards.

'You are quite stubborn at times,' he said, as he ascended the stairs next to her.

'How else do you think I got through officer training?'

'Are you referring to your lowly accent?' he said. 'I had noticed. You should make more of an effort to hide it.'

'That's exactly what the others in my class used to say, when they weren't making fun of me.'

'You are from Naeth, aren't you?'

'Yes.'

'I also hale from Naeth.'

'I know. You are not the only one who can judge accents, Travers.

However, you are not from the same part of Naeth as me. You are from the rich suburbs out in the foothills to the east of the city.'

'Well done. And you are from?'

'The harbour district.'

'Ah.'

'Do you still want to rub ointment into my back?'

He eyed her. 'Yes. May I?'

'No.'

'Is there someone waiting for you back East?' he said. 'You have no ring on your finger, so I had assumed that you weren't married.'

'I'm not married; and there is no one waiting for me.'

'I see.'

They reached the front door of her apartment, and she took out her key. She unlocked the door and pushed it open; and Travers gasped at the view through the balcony windows. He walked past her and strode out on to the wide balcony, then laughed.

'This is something; truly magnificent,' he said. 'Little Lord Kheran must hold you in high esteem, Lieutenant.'

Cisca closed her front door, then went out and joined him on the balcony.

She placed her hands on the railings and gazed out at the still blue waters of the Cyasarta inlet.

'What did you mean by "I see"?' she said.

He turned his attention back to her. 'Excuse me?'

'When I told you that I had no one waiting for me across the ocean, you said, 'I see".'

He smiled. 'I was making a simple deduction. If you have no one special, and yet you would prefer me to keep my distance, then I must assume that I am not your type. Do you have a type, Lieutenant?'

'I'm not sure,' she said. 'However, I imagine that he would not leap from friendship to offers of intimacy quite so quickly. I know almost nothing about you, Lieutenant Travers, except that you belong to a social class far higher than my own. I cannot believe for one moment that your mother would be happy with such a match.'

He laughed. 'One would think from your words that I had offered to marry you. We are both single Aucterians, far from home; both officers in the Dominion armed forces, stranded on this little lump of rock amid the great ocean. Could we not comfort each other for a while?'

'You have just confirmed my suspicions about you, Lieutenant,' she said. 'No. I think I will wait for someone who loves me. Good day, Travers.'

He nodded, though his eyes remained on the view. 'Very well. I shall respect your wishes. Friends?'

'I could manage friends,' she said.

'Then I shall no doubt bump into you around the palace,' he said. 'I will see myself out.'

Cisca stayed on the balcony until she heard the sound of her apartment door close, then her shoulders sagged. She walked into her rooms and lay down upon her bed, her limbs and back aching. She tried to imagine what would be happening if she had accepted his offer. Would it have been so terrible? She was an adult, and she had known of several young officers in the dragon capital on Inopei who had paired off together without ever being in love. Was she naïve to expect more?

There was a tap at her door and she got back to her feet, relieved to have something to take her mind off her wandering thoughts. She walked to the door and opened it, then stood at attention and saluted in the presence of two high-ranking Dragon Corps officers.

'At ease, Lieutenant,' said a major.

'We have been meaning to introduce ourselves,' said a lieutenant-general. 'This is Major Polarn, and I am Lieutenant-General Foley. May we come in?'

'Of course, sir,' she said, opening the door wider for them to enter. 'Would you care for a drink?'

'Thank you, no,' said Foley. 'Was that Lieutenant Travers we saw leaving your apartment just now?'

Cisca's cheeks burned. 'Yes, sir. He is just a friend, sir.'

The two senior officers smiled at each other, and Cisca bit her tongue to suppress what she wanted to say.

'May we sit?' said the major.

Cisca gestured to the long couch, and the two officers sat.

'So, Lieutenant,' said Foley, 'notwithstanding the problems you had in Lord Noxon's service, how have you been getting on in Igatz?

Cisca took a seat opposite the two men. 'Very well, thank you, sir.'

'Good, good. And Lord Kheran? Have you been enjoying your new placement?'

'Yes, sir.'

'Excellent. That is why we are here. Lord Kheran seems to have taken a real liking to you, Lieutenant. To be honest, it has, on occasion, been somewhat challenging to find the young lord a suitable member of the Dragon Corps to keep him company; but you appear to be doing a splendid job.'

'Thank you, sir.'

'If you keep this up, Lieutenant, then I daresay that you may be able to overcome the recent blot in your record.'

Cisca smiled.

'Can you be discreet, Lieutenant?' said the major.

'Yes, sir.'

The two senior officers glanced at each other, and the lieutenant-general nodded. The major reached into a pocket and withdrew a set of keys. He studied them for a moment, then gave Cisca a piercing glance.

'It is imperative,' he said, 'that these keys do not fall into the wrong hands. We are showing a great deal of trust in you, Lieutenant – trust that one might not assume you deserve, based upon your recent troubles. However, Lord Kheran has made his feelings known to us, and so here we are.'

He held the keys out in front of him, and Cisca extended her hand. He pulled them back, just out of her reach.

'You are not to confide in anyone that you possess these keys,' he said, 'nor are you to allow them out of your sight for a single moment. Is that understood, Lieutenant?'

'Yes, sir. What are the keys for?'

'They allow direct access to Lord Kheran's quarters. When you turn up for duty each day, you shall no longer have to wait for courtiers to tell Lord Kheran that you have arrived. Instead, you are to proceed into his chambers without requiring an escort. Do you feel able to assume such a responsibility?'

'Yes, sir. Thank you, sir.'

The major dropped the keys into Cisca's palm.

'Do not let us down, Lieutenant,' said Foley, his eyes narrow.

'I won't, sir.'

The two officers stood, and Cisca got to her feet, her hand clutching the set of keys.

'Two last things,' said the major. 'Firstly, you are not to breathe a word of this to anyone; and that includes Lieutenant Travers. If we discover that you have let slip that you are in possession of these keys, then you can expect the full wrath of the Dragon Corps to fall upon you.'

'Understood, sir. What was the other thing?'

'There is a little get-together this evening in the officers' hall,' said Lieutenant-General Foley, 'for a few drinks and perhaps some dancing. There will be several town dignitaries and worthies present, and it is our job to make them feel welcome. Dress uniforms are required, as is your attendance, Lieutenant. Be there one hour after sunset. Your days of hiding away from your colleagues are over.'

Cisca swallowed. 'Yes, sir.'

The major eyed her for a moment, then the two officers strode to the door. Cisca let them both out, closed the door, and exhaled. She peered at the keys in her hand. Access to dragons of Lord Kheran's rank and status was rarely handed out to officers as junior as she was, and she knew that only his personal insistence would have persuaded the Dragon Corps to have obliged. Her hand shook a little. This was her opportunity. If she could prove her reliability and discretion to the senior officers based upon the Serpent Isle, then her career might have been saved. She sent a silent prayer of thanks to the dragon gods that she had turned down Lieutenant Travers's advances. If he had been in her apartment applying ointment when the major and lieutenant-general had arrived, then... then... No. It was best not to think about that.

She walked out on to her balcony and gazed down at the large sundial on the lawn below her. Lord Kheran's lesson would soon be finishing, and she had yet to clean herself up and have some lunch. She smiled. She would thank the dragon child for the great honour and privilege he had bestowed upon her, and then, afterwards, she would steel herself and get ready for an evening of mingling with the officers she had so far been avoiding. She would drink but not get drunk, talk to everyone without saying too much, and dance without making a fool of herself.

Who knows, she thought – she might even enjoy herself.

CHAPTER 9
THE DANCE

Igatz, Serpent Isle – 1st Nethinch 1588

Leona frowned across the interior of the carriage at the naval officer. He was an upper-class Aucterian, and she found it hard to believe that he could possibly share the same motives and aspirations as the colonel; and yet, Friel was laughing along with him as if they were the best of friends.

'And then?' said the colonel.

'And then she turned me down,' said the naval officer. 'I must be out of practice – I genuinely believed that the ointment would have done the trick.'

'Oh dear, Travers,' said Friel. 'How did you part?'

'With a vague promise that we would be friends,' he said. 'I shall keep up the pressure on her, and I'll wear her down in the end.'

'You don't need to sleep with the girl,' Friel said; 'you just need to ensure that she trusts you.'

'Perhaps, but she is rather beautiful, as you will see tonight. I shall make a point of asking her to dance. Should I introduce her to you, Colonel?'

'No,' he said. 'It would be better if she thinks that we don't know each other. How often does she see Lord Kheran?'

'Every day. That little dragon is besotted with her.'

'Does she have access to his private quarters?'

'I don't know. A curious thing happened when I left her apartment, though. Two senior officers from the Dragon Corps were on their way to see her. If I had to guess, then they were there on official business, rather than for a friendly chat. Poor old Cisca has had a torrid time.'

'You did well to complain about her behaviour to Lord Noxon,' said Friel. 'Had you not done so, then she would probably be on the boat heading back to Inopei. Keep up the good work, Travers. It sounds as though Cisca will be essential to our plans.' He turned and tapped on the driver's window. 'Pull over, my good man.'

Travers frowned as the carriage halted by the side of the road. 'We are still a ten minute walk from the palace, Colonel.'

'I know,' said Friel, 'but I am not taking any chances; not now, not when so much is at stake. We shall arrive separately, and we shall studiously ignore each other for the duration of the evening. Make sure you ask Cisca to dance while I am close by, so that I can identify her.'

Travers nodded, then the driver opened the door and the naval officer stepped down to the lamplit cobbles. The driver closed the door, and Friel leaned back in his seat.

'What an awful man,' said Leona, as the carriage got underway again.

Friel shrugged. 'Did he lie?'

'Not to us,' Leona said; 'but he's tricking that girl. He's making her think that he likes her, when he's just using her.'

'That girl, as you put it,' Friel said, 'is an officer in the Dragon Corps. In other words, she is our enemy.'

'Yes, but I can't help feeling sorry for her.'

'Leona, people are going to die in the next few days – good people, bad people; the innocent and the not so innocent. If the worst that happens to Cisca is a few hurt feelings then she can count herself lucky.' He gazed out of the carriage window. 'I never thanked you for standing by me at my mother's funeral in Fidalaimos; so, thank you.'

'I... of course, sir. I wouldn't have been anywhere else. Do you want to talk about it?'

'Not right now. In a few minutes, I will be smiling at people I loathe and pretending to have a good time. The last thing I need to do is dwell on what happened to my mother. Perhaps when we return to my town-house later tonight. I have a lot bottled up, Leona. Too much. Will you indulge me? If I unburden myself, there will likely be a few tears.'

'I'm here for you, sir.'

He nodded. 'You may have to dance with a few Dominion officers.' He turned and shook his head at her. 'Perhaps I should have dressed you a little more conservatively. You are looking so pretty tonight that I fear you will have a queue of young Aucterians seeking your hand.'

Leona glanced out of the carriage window. 'Would any wish to dance with a Zamatan, sir?'

'Dance? They will be hoping to get you into bed, my sweet Leona. It will take a monumental effort on my part to pretend that I don't hate them; and you will also have to suppress your true feelings. It would be wise if you didn't drink too much.'

Leona nodded, then she continued to gaze out of the window. The colonel had been keeping his emotions to himself since his mother had died in the village, but he seemed more vulnerable than usual. The funeral had been hard to endure. The colonel's younger brother and sister had been there, along with several nephews, nieces and cousins, and many had eyed Leona in a manner that made her suspect they thought of her in the same way that Reyn had. The only relatives who hadn't been there were Lahnos, who had been ordered to remain in the colonel's cottage; and Bauchlie, Friel's renegade son. Leona had half-expected either or both to make a surprise appearance, but, to her relief, neither had obliged. As the new head of the Laimos family, the colonel had said a few words by the graveside, but to an untrained ear they had sounded cold and aloof, and they had left the village shortly afterwards, taking a carriage and two ferries back to the comfort of Igatz. She wondered if the rest of the family were gossiping about her.

They probably thought that the colonel didn't care about them, or the village, but Leona knew that wasn't true.

The carriage reached the entrance to the Dragon Palace and stopped by the strong iron gates. A squad of well-armed Bullan soldiers were posted there, checking the invitations of everyone trying to enter, and Leona saw their driver hand over a white envelope. Two Bullan peered through the carriage windows, then waved them on, and the carriage wheels crunched over the gravel of the long driveway. Several other carriages were already lined up under the tall lamps lighting the front of the Dragon Palace, and there was a heavy presence of soldiers patrolling the gardens. Aucterian merchants in fine clothes were mingling with Dominion officers in their best uniforms as they made their way into the white marble building, all under the watchful eye of the Bullan.

'Are we the only Zamatans here?' said Leona, as their carriage drew to a halt.

'Quite possibly,' said Friel. 'Lord Rufus, the acting Governor, wishes everyone to believe that life is carrying on as normal, as though the death of the dragon god has not shaken the foundations of Dominion rule.' He took a breath. 'Remember, this is all part of the game. As soon as we step down from the carriage, I shall play the role that I have been assigned, and you shall play yours. Are you ready?'

'Yes, sir.'

The driver opened the carriage door, and Friel smiled broadly.

'Thank you, my good man,' he said, as he stepped down to the gravel.

The driver raised a hand, and helped Leona to the ground, where she smoothed down the front of her dress. A warm wind brushed over her exposed shoulders and neck, and she suppressed a shiver. The colonel walked ahead of her, and she followed two paces behind; and they joined the procession of people entering the palace. Upper class Aucterian accents drifted by on either side, and Leona wondered what people would do when they heard her speak. Two rows of courtiers funnelled the guests through the marble hallways and into a large hall, where a musical band was playing something at a discreet volume – loud enough to dance to, but quiet enough so that no one had to shout to be heard. A waiter went by with a tray of crystal glasses, and Leona took one. Then she turned, and realised that the colonel had gone. She looked through the crowds, and caught sight of him talking to a robed merchant with thick gold chains around his neck. Leona bit her lip, then walked on. She passed a group of young Dominion officers who were laughing together in their fine dress uniforms, and took a place by the side of the hall. Perhaps if she kept to herself then no one would bother her.

'Good evening,' came a voice from her right.

She turned, and saw two handsome young naval officers approach.

'I don't believe I have ever seen you here before,' said one.

'This is my first time in the palace,' said Leona.

The two officers' eyes widened.

One smiled. 'Is that a rural accent, or...?'

'It is a Kaugatz accent,' she said.

They laughed.

'I didn't think we allowed Zamatans into the palace,' said one. 'Are you working here tonight?'

'No.'

'Then?'

'I am Colonel Friel's assistant.'

'Colonel Friel?'

'He's a notorious lawyer,' said the other officer. 'You must have heard of him. He's militia. Half of the naval staff in Handshore owe him a favour.'

'Do you mean Colonel Laimos?' he said.

'That's the one.' He glanced back at Leona. 'And would Colonel Laimos be angry if I asked you to dance, Miss...?'

'My name is Leona,' she said, 'and no, he wouldn't be angry.'

He extended an arm. 'Then may I?'

She looked for somewhere to leave her glass, and the other officer plucked it from her hand. The first officer led her out on to the dance floor in the centre of the hall, where a few other couples were already dancing. The officer took her right hand in his left, then placed his other on to her waist.

'So,' he said, as they began to turn, 'what does being Colonel Laimos's assistant entail?'

'I do all kinds of things for him,' she said.

'I bet you do. Pays well, does it? Your dress is worth a small fortune, and your jewellery certainly didn't come cheap. You are the best dressed Zamatan I have ever laid eyes on; I had no idea you cleaned up so well.'

She smiled. 'Do you work at the base?'

'Yes,' he said. 'I have been stationed in Handshore for almost a year.'

His hand strayed a little too low from her waist, and she moved it back up.

'Tell me,' he said, 'what do you lot think about the present situation, eh? You are the first Zamatan I have spoken to, apart from the servants on the base, but all they say is, "yes, sir".'

'By situation, I assume you are referring to the passing of His Majesty King Gahad?'

'I am indeed.'

'I think it is a dreadful shame.'

He eyed her, then smiled. 'That's the understatement of the century. There will probably be a war. After all, the Dominion can hardly allow those Gunstian bastards to get away with killing our king. How will the Zamatans react if we invade Gunst? Can we expect any trouble from you?'

'I wouldn't know,' she said.

'No, I doubt you would. No offence, but I hardly think Colonel Laimos hired you for your tactical acumen, not when your other assets are so... arresting.'

Leona tried to smile, but the effort was making her face hurt.

The music changed, and the dancing partners came apart and bowed to each other.

'Thank you for the dance,' Leona said.

'It was my pleasure,' the officer said. 'Perhaps later, we can dance again?'

'Perhaps,' she said.

He escorted her back to the side of the hall, where the other officer handed her the glass he had been holding. Both inclined their heads a fraction towards her, then strode off. Leona exhaled, then took a sip of her sparkling wine. To her left, she noticed another woman standing alone. Their eyes met, and Leona gave her a slight smile.

'You look as though you find this as tiresome as I do,' the woman said.

'Do I?' said Leona. 'Damn it. I was trying to make it seem as though I was having the time of my life.'

The woman laughed. 'I think we both need to practice our smiles.'

'Are you a naval officer?' Leona said.

'No. Dragon Corps.'

'Your uniforms all look the same to me,' Leona said, then she cursed her stupidity. The woman hadn't seemed to have noticed her accent, but now she would surely guess that she was Zamatan.

The woman raised an eyebrow, but said nothing.

Two more officers approached, and bowed.

'May we have this dance with you both?' said one.

'No,' said the Dragon Corps woman. 'We were in the middle of a conversation.'

The two young men frowned, glanced at each other, then moved on.

'Was that wise?' said Leona.

'I don't care,' said the woman. 'I was ordered to come here, and I will be on my best behaviour; but that doesn't mean I wish to dance with everyone who asks. Who did your hair? It's nice.'

'Thank you. My employer knows several of the town's best hairdressers, but I can't remember the name of the woman who did it.'

'Your employer?'

'Yes.'

Another naval officer approached, and bowed before the woman from the Dragon Corps.

She narrowed her eyes at him. 'Well, look who it is.'

Leona glanced at the officer, then her features froze.

'Good evening, Lieutenant Cisca,' said Travers. 'I would say that you are looking wonderful this evening, but I seem to recall seeing you in a dress uniform several times already since you got here.'

'Are you enjoying yourself, Travers?' she said.

He shrugged. 'These events are more of a chore than anything else. How are the bruises?'

'Bearable, thank you.'

'My offer still stands.'

'I thought you said you would respect my wishes?'

'I do, but that doesn't mean my feelings have changed.' He extended an arm. 'Would you care for this dance? Please say yes. If you do, then I promise I won't bother you for the rest of the evening.'

Cisca smiled. 'Well, in that case, how can I refuse?'

Leona said nothing as Travers led Cisca out on to the dance floor, but inside, her stomach was churning. She wanted to shout out, to warn Cisca that Travers was trying to entrap her in his plans. No, she thought – they weren't Travers's plans, they were the colonel's, and Leona was complicit. Her heart sank as she watched Travers lead Cisca across the dance floor, their graceful movements honed by years of officer training. She saw the colonel watching them both from the other side of the hall, then his attention went back to the group of merchants he was talking to.

'Good evening,' said a young officer to her left. 'May I?'

Leona nodded. She gave her empty glass to a waiter and took the officer's hand. They walked on to the dance floor, took their positions, and began to move to the lilting music.

'Might I say how beautiful you are looking?' the young officer said. 'Your eyes called me from across the hall.'

Leona smiled.

'And that smile,' he went on. 'You are the most beautiful woman here tonight. Who did you come with?'

'My employer brought me here,' she said.

The officer came to an abrupt halt, and released her hand and waist.

'Is something wrong?' she said, conscious that many had turned to watch.

'Are you Zamatan?' he said in a loud voice. 'Have I been dancing with a servant?'

'I am not a servant.'

'What then – a prostitute? How dare you try to ensnare me? Have you no shame?'

He turned and strode away, leaving Leona standing alone in the middle of the dance floor. She overheard a few muffled laughs and lowered her gaze, fighting every instinct to hurl abuse at the officer who had insulted her. She had a role to play, she told herself, and that role included being humiliated. Bring on the revolution, she thought; let it crush the Aucterians and their damned arrogance.

She turned, and saw a few naval officers laughing at her. Her fists clenched involuntarily, and she strode towards them.

'Do you have something you wish to say?' she said to them.

One of them pointed. 'I think you might be in the wrong place. The kitchens are over there.'

She pulled back her hand, ready to unleash a punch, and someone grabbed hold of her arm.

'I think my assistant might have had a little too much to drink, gentlemen,' said Friel, a smirk on his lips. 'My apologies. Let me call her a carriage.'

'Leave your little whore at home next time, Colonel,' said a naval captain, as the others laughed.

Friel said nothing as he led Leona away, his fingers tight around her arm. He walked her through the crowds of rich Aucterians and out of the hall.

'Are you sending me home?' she said.

Friel said nothing. He kept walking, until he had led her out into the balmy evening air. With his face a mask of calm assurance, he flagged down their carriage, and their driver opened the side door.

'Get in,' said Friel.

She glared at him, and climbed up. Then, to her surprise, he got in next to her, and closed the door.

'Take us home,' he called to the driver.

The driver nodded, then took his seat up on the bench, and the carriage began to move off.

'Are you angry with me, sir?' Leona said.

Friel shrugged, though his eyes tightened. 'Not as angry as I would have been had your fist connected with that young officer's face,' he said. 'What happened to your self-control?'

'I couldn't help myself,' she said. 'I should have walked away. I'm sorry.'

He turned to her. 'For two years,' he said, 'I have been attempting to train you; to turn you into someone able to mask their true feelings from the outside world – and all it took was a few rude insults from a couple of arrogant officers and you nearly found yourself in prison. Do you know the penalties that befall Zamatans who strike Aucterians? You would have been flogged.'

'I failed you, sir.'

Friel leaned back into his seat and closed his eyes. 'You almost did. You are correct – you should have walked away, but I should have known better. Perhaps you are not ready to be placed into such situations. Still, I think we got away with it. Those we left behind at the dance will no doubt be gossiping about my impetuous young assistant, but I don't believe that any lasting damage has been inflicted upon our cause.'

'Then I didn't completely ruin the evening?'

'No. You didn't. It was a success. Thanks to Travers, I identified the Dragon Corps officer who is caring for Lord Kheran, and that was my primary objective.' He opened his eyes again. 'I have also realised your limits. Damn it, Leona – after everything I have accomplished, I was almost undone because of you. Years of patient preparation; years of compromising my integrity, and all it took was one man to call you a whore, and you were ready to destroy everything I have built. If you aren't careful, you will become a danger to me, Leona; a risk. A weakness. How did it come to this? You need to do better, girl.'

'You are not my father,' she said.

Friel raised an eyebrow, but said nothing. Leona turned and gazed out of the window. They had left the palace grounds and were travelling through the wide streets of central Igatz, and she looked at the tall buildings, their ornate façades illuminated by the rows of iron streetlamps. It was his mother's death, she decided – that was what had caused the colonel to lash out at her with his anger. She frowned, wondering if that was true. Part of her had hoped that the colonel had intervened because he cared about her, but her long-held suspicions about his motives seemed clear – she was a useful assistant to him; nothing more. He cared more about her Gift than he did about her.

The carriage took a left at the main square, and entered an area of large townhouses. The streets had been quiet since King Gahad's death had been announced, and that night was no different. The colonel said nothing for the remainder of the journey, and their driver halted in front of his townhouse. He dismounted from the driver's bench, and opened the side door.

Friel stepped down to the smooth pavement and climbed the steps to the front door. The driver shared a glance with Leona, then helped her down.

'I shall put the carriage away for the night, sir,' the driver said, but the colonel wasn't listening. He unlocked his front door and disappeared into the darkness of the interior.

'Is he all right?' said the driver.

'Could you hear what we were saying?' Leona said.

'I try not to overhear your conversations, miss,' he said, 'but sometimes I can't help it.' He smiled at her. 'Despite his words, I know that the colonel is fond of you. I'll see you in the morning.'

Leona smiled back at him, then ascended the steps to the open door. She entered the house and closed the door behind her, sliding the large bolts into place. She lit a couple of lamps, and carried one through to the main drawing room. The colonel was sitting on a couch with his head in his hands.

'Get me a drink,' he said. 'No wine; I need to get rapidly and thoroughly drunk.'

'Yes, sir.'

She went through the ground floor of the townhouse, lighting a few more lamps along the way. She reached the colonel's study, and opened the door.

Sitting in the colonel's armchair was a man, his features shrouded in shadows. Leona cried out, and almost dropped the lamp.

'You must be Leona,' said the man, his voice almost a growl.

Leona put a hand to her mouth. The man stared back at her, and she saw the faintest resemblance to the colonel upon his features.

'Is he home?'

Leona said nothing.

The man shook his head and got to his feet. He was tall and well-built, and had a scar that ran down his right cheek. He eased Leona to the side and walked out of the study, a bottle of brandy in his right hand. Leona stared after him, aware that she should be raising the alarm, but something about the man's presence had terrified her. She snapped out of her stupor and ran after him, but he had already reached the drawing room by the time she had returned there. She hurried in, and saw the colonel on his feet. Face to face, the strange man was several inches taller than the colonel, and each was eyeing the other in silence.

'He was in the study!' Leona blurted out.

The colonel nodded.

'I'm ready,' said the man. 'Are you?'

'I am,' said the colonel.

'When?'

'Tomorrow.'

The man nodded, then he sat on a couch and opened the bottle. He glanced at Leona. 'Get me a glass.'

Leona stared from the man to the colonel.

'Get one for me, too,' Friel said; 'and one for yourself.'

'Can we trust her?' said the man.

Friel nodded. 'The glasses, Leona. I am not going to drink from a bottle.'

Leona raced back out of the room. She rushed along the quiet passageways to the kitchen, collected three glasses, and hurried back to the drawing room.

'The weapons have been distributed,' the man was saying as she returned; 'but not to the Gunstians. At sunset tomorrow, if we are agreed, the uprising will begin in Kaugatz.' He eyed Leona with suspicion.

'Did I not say that we can trust her?' said Friel, taking a glass from her.

'You didn't trust her when you visited me in Gatzoun Medamuna,' the man said.

'Pour the damn brandy,' Friel said.

Leona sat, and the man filled their glasses with the rich golden liquid.

'Does she know who I am?' he said.

'She does,' said Friel.

'You're Bauchlie,' she said.

He nodded. 'Everything you have heard about me is true, girl. If you betray us, I will kill you.'

'She will not betray us,' said Friel; 'and if you kill her, then I will do the same to you.'

'You must be getting soft, father.'

'I am merely protecting my assets,' Friel said. 'Now – the plan. I assume the boat from Gunst arrived on time?'

'It did.'

'And did they keep their word?'

'They did, for once. Gunst is your responsibility, father. You have made them promises that I shall not honour.'

'I did what I had to do, son. Leave the Gunstians to me. Are you clear on your responsibilities?'

'I am. All I need is a way into the palace.'

The colonel smiled. 'I have taken care of that.'

'And access to the dragon child?'

'I have taken care of that, too.' He raised his glass. 'A toast.'

'To freedom?' said Bauchlie.

'No,' said Friel; 'to my mother.'

'The grandmother who never knew of my existence?'

'We all have regrets, son, and not telling my mother about you is one of mine.'

Bauchlie turned his heavy glance to Leona. 'Let us hope that this girl does not turn out to be another regret.'

Friel smiled. 'You know,' he said; 'perhaps it is time to let you into a little secret regarding my young assistant.'

CHAPTER 10
SWEPT ALONG

Fidalaimos, Serpent Isle – 2nd Nethinch 1588

'You know why I'm angry,' said Lahnos. 'My grandmother died, and I was forbidden from going to her funeral.'

Reyn narrowed her eyes.

'Don't you believe me?' he said. 'Do you think I'm lying to you?'

Reyn poured herself another glass of lemonade, and stretched her legs out on the veranda deckchair.

'Well?' Lahnos said. 'Are you calling me a liar?'

'No,' she said. 'I'm not saying that you're a liar. I believe that you're upset about the funeral, and about your grandmother's death.'

'Then?'

She turned to him. 'I just think that there's more to it. I know you, Lahnos, and I know your moods better than you do. Something happened in your grandmother's house that you're not telling me about; something that has been weighing on your mind.'

Lahnos glanced away from her, his fury simmering.

'You told me that you argued with your brother,' she went on, 'and then you told me that you argued with your grandmother.'

'And then she died,' he said. 'It was my fault. I didn't mean it, but it was still my fault. If my elbow hadn't hit her, she would still be alive. And you wonder why I'm angry.'

'Look at me,' she said. 'Don't turn away. Look at me and tell me that nothing else happened.'

'I don't understand why you are so obsessed with this.'

'Look at me. If you tell me that nothing else happened, then I will believe you; and I will never bring it up again.'

He stared at her. How did she know? He had told her nothing about the moments after his grandmother's death and yet, somehow, Reyn had discerned that he hadn't been completely honest with her.

'I'm waiting,' she said.

Lahnos lowered his gaze, then he turned away again, his eyes on the orange groves to the rear of Uncle Friel's cottage.

'I… Shit. You won't believe me.'

'Don't you dare say that to me,' she said. 'I thought we were in this together, Lahnos.'

'Before I tell you,' he said; 'I need to know – are you Gifted? I mean, like Leona? How did you know I was keeping something from you?'

'I don't need to be Gifted; your face tells me all I need to know.' She gave him a half-smile. 'You're not very good at keeping secrets, Lahnos.'

'I… I'm a death-reader, Reyn,' he said. 'I am Gifted.'

Reyn said nothing for a long moment, her eyes piercing him.

'Do you believe me?' he said.

'Yes. What happened?'

'I saw… things. Memories. My grandmother's memories. I saw her as a child, then I saw my parent's wedding.' He closed his eyes as they began to well. 'And I saw my mother being murdered.'

She took his hand. 'Oh, Lahnos; my poor baby.'

'It was awful,' he said. 'Men dragged her out of the house. I'm sorry; I should have told you, but… it all seemed too much to take in. My father might still be alive. He disappeared without a trace. He might be alive, Reyn.'

She reached out and embraced him, and he sobbed in her arms. 'It's all right,' she said; 'everything is all right.'

'And then,' he went on, 'I heard her voice.'

'Whose voice? Your grandmother's?'

'I think so. Who else could it have been? She spoke to me, and healed my mind. And then I woke up to see Uncle Friel looking down at me. He knew, Reyn – he knew before I had a chance to tell him. How?'

'I don't know. Theodora gave us Thirteen Gifts. Maybe Friel is also Gifted. Can you remember what all the Gifts are? I can't. Maybe one gives the power to sense other Gifted folk.'

'I am a freak,' he said.

She pulled back a little and looked at him. 'Never say that. The Gifts are just that – Gifts. Theodora gave them to the people of this world to help us. I hate it when people call them curses, or say that the Gifted are monsters or freaks. Do our horns make us freaks? Does my tail make me a freak? Promise me that you will never say that again.'

He stared at her.

'Promise me,' she said. 'I'm serious.'

He nodded. 'I promise.'

'We will still need to keep it a secret,' she said, wiping the tears from his face. 'Others won't understand. Most people are scared of things they don't understand. I remember hearing stories about the Dominion hunting down the Gifted.'

'That's why they killed my mother.'

'Yes,' she said, 'but that's not what I meant. I wasn't talking about the idiot Aucterian farmers – I meant the rulers of the Dominion. The dragons, and the Gunstians, too. People like you and Leona are useful to them. It makes sense now – why your Uncle Friel brought you here. If he could sense that you were Gifted, then he could also sense the same about Leona. What did he say?'

'Not much. He mentioned that he had known of two others who were also death-readers, and that they had both worked for the Dominion.'

'And now he wants you to work for him, just as Leona works for him.'

'I understand why Leona's Gift could be useful to him, but death-reading? How could that be useful?'

'Come on, Lahnos; think. Imagine you were interrogating someone; no – imagine Friel was interrogating someone. Why torture them to reveal the truth when you could just kill them? Friel wants a revolution, doesn't he? What if he needed information about the Bullan garrisons, or... I don't know, about the plans of the Northern Fleet? He captures an officer, and executes them – and then you read the information he needs.'

'My Uncle Friel wouldn't do that.'

Reyn narrowed her eyes. 'Are you sure? I mean, completely sure? He wouldn't be a very successful revolutionary if he wasn't prepared to execute someone.' She chewed her lip. 'I wonder if you being sent here has something to do with what your uncle is planning. Every Zamatan in Kaugatz has heard the rumours. The people there are ready to fight back against the Dominion – all it would take is a spark to light the fire; and maybe Gahad's death is what your uncle has been waiting for.'

'But my uncle couldn't have possibly known what was going to happen to King Gahad.'

'No; but he has been waiting for something, and this could be it. Gahad's murder might be the excuse he needs.'

Lahnos stared out at the orange groves, as a sinking realisation gripped him. Reyn was right. Friel hadn't rescued him from prison to be nice, or because he was acting in his nephew's best interests; he had done it because he viewed Lahnos as a useful asset to his crazy cause.

'And I've been thinking about the so-called deal he made with the Bullan to get you released,' Reyn went on. 'Does it make any sense? Why would there be a law that exiled someone to a different part of the island? Zamata may seem huge to us, but it's tiny compared to the rest of the world. You could walk from one end to the other in a single day.'

'Do you think he was bullshitting us?'

'What do you think?'

Lahnos said nothing.

'Leona was being cagey with us about something else,' Reyn said. 'If

I'm right, then she would have known that Friel was lying to us. He wants you out of Kaugatz for something, but the deal was a lie, and she knew it.'

'That little bitch.'

'Don't blame her. She's sworn to keep Friel's secrets – she told us that herself. It's your uncle who is to blame. I didn't want to say anything to you about this before now, because I didn't understand his motives; but it's clear – he wants to use your Gift in the coming revolution. Are you going to let him?'

Lahnos chewed his lip. 'You know, I'm getting tired of sitting around this *cottage* every day.'

'Me too.'

'Shall we go home?'

Reyn smiled. 'I think that might be a good idea. We'll need to be careful, though. Your uncle has spies everywhere. All it would take is for someone to tip him off, and he'll guess what we've done.' She nodded towards the carriage that sat by the edge of the driveway. 'We can't take that. The driver works for Friel, and he would refuse to go back to Kaugatz; and if we steal it, then he'll report us.'

'We can get a boat from Wayston,' Lahnos said. 'We can slip out of the house and take an old track I know that leads down to the coast. We could be in Wayston harbour in under an hour. We'll need money to pay a fisherman to drop us off in the hills overlooking Kaugatz, and then we could be home by sunset.'

Reyn nodded, then hesitated.

'What is it?' he said.

'You might have to compromise on your principles,' she said.

'What principles? I don't mind stealing something from the house to pay our way.'

'Not that principle,' she said. 'I'm talking about your horns.'

'Oh.'

'You know that if anyone sees them, then the news will reach Friel. I'm sorry, Lahnos, but you're going to have to hide them.'

'How?'

'We'll take that track you mentioned,' she said, 'but when we get to the outskirts of Wayston, you will stay behind, and I will go on ahead to hire a boat. Then, we'll collect you from a quiet part of the coast. That way, only the fishermen will know, and we'll pay them enough to buy their silence.'

'What's to stop them robbing you and leaving you floating in the Hansarta?'

'Easy – you keep the money. They don't get paid unless they pick you up. Trust me, Lahnos. I can handle this.'

'I know, but it won't stop me worrying about you.'

She kissed him. 'You are everything to me; everything.'

'I love you.'

'Then let's raid the house for valuables and go.'

They packed a bag with silver cutlery, and sneaked out of the garden by climbing over a fence. Friel's driver was sitting on the front porch of the mansion, and Reyn and Lahnos sneaked past, using the orange groves as cover. Lahnos led them west for five minutes, and they came to an old goatherd's track that he remembered from his youth. The sun was high in the sky as they trekked down the southern slopes of Mount Medamuna, and both were sweating freely by the time they reached the wheat fields along the narrow coastal plain. They walked for a mile and a half between the rows of wind-break trees that ran next to the patchwork of fields, until the clear waters of the Hansarta inlet were spread out before them.

'Wayston is ten minutes to the east of here,' Lahnos said, as Reyn pulled a head scarf over her hair and horns. 'The harbour is small, but there should be a few boats tied up. If you go to the tavern on the quay-side, you'll find plenty of fishermen sitting outside with their little cups of coffee.'

She nodded. 'How much is the silver worth?'

'I'd guess about three hundred in gold,' he said. 'Offer them two hundred, and see if they'll take that.'

Reyn smiled at him. 'I know how to haggle, Lahnos. Where will you be?'

He pointed at the coast. 'Platzog Cove,' he said. 'They'll know it. There's a small beach there, and I'll be waiting in the trees. I'll see you approach, and swim out to meet you.'

They kissed, then Reyn turned and began to walk towards Wayston. Lahnos watched her leave, then he walked down towards the crystalline Hansarta. The little beach was deserted, and he sat under the branches of an old gum tree. The sun was blazing hot, and he rested in the shade as he thought about his Uncle Friel. He needed time to work it all out in his mind, he decided. His decision to leave had been quick, and they had acted upon it without delay. A bitter feeling of betrayal crept over him – was there no one except Reyn that he could trust? For a few days, Uncle Friel had seemed different from the rest of his family – was he no better than the others? He was certainly more cunning than his Auntie Fenna and Uncle Frickel; more worldly, and more calculating, but what did that matter if he couldn't be trusted?

The fishing boat arrived an hour later, and bore Lahnos and Reyn across the Hansarta. The men on board had stared at the horns on Lahnos's head, but each assured him that they would say nothing, and he had handed over most of the silver he had stolen from the mansion. The sun was starting to lower in the western sky when the boat beached by the high dunes on the other side of the Hansarta, and Lahnos and Reyn resumed their trek. They walked through the vast olive groves that clung on to the low terraced hills to the north of Kaugatz, and then descended into the narrow streets of the town they called home.

Kaugatz seemed quieter than usual, and not just because of the spring heat. The markets had remained closed after their mid-afternoon hiatus, and only a few black-robed Gunstians seemed to be out on the streets, gathered by the corners of the larger junctions, and speaking together in their own language.

'This isn't right,' said Lahnos. 'Something is different.'

Reyn nodded, her eyes tight as she glanced down the deserted streets. 'Everyone is indoors,' she said. 'Maybe there's a curfew.'

'Maybe,' Lahnos said, 'but if that was the case, then you'd expect to see more militia out and about. I haven't seen a single one of those collaborating bastards since we got here. Is it finally happening? Is the uprising beginning?'

Reyn said nothing, but her expression darkened.

They passed the main road that bisected the town of Kaugatz from east to west, and entered the familiar streets close to the little part-Bullan enclave. A few children stared at them as they walked past, then an adult called them inside, and they scattered. An old part-Bullan woman with her horns shorn off was sitting at an intersection that marked the beginning of the area of rundown tenements where their kind lived, and she peered towards the setting sun as Lahnos and Reyn approached.

'What are you doing outside, dears?' she said to them.

Lahnos frowned. 'What is everyone doing inside?'

The old woman said nothing for a moment, her eyes hard as she evaluated them.

'We've been out of town for a few days,' said Reyn. 'Is something happening?'

'Out of town?' she said. 'Where?'

'I've lived here for four years,' said Lahnos. 'You know who I am. Why are you questioning us like this?'

'I know who you are,' the old woman said. 'You're Lahnos. Where have you been?'

'My grandmother died,' he said, 'and I was back in my old village.'

'Go to the funeral, did you, son?'

'What do you think? My family couldn't wait to see the back of me. All the same, my grandmother looked after me when I was little, and I could hardly ignore her death.'

'That's not the story I heard, Lahnos,' the old woman said. 'We heard you were in prison. We heard you were arrested in Igatz.'

'I was only in for a couple of days,' he said, 'and then my uncle picked me up and took me to the village. Look; I'm starting to get a little annoyed by these questions. Be straight with us – what do you suspect? What do you think we've done?'

The old woman said nothing for a moment, then she glanced at the empty streets. 'The Bullan had you, or so I was told. Sometimes, the Bullan release folk early, if they agree to act as informers.'

Lahnos's temper almost boiled over. 'You think I'm a damned informer? You think I would sell out my own people to get out of jail a few days early? I've served my time before; everyone knows it. I've been arrested over a dozen times, and I've never once made a deal.' He pointed a finger in the old woman's face. 'The last few times I've been locked up, the Bullan never even bothered to ask me to become an informer, because they knew exactly what I would say!'

Reyn began to pull his arm back as the old woman remained silent, her face impassive and unimpressed.

Two part-Bullan men emerged from a nearby tenement. Lahnos clenched his fists as they approached, and took a step away from the old woman.

'Lahnos Laimos,' said one of the men. 'You're back.'

'He says he was at his grandmother's funeral,' the old woman said.

'That's not what I said,' Lahnos cried. 'Do you think they would allow me to attend the graveside? My family hate me.'

'He's telling the truth, Granny Lupin,' said the man. 'Only, he's supposed to still be in Fidalaimos.'

Lahnos fell silent.

'What are you doing back here, son?' said the man.

'I wanted to come home,' he said. 'Will someone tell me what is going on?'

'Come with us,' the man said. 'Now.'

'Why?'

'We're not asking, Lahnos. Come with us, or get out of our territory.'

Lahnos and Reyn glanced at each other. The two men gestured to the tenement, and Lahnos exhaled.

'Fine,' he said, 'but there had better be a damn good explanation for this.'

Lahnos and Reyn followed the two men into the tenement, and they were swallowed up within its thick shadows. They were led to a squalid apartment on the second floor, where eight heavily-armed part-Bullan were sitting on broken furniture. Two had their eyes on the street, while the others turned to watch Lahnos and Reyn be led inside.

'Do you want to fight, Lahnos?' said one of the men who had been outside.

'Don't ask him that,' said the other; 'ask him why he's not in Fidalaimos. We were told he was there for a good reason and that he wouldn't be coming back.'

'Who told you that?' said Lahnos.

'You're not stupid, son,' said the second man. 'Who do you think?'

'My uncle?'

The men nodded.

'And what has my uncle got to do with what's going on? What is going on?'

'Why did you come back?'

'Because I was sick of sitting on my arse. My uncle told me nothing. He dropped me off at his cottage, then went back to Igatz. What were we supposed to do – sit there until our horns fell off?'

The men in the room glanced at each other.

'I say we let him fight,' said one. 'We all know he's handy in a brawl.'

'His uncle will have something to say about that,' said another.

A third sighed. 'He's here now, whether the colonel likes it or not.'

'We'll have to inform him,' said the second man. 'He'll find out one way or another, so it's best if he hears it from us. It'll have to wait until the morning, though – there will be no more ferries running tonight.'

'Why not?' said Reyn. 'I want to hear you say it.'

'Be quiet, girl.'

Reyn bristled. 'Don't you tell me to be quiet. I've stood back and said nothing while you all dithered and argued. We all know the rumours – is it finally happening?'

No one responded.

'It's happening tonight, isn't it?' Reyn went on, her voice flattening. 'Sunset?'

One of the men nodded.

'Are we attacking the two Aucterian enclaves in Kaugatz?' Reyn said. 'And the ferry terminals? What about the Bullan guard posts? And the militia stations? All of them?'

'We can't let her leave,' said one of the men.

'Why?' Reyn cried. 'Who do you think I'm going to tell? I'm Zamatan, just like you. I have horns and a tail. I'm part-Bullan – do you think I would betray my own folk? Give me a damn weapon; I want to be a part of this.'

'Is it true?' said Lahnos. 'Are we taking control of Kaugatz?'

'The colonel told us that your heart wasn't in the fight,' said one of the men. 'He told us you weren't ready.'

'Damn my uncle,' Lahnos cried. 'He had no right to tell you that.'

'Was he wrong, lad?'

Lahnos's heart raced, and he made a decision. 'Yes. He's wrong. For some reason, my uncle is trying to protect me, but he's wrong. I'm ready. If we're taking this damn island, then I refuse to sit it out. This morning, Reyn and I were sipping lemonade on a veranda, completely unaware of what was happening here – but this is our home, and I intend to fight for it. We both intend to fight for it, whether you agree or not.'

'Will you take orders, lad?' said one of the sitting men, who had two blunt horns coming out of his head. 'We don't need rogue elements. We have a plan, and we're going to stick to it.'

'Where do you want us?' said Lahnos.

The men gazed out of the window at the setting sun.

'It's too late to relocate them now,' said the sitting man. 'I'm calling it. If the lad wants to fight, then he can join our attack on the ferry terminal opposite the Handshore Naval Base.'

'And what about the colonel?' said another man.

'I'll take responsibility,' said the sitting man. 'Arm Lahnos. The girl will have to stay here.'

Reyn frowned. 'But…'

'Those are my orders,' said the sitting man. 'Blood will be spilled this night, and I'm not having girls butchered under my watch. It's either that, or we lock you both in the basement until the colonel gets here.'

Reyn took Lahnos's hand. 'This is bullshit.'

'I know,' he said, 'but what choice do we have?'

She nodded, though her eyes remained defiant as she glared at the sitting man. 'All right. I can obey orders. Just make sure that you do it right.'

The sitting man laughed.

The sun set at that moment, and a low din of banging pots and pans started to rise up from the dense streets of Kaugatz.

'That's the signal,' said the man in charge, as he got to his feet. 'Everyone out. And before I have to ask again, would someone give the damned boy a weapon?'

One of the men handed Lahnos a war axe, then the others started hurrying from the room. Outside, the din was growing louder as the part-Bullan emerged onto the streets. Someone shoved Lahnos in the back, pushing him towards the door.

Reyn gripped on to his hand. 'Come back to me,' she said.

'I will,' Lahnos said, then he pulled his hand free and followed the other men down the stairs.

'How many part-Bullan are taking part?' he asked, as they ran down the steps.

'Over a hundred,' said one of the others. 'We're joining a group of ordinary Zamatans in the attack on the terminal.'

'And how many militia and Bullan are there?'

'A few companies; maybe more.'

They emerged into the fading light of dusk and fell in with a large mass of part-Bullan as they headed south towards the shores of the Cyasarta inlet. The old woman who had been keeping watch on the intersection was still there, and she waved at the men as they passed.

'Go get them, boys!' she yelled.

The part-Bullan reached another junction, where a large crowd of armed Zamatans were waiting. The leaders of the two groups conferred for a moment, then they all began to move off, a surging mass of humanity heading towards the little harbour that controlled access to Igatz. Some were holding flaming torches, and Lahnos felt his emotions rise – a mixture of nervous anticipation and a sickly realisation that people were about to die. The noise grew and grew as the crowd flooded down the streets towards the inlet, and Lahnos heard a scream of fear and agony from somewhere off to his left.

The crowd roared as the ferry terminal came into sight at the end of a long straight road. A line of armoured Bullan soldiers was blocking the street, supported by dozens of Zamatan militia armed with crossbows and shields.

'Kill them all!' someone shouted. 'Bullan and militia; kill them all! For Zamata! Zamata!'

The crowd roared again as it raced towards the soldiers and militia guarding the ferry terminal.

Lahnos hesitated for a split second as he stared at the thick line of Bullan. What was he doing? Was he insane? There was about to be a bloodbath, and his feet seemed frozen to the ground. His uncle had been right – he wasn't ready.

I am with you, Lahnos, said a voice in his head, the same voice that had comforted him after he had seen the memories of his grandmother. *I shall be watching over you. Be brave, and strong; and fight to protect the ones you love.*

Lahnos felt his fears ebb away. He gripped his axe, roared along with the others, and charged.

CHAPTER 11
THE FOUNDATIONS OF FAITH

Igatz, Serpent Isle – 3rd Nethinch 1588

Cisca turned over in bed, her eyes opening. Something had disturbed her sleep, a noise from somewhere. She yawned. Her eyes started to close again, then she noticed a strange flicker of light seeping between the shutters that barred the balcony doors. She watched the light for a moment as it created a pattern on her ceiling and walls, then she pulled the cover from her and swung her feet off the bed. It was probably nothing, she thought, as she pulled on a dressing gown, but her curiosity drove her towards the balcony. She opened the door, and gasped. The night sky seemed to be glowing. She walked out into the warm air. Her view was of the Cyasarta to the east, while the light seemed to be coming from the other direction. She turned, but could see nothing over the bulk of the palace. Was Igatz on fire? Surely the bells of the town would be ringing if that were the case. She turned back, and saw flames reflecting off the waters of the inlet. She leaned over the balcony and craned her neck to the left. Smoke and fires were rising above the suburbs of Kaugatz on the far side of the Cyasarta, and a low rumbling din reached her ears.

She needed to remain calm. Perhaps fires were common in the dense streets of Kaugatz. Her military instincts took over, and she walked back into her room. She shed the dressing gown, lit a lamp, and pulled on her uniform, in case she was called for duty. She brushed her hair in front of the dresser mirror, then tied it back.

She yawned again. It was past midnight, by her reckoning, but with no moon at that time of the month, it was hard to tell. Should she wait, or should she leave her apartment to find out what was happening? She thought through what she had been trained to do. Wait, she thought. Her superior officers needed to know where she would be, and they would summon her if she was required. She extinguished the lamp and lay down on the bed. Her attention drifted, then her eyes opened again as a flash of light made the sky glow. What was the worst that could happen? Perhaps the Gunstians had invaded the island, but they would have had advance notice of that, and it seemed foolhardy to have launched an attack in the middle of the night. Besides, the intelligence report that she had read had the Imperial Gunstian Fleet a thousand miles to the south of the Serpent Isle.

A shout rose up from the gardens – a guttural order voiced in the language of the Bullan, a language that they refused to share with outsiders. Cisca wondered what it meant. She had slowly become accustomed to the presence of the strange Bullan soldiers on the island, but they still had the power to unnerve her. Their tails in particular she found to be grotesquely fascinating.

Someone thumped on her door and she responded without thinking. Her feet touched the floor of her room, and she hurried to the door and opened it.

She saluted. 'Sir.'

The Dragon Corps major eyed her. 'You're up, I see. Good. Get yourself down to the main audience hall immediately while I summon the rest of the officers.'

'Yes, sir.'

The major strode away before Cisca thought about asking for the cause of the disturbance. She was still half asleep, she realised, as she collected her keys and locked her apartment door. Please let there be coffee in the audience hall, she silently begged the dragon gods. She passed courtiers lighting lamps in the palace corridors, and hurried down the stairs to the main section of the palace. Bullan soldiers were clustered in the central hallways, talking among themselves in low voices, while human officers from the Dominion Navy and Dragon Corps were making their way to the audience hall. Cisca looked for Travers among the crowds, but saw no sign of him. The audience chamber was in semi-darkness when she entered, with courtiers trying to light the enormous chandeliers that hung suspended on chains from the domed ceiling, while up on the low central platform, Lords Rufus and Meer were standing, their reptilian eyes on the assembling human officers. Cisca found a place at the rear of a large group of naval officers and stifled another yawn.

Lord Meer glanced down at Lieutenant-General Foley. 'Are there more humans to come?'

'Some are still being awoken, my lord,' said the officer. 'It shouldn't take too much longer.'

'I have waited long enough,' said Lord Rufus. He raised his long neck. 'Humans!' he cried out, his voice filling the hall.

The officers froze, and every eye turned towards the acting Governor of the island.

'You have been summoned into my presence as a precaution, nothing more,' Lord Rufus went on. 'Lord Meer – please inform them of the situation.'

'Yes, my noble lord,' said Meer. His glowing eyes scanned the hall. 'Yesterday, at sunset, lawless criminals in the town of Kaugatz started a riot. The town has seen riots before, but this one was different – this one was clearly coordinated. Foreign forces are at work, stirring up discontent among the benighted native inhabitants of this blessed isle. By midnight, two of the four ferry terminals that link Kaugatz to the rest of the Serpent Isle were in the hands of the rioters, while the two Aucterian enclaves were placed under siege. Bullan forces have been attacked at more than a dozen locations, according to what can only be described as a carefully-prepared plan. That this is the work of Gunstian agents is clear. Worry not, though, for order shall be restored. Fresh Bullan companies are being shipped across the Cyasarta from Igatz as I speak. They will defend the Aucterian colonists and subdue the rioters. They have been ordered to give no quarter, for the rapacious and subversive rebels deserve none.' He fell silent for a few moments, as the officers in the hall digested his words.

'However,' the dragon went on, 'this is not a rebellion. It is merely a riot. The Zamatans love the Dominion, and none of you shall use the word *rebellion* to describe tonight's events. Rebellions do not occur upon the Serpent Isle. What is taking place is criminal, not political. Order will be restored by dawn, and then the guilty shall be condemned and executed for their crimes. For the remainder of this night, all officers shall report to their posts, and there they shall remain until further notice. You are dismissed.'

The two dragons stepped down from the platform, and the humans cleared a wide path for them as they strode from the hall. Cisca noticed a few courtiers brewing coffee by the side of the circular chamber, and joined the queue to receive a cup. The atmosphere was subdued, and many of the officers appeared dazed after being awoken in the middle of the night. The queue shuffled forwards, and Cisca took a cup of scalding hot liquid from a courtier, then moved to the side.

'Can you believe this bullshit?' whispered someone to her left.

She turned, and saw Travers standing next to her, looking fresh and alert. She sipped coffee from the cup.

'Kaugatz is burning,' Travers went on, 'and the dragons are worried about us calling it a rebellion?'

'I'm sure Lord Meer knows best,' Cisca said.

'Oh, you're sure, are you? Dragons always know best – is that what you were taught in the academy?'

'It's what you were taught, too.'

Travers shrugged. 'I'm going back to bed.'

Cisca frowned at him. He didn't look as though he had been to bed at all that night.

'We were ordered to go to our posts,' she said.

'I'm not on duty just now,' he said. 'I have no post to go to. And what about you? Why aren't you rushing to your post?'

'I will, as soon as I have finished this coffee.'

'Off to see Lord Kheran, are you? For all the good it will do. The dragon child is probably sleeping.'

'I hope he is,' she said. 'If he's awake, then he might be frightened, and I don't want that. It's better if he sleeps through it.'

'I'll walk with you to see the young lord's courtiers,' he said.

'Why?'

'Well, you'll need to request access to Lord Kheran's quarters; otherwise you won't get in.'

'That's not what I meant. I meant why would you want to walk with me?'

'Is this about the dance? I apologised for coming over a bit strong. I thought we were friends?'

Cisca narrowed her eyes. 'You seem a little agitated this evening, Lieutenant. Are the riots that bad? Should we be concerned?'

He leaned in closer. 'I have never seen anything like this since I arrived on the damn island. Dozens of Bullan have already been killed or injured, and I was told that over a hundred Zamatan rioters are lying dead in the streets. And as for the militia...'

'What about them?'

He shrugged. 'I'm hearing mixed reports. Some say that the militia based in Kaugatz are doing their duty and fighting the rioters, while others say that they have laid down their weapons. Others still are saying that entire units have switched sides.'

'How do you know all this if you were in bed?'

Travers smiled. 'You have me there. All right, I confess that I wasn't in bed. I couldn't sleep. My room looks to the west, and I have been watching the flames rise over Kaugatz since sunset.'

Cisca finished her coffee and placed the empty cup on to a courtier's tray.

'I need to go to work,' she said.

'I'm not stopping you, Lieutenant.'

She strode towards the arched exit that led to Lord Kheran's quarters, then found Travers walking alongside her. She rolled her eyes, but said nothing.

'And that nonsense about the Gunstians,' Travers said. 'I can scarcely believe that Lord Meer had the gall to blame them for what the Zamatans are doing.'

'It sounded like a plausible explanation to me,' Cisca said.

'Well, you are still new here, and so I will overlook your ignorance of such matters.'

'You are too kind,' she said.

'Thank you.'

'I really do need to get to work, you know,' she said, as they approached the doors to Lord Kheran's quarters.

'I know.'

'Then why are you following me?'

'I thought you needed the company. I'm at a loose end and, to be honest, I don't want to sit alone in my room to watch Kaugatz burn. Do you need a hand with anything?'

Cisca came to a halt by the human-sized entrance doors that led to Lord Kheran's chambers. The keys for the doors were in her pocket, but she was under orders not to reveal that she possessed them, and was starting to feel a little uncomfortable with Travers's presence.

'Well?' he said. 'Can I assist in any way?'

'I don't want to sound rude,' she said, 'but would you please leave me alone?'

'Why?' he said. 'I'm not doing anything wrong, am I? All right – I admit it – I'm a little bit scared by what the riots could mean, and I would rather not be on my own.'

'You're scared?'

'Is that so hard to believe? Do you know what those rioters would do to us if they reached Igatz?'

'They won't reach Igatz,' she said. 'The Bullan will restore order.'

'If only I had your confidence.'

'Travers – I need to go to my post.'

'And I am not preventing you from doing that,' he said. 'Go on – go to your post.'

Cisca's anger flared, and she struggled to keep her composure. With Travers lingering by her shoulder, she would have to request access to Lord Kheran's quarters in order to conceal from him the fact that she had the keys in her pocket. She approached the double doors and rapped on them with her knuckles.

'How long do they usually take to answer?' Travers said.

Cisca shrugged.

'I get the feeling that I am starting to annoy you.'

'Whatever gave you that impression, Travers?'

They waited by the entrance as Cisca's impatience grew. At length, one of the double doors opened and an old courtier peered out at her.

'Why are you wasting my time, Lieutenant?' the courtier said. 'You know you can...' His voice tailed away as he noticed the presence of Travers. He frowned. 'You had better come in.'

'Good night, Lieutenant Travers,' Cisca said, then she followed the courtier into a lamplit hallway.

'Why did you bring that naval officer to the doors of Lord Kheran's quarters?' the courtier said, as he locked the door behind them.

'I didn't bring him,' Cisca said. 'He followed me. He refused to leave me alone.'

The courtier's eyes narrowed. 'Does he know that you have...?'

'He probably does now,' Cisca snapped, 'after your little indiscretion by the door.'

'My humble apologies, ma'am,' said the courtier, his face falling. 'Lord Kheran is... upset by the fires and the noise, and I may have allowed my frustration to get the better of me. Do you intend to report this incident to Lord Meer or Lieutenant-General Foley?'

Cisca rubbed her face. 'Just take me to Lord Kheran.'

'Yes, ma'am.'

The courtier led her along the hallway, and they entered a large chamber full of supplies. Everything the dragon child required was stored somewhere within the racks of shelves and crates – food, toys, grooming implements, cushions, and a multitude of mops, pails and brushes. They passed through the chamber and walked into a vast hall, where Lord Kheran was lying upon a heap of soft mattresses and blankets. He turned his head towards them.

'Where have you been, Cisca?' he said, his voice low and wavering.

'I came as quickly as I could, my lord,' Cisca said, bowing before the royal child.

'Is it true?' he said. 'Is Kaugatz burning?'

'There is some trouble, my lord,' she said, 'but the brave Bullan soldiers will deal with it.'

'Is Igatz safe?'

'Yes, my lord; perfectly safe. The ships of the fleet will prevent any of the rioters from crossing the Cyasarta.'

'They don't need ships. Igatz is not an island, Cisca. The bad humans could walk here.'

Cisca strode up to the dragon, and placed a hand on to the side of his head. She scratched his silvery scales.

'One Bullan is worth twenty rioters,' she said. 'We're safe.'

'Do you promise?'

'Yes.'

The dragon child closed his eyes and laid his head onto the mass of cushions and blankets. Cisca sat down upon a mattress, her legs crossed beneath her, and kept her hand on the dragon's head.

'Your mother would be very proud of you,' she murmured; 'for being so brave.'

'I like you,' he said. 'I'm glad that Lord Noxon left you here.'

'You know, my lord – so am I. Perhaps Lord Meer did me a favour when he complained about me.'

The dragon opened an eye a crack. 'Lord Meer didn't complain about you, Cisca. I know he threatened to, but he was only teasing you. It was a human who did it. A man.'

'A man?'

'Yes. I was there. The man told Lord Noxon that you had said rude things about him, and Lord Noxon got very angry.'

'Do you recall the man's name, my lord?'

'No. I wasn't paying attention, and you all look the same to me. Well, not all of you. I recognise you by your eyes. You have kind eyes, Cisca.'

Cisca frowned. Had one of her colleagues in the Dragon Corps betrayed her? Perhaps it had been one of her superior officers from the voyage out from Inopei; someone who had taken a dislike to her, or someone who had taken umbrage at her lowly accent. Her thoughts went to Travers, but she couldn't fathom any possible motive for him to have acted in such a manner, and she dismissed the notion.

'Would you read me a story?' said the dragon.

'Of course,' she said. 'Which one would you like?'

'Something from the *Tales of Gahad the Mighty*,' he said. 'I like those.'

Cisca pulled herself to her feet, stretched her legs, then walked back to the large supply room. An old Aucterian servant was there, sorting through the sacks of dragon food, and she glanced at Cisca as she entered.

'Have you heard, ma'am?' she whispered. 'The rebels have taken another ferry terminal, and two thousand Aucterian colonists are now cut off in Kaugatz.'

'Which terminal?' Cisca said.

'The one opposite the Fortress of Atzoun, ma'am. That only leaves one harbour in Kaugatz still in our hands – the one closest to this palace. If they take that, then...'

'Stay calm,' said Cisca. 'You shouldn't be paying heed to any rumours. And we should call them rioters, not rebels.'

'Yes, ma'am. Sorry, ma'am. Where did they get all of their weapons from? The Zamatans aren't supposed to have any.'

'Everything will be clearer when the sun rises. Get back to work.'

The servant bowed her head. 'Yes, ma'am.'

Cisca went to a bookshelf and pulled down the large volume that Lord Kheran had requested. She glanced back at the servant, but the old woman had her gaze lowered as she arranged the sacks of food.

Cisca walked back into the dragon's chamber, and re-took her position on the mattress by his head.

'Right,' she said, trying to sound cheerful. 'Which tale would you like to hear? The one about His Majesty's arrival upon this world? What about the one when King Nathaniel the greatest of the gods turned King Gahad into a dragon?'

'Do you believe that?' said Kheran.

Cisca blinked.

'Are these stories all true?' the dragon child went on.

'I... I don't know for certain, my lord. They are the stories every child in the Dominion learns at school, but it all happened such a long time ago.'

'One thousand, five hundred and eighty-eight years ago.'

'Yes. Only His Majesty King Gahad has lived that long... I mean...'

'I know what you mean, Cisca. It's all right. I sometimes forget that he is dead, too. I thought he would live forever.'

'I also thought that, my lord.'

'The demon witch killed him; that's what my father told me. Cisca – what is a demon witch?'

'I think it means someone who has the old powers. The Gifts of Theodora. Some people say that the Gunstians still have Gifted men and women living among them. I think the demon witch might be one of them.'

'What if she comes here, Cisca? She might already be here – she might be leading the riots in Kaugatz. Will she kill me if she comes? If she killed King Gahad, then what could I do to stop her? What could my father or Lord Meer do?'

'No one is going to hurt you, my lord,' Cisca said.

'In the *Tales*, King Nathaniel gave this world to King Gahad, and told him that it was his.'

'Yes; that's right.'

'But it's not true, is it, Cisca? The Dragon Dominion has tried to conquer Gunst, but we failed. They beat us. How could Lord Nathaniel be wrong?'

'I don't know if he was wrong, my lord. Maybe, to King Nathaniel, two thousand years is a short time. Maybe a million years is a short time to the ever-living gods.'

'A little while ago, we all called King Gahad an ever-living god.'

'Yes. I know.'

'We were wrong.'

Cisca bowed her head.

'Before King Gahad arrived on this world,' Kheran went on, 'there were people already living here. There were people in Inopei, and people in Aucteran. What happened to them all?'

'I don't know if I am the right person to tell you, my lord.'

Kheran stared into her eyes. 'If you don't tell me, no one will. I have already asked my mother and father this question, but they refused to speak of it. Why? I order you to tell me, Cisca.'

Cisca's mouth dried up.

'Tell me, or leave my quarters,' the dragon said.

'All right,' she said. 'I will tell you.' She closed her eyes, so that she wouldn't have to endure his stare. 'When King Gahad arrived on this world, he wasn't alone. He brought many dragons with him, and he brought thousands and thousands of humans to live here. At first, the new humans lived alongside the ones who were already here, but the old humans slowly grew more angry, as the new ones spread all over Inopei and Aucteran. There was fighting between the two groups, and then, a thousand years ago, King Gahad came to a decision. He... His Majesty ordered that all of the old humans... he decided that it would be better if...'

'Yes?' said Kheran. 'What did he decide? What happened to the old humans?'

'The dragons killed them all, my lord.'

Kheran fell silent.

'Every human who lives in Inopei or Aucteran today is descended from the settlers King Gahad brought with him,' Cisca went on. 'The only native... people who still live in the eastern half of Athumia are the Bullan. All of the original humans have gone.'

'Now I see why the Gunstians hate us so much,' Kheran said. 'They think that we want to do the same thing to them.'

'The Dominion has changed since those days, my lord,' Cisca said. 'Look at Irlan and Elso – we conquered those regions over a century ago, and we have allowed the natives there to live. And upon the Serpent Isle, too. Not only have we let the native Zamatans live in peace, but we even leave the local Gunstian islanders alone. We have built them schools and roads, and allow them to keep their customs and traditions. I think...'

'Yes? What do you think, Cisca?'

'What I was going to say might sound blasphemous, my lord, and I wouldn't wish to offend you.'

'You have already told me that my ancestors murdered every native human in the East. What could you say that is worse than that?'

Cisca took a breath. 'All right. I think that King Gahad realised that he had made a mistake. I think that he changed his mind, and decided that killing the inhabitants of this world was a bad thing to do.'

'Are you saying that the mighty and ever-living King Gahad made a mistake? The *Tales* say that it is impossible for King Gahad to make a mistake. I mean, that it was impossible.'

'Are you angry with me, my lord?'

'No. I know that the *Tales* are wrong. If they were right, then King Gahad would not be dead. Why do the *Tales* say nothing about the Gifted?'

'I don't know, my lord.'

'Guess.'

Cisca rubbed her face. 'Well, I think it might be because the Dominion didn't want us to know about them. Every Gifted person in the East was killed a thousand years ago, and perhaps they wanted us to forget about them.'

'When you say *Dominion*, you mean the dragons, don't you?'

'I love the dragons of this world, my lord. I worship and obey them. I am in their service, and would never be disloyal.'

'But you think we make mistakes?'

Cisca said nothing, as a base fear gripped her.

'You think King Gahad made a mistake when he killed all of the humans in the East,' Kheran went on. 'If you think His Majesty could make mistakes, then what about every other dragon? None of us are as mighty or as wise as King Gahad was. Lord Noxon, for example – he made a mistake when he left you here. He was also rude and nasty, and I didn't like him.'

'I don't know what to say, my lord.'

Kheran pushed his head forward and nuzzled her. 'You are the only human who has ever been honest with me. Cisca, you are dear to my heart. Never leave me.'

She raised her arms and embraced his face. 'You are also dear to me, my beautiful dragon. I will never leave you.'

They remained in that position for a long time, each with their eyes closed. Despite the kind words Kheran had spoken, Cisca's heart was full of turmoil. She had come closer to rejecting her own beliefs than at any other point in her life, and it had left her feeling sick and confused. If the dragons could make mistakes, then how could they be gods? What did it mean to be a god? Gahad's death had sent a tremor throughout the world, and had shaken the foundations of Cisca's faith. She started to sob for the dead dragon king, as the implications of his demise finally became clear to her. Was the Dominion based upon a lie?'

'Why are you weeping, Cisca?' said the dragon child.

'For Gahad,' she said.

A low cough came from the corner of the chamber, and Kheran lifted his head.

'Why are you disturbing us, human?'

'My humble apologies, my blessed lord,' said Major Polarn from the Dragon Corps. 'I have news that you should hear.' His eyes flickered over to Cisca as she wiped the tears from her cheeks. 'News regarding the present troubles.'

'Yes?' said Kheran.

'The Bullan reinforcements have struggled to gain a foothold upon the shores of Kaugatz,' the major said, 'and therefore Lord Rufus has decreed that Lord Meer will fly out in person to subdue the riots. He will be leaving at dawn's first light, my lord, and your blessed father wished for you to know.'

'Lord Meer will be fighting the rioters?' said Kheran.

'Lord Meer shall be destroying them, my lord,' said the major. He glanced at Cisca again, but his eyes betrayed no emotion. 'I shall leave you now. Good night, my lord.'

The officer bowed, then turned and walked from the chamber. Cisca swallowed, as she tried to imagine the carnage a fully-grown dragon could inflict upon the town of Kaugatz.

'Lord Meer is going?' said Kheran. 'Is it right for dragons to slaughter humans? I thought you said the Dominion had changed, Cisca.'

'I thought it had, my lord,' she said. 'It seems that I, too, was wrong.'

CHAPTER 12
TSALLON ANURA

Kaugatz, Serpent Isle – 3rd Nethinch 1588

Leona gazed out from the ancient battlements of the monastery of Tsallon Anura as the sun appeared over the horizon to her left. On the other side of the Cyasarta inlet, she could see one of the enormous breakwaters that marked the edge of the Handshore Naval Base. Dominion warships were visible in the growing light, patrolling the inlet between Kaugatz and Igatz. Behind her, smoke was billowing up from the dozens of fires raging through the town of Kaugatz, and she could hear the cries of wounded Zamatans in the grounds of the old monastery. The colonel had made Tsallon Anura his headquarters when they had arrived in Kaugatz just before sunset on the previous day, and from there he had orchestrated a night of bloody violence and horror that Leona had scarcely believed possible. The colonel had kept her far away from the fighting, but she had seen the rows of mangled and butchered corpses, along with the hundreds of wounded who had been brought to the relative safety of the monastery.

'The night is over at last,' the colonel said to her left.

'It was the longest night of my life, sir,' she said.

'You should get some rest.'

'I will rest when you do.'

The colonel smiled. 'That might be a while from now. The dawn shall bring the Dominion's response, and we shall need to be prepared.'

'But the Bullan have been counter-attacking all night, sir,' Leona said. 'What other response can we expect?'

The colonel said nothing for a moment as his dark eyes gazed at Igatz in the distance. 'We shall see.'

'Is all this worth it, sir?'

'Yes.'

'Are you certain?'

'How could it be otherwise?' he said. 'I have been planning this my entire life. Every deal, every compromise, every betrayal – they have all led here, to this moment. Zamata shall be free, Leona.'

A young rebel fighter with a mace and a red armband ran up the stairs to the battlements and bowed his head before the colonel.

'I asked for a moment's rest,' Friel said. 'This had better be important, lad.'

'Sorry, sir. I was told that you would want to hear this. The part-Bullan have reported from their district, sir. They say that Lahnos Laimos is there, fighting alongside the others. He took part in the battle for the central ferry terminal.'

Friel's composure dissolved into anger. 'My nephew is in Kaugatz?'

'That's what the report says, sir.'

'That stupid little... I will throttle the ungrateful wretch when I get my hands on him.' His eyes widened. 'Is he injured? Is he alive and well?'

'The report states that he survived the battle intact, sir. It also says that he fought bravely, and killed a Bullan soldier.'

The colonel put a hand to his eyes.

'Am I dismissed, sir? May I go?'

'Not yet,' said Friel. 'I want a message sent to the part-Bullan leadership. Lahnos is to be brought here to Tsallon Anura, with all possible speed. If a girl by the name of Reyn happens to be with him, then she is also to be brought here. Ensure they have an armed escort for the entire journey. If either die, I will be holding someone responsible; do you understand?'

The fighter bowed his head. 'Yes, sir.'

'Good lad. Off you go.'

Friel glanced at Leona as the young man ran back down the stairs.

'There were no lies, sir,' she said.

'Damn it all,' Friel muttered. 'After the trouble I endured to get that idiot boy as far away from danger as possible, and he walks right into it.'

'Perhaps, sir, if you had been honest with him in the first place, then...'

Friel snorted. 'Then what? He would have refused to come with me. He would have remained in jail in Igatz, or worse, he would have stayed in Kaugatz. I should have broken the boy's legs.' He shook his head. 'Now every part-Bullan in the rebellion knows that my own nephew has defied my orders. I shall have to make an example of him, Leona. If I don't, then what's to stop the others from thinking they can disregard my commands?'

'At least he ran towards the fighting,' Leona said. 'That shows spirit, sir. It would be far worse if he had fled in the other direction. He's young – you can put it down to his irrepressible sense of patriotism. And he killed a Bullan soldier. There are many ways that you could turn this to your advantage.'

The colonel smiled. 'His "irrepressible patriotism", eh? If only that were true, Leona. Lahnos cares about the part-Bullan, but his heart isn't with the cause. He has spent too many years getting nothing but abuse and grief from his fellow Zamatans to have any real sense of empathy with them. If I even start to suspect that Lahnos will drive a wedge between the native peoples of this island, then I will have to take action. One of my greatest achievements in this rebellion so far was persuading the part-Bullan to join the fight, and then persuading the other Zamatans to allow the part-Bullan to join the fight. I cannot permit Lahnos to jeopardise that.'

Another rebel fighter climbed the stairs bearing a tray with two small cups and a bowl of bread. He bowed before the colonel.

'Gifts from the monks, sir. Coffee and bread.'

Friel smiled. 'The monks? Are we sure they haven't poisoned it?'

The rebel fighter hesitated, his eyes wide.

'It was a joke,' said the colonel. 'I shall take the coffee, even though this will be my tenth cup since sunset. Give the bread to the injured men, and be sure to thank the monks for me.'

'Yes, sir.'

The colonel lifted the two cups of coffee from the tray, and the rebel fighter bowed his head and retreated down the stairs. Friel handed one of the cups to Leona.

He smiled. 'I forgot to ask if you were hungry, Leona.'

'I'm too anxious to be hungry, sir.' She lowered her gaze as she sipped the hot coffee. 'How many died last night?'

'It will be a while before we have an accurate figure.'

'In your best estimation, then, sir?'

Friel shrugged. 'This is purely guesswork, based upon the bits and pieces of information I have received, and then extrapolated across all of Kaugatz; but I would estimate around three hundred Zamatan civilians, the same number of Aucterian civilians, perhaps a hundred and fifty members of the Zamatan militia, and... up to a hundred Bullan? The wounded will come to approximately three times that figure, or thereabouts. As you said – it was a long night.'

A rebel officer mounted the stairs.

'Sir,' he said, 'I am fielding urgent questions from various districts of Kaugatz, and I need to provide some answers. Can we expect you back at your post soon?'

'After I have drunk this coffee, Captain,' said Friel. 'But you can supply me with the most pressing issues here and now, and I shall give you a decision for each one.'

'Thank you, sir. Firstly, the commander in charge of assaulting the eastern ferry terminal has requested reinforcements. Three companies of Bullan have dug in along the perimeter of the harbour, and the commander says that he does not have enough men to take the position.'

Leona and Friel glanced to their left. The only Kaugatz ferry terminal still in Dominion hands was a little over half a mile from the monastery of Tsallon Anura, and the faint sounds of battle were just audible.

'He can have the reserves in the central district,' Friel said. 'They amount to an extra eight hundred fighters. I want that terminal taken today.'

The captain nodded. 'Yes, sir. Secondly, we now have almost two thousand Aucterian civilians corralled in their southern enclave, sir. They have surrendered, and have been disarmed, but the local commanders are saying that they have no fresh water or spare food to give to them. Should we divert supplies from other districts to feed them?'

'No,' said Friel. 'Have the Aucterian civilians driven out of town. They can walk to Igatz. Inform the units guarding the southern land approaches to Kaugatz to let them pass unmolested. They can take one item of luggage each, but I want them all out by sunset at the latest. There are to be no reprisals, and no massacres. If the Aucterians cooperate, then they are free to leave.'

'Yes, sir. Thank you, sir. That was all for now.'

'I shall be back in the temple offices in ten minutes, Captain.'

The officer bowed, then hurried away.

'You're making the Aucterians walk all the way to Igatz, sir?' said Leona. 'That's, um...'

'About sixteen miles by land,' Friel said. 'They'll live. The Aucterians in the eastern enclave present a bigger difficulty – at least those in the southern enclave are already on the edge of town. The only way to get the eastern lot back to Igatz is by boat, and...' His voice tailed away.

'What it is, sir?'

Friel said nothing, a hand up by his eyes as he squinted at the sunrise to the east. A bell rang out from a high spire in the monastery grounds, and dozens of rebel fighters stopped what they were doing.

'Sir?' said Leona.

'Oh shit,' muttered Friel. He turned, and raced down the stairs.

Leona stared at him, then followed, her boots clacking off the ancient stone steps. Friel ran to a group of officers, and grabbed one by the shoulder.

'Get your teams into position, Lieutenant!' the colonel cried. 'Now, now!

The young officer's eyes widened, then he saluted and sprinted away.

'Raise the flags,' Friel called out to another officer. 'I want the old flag of Zamata flying from the highest points of Tsallon Anura. Go!' Friel turned. 'Get the wounded into the monastery buildings, and order every able-bodied fighter to seek cover!'

He turned again, his eyes wild, and saw Leona.

'What's happening?' she said, her voice straining.

He gave her a look that bordered on madness, then he raised his arms in the air. 'Dragon! Dragon attack!'

He grabbed Leona by the arm as dozens of rebel fighters began running through the grounds of the monastery.

'The dragons won't attack us,' said Leona, as Friel dragged her towards the high curtain wall. 'We worship them. They are our gods.'

A large shadow passed overhead.

'Get those damn flags up!' Friel cried. 'Get that beast's attention.'

The shadow passed again, and Leona glanced up. Above her, the enormous bulk of a green dragon was hovering over the monastery.

'That's it, you big bastard,' Friel whispered. 'Look at us; ignore the rest of Kaugatz.'

A large standard was raised from the tallest spire of the monastery, a spread of blue and white fabric. The dragon's eyes gazed at it, then its mouth opened. A great burst of flames surged from the dragon's jaws, enveloping the ancient tower from where the flag had been displayed. The dragon moved its head down, and the flames went from the top of the spire to its base. The stones of the tower glowed red hot, and it began to split and fragment. There was a great grinding sound that drowned out every other noise, and the tower collapsed, spilling hundreds of tons of masonry into the grounds of the monastery. Lines of injured rebel fighters were hit, their bodies pulverised by the falling rock, then the dragon came in lower and sprayed fire along the length of the curtain wall where Friel and Leona had been standing just moments before. Several fighters fell screaming, their flesh, clothes and hair incinerated. Leona felt her knees sag, and Friel dragged her to an alcove by one side of the old stone cloister.

'Keep your head down,' he yelled at her.

The dragon turned again, his attention caught by a few crossbow bolts that had struck his right flank. He raked his huge claws out, and the talons ripped through two fighters, tearing their bodies to pieces.

'Who dares rebel against the blessed Dominion?' the dragon roared, as the conflagration engulfing the ancient monastery grew around him.

'Where is that damned lieutenant?' Friel hissed. 'If he has run away I will rip his head off with my bare hands.'

The dragon gazed around at the death and destruction he had caused, then he began to ascend back into the air.

'No!' Friel cried. 'Get back here, you damned lizard.'

The colonel raced out from the alcove, his arms waving above his head.

'I dare!' he cried. 'Lord Meer, I dare rebel! Do you hear me, you bastard? I dare!'

Leona stared at Friel from the alcove, her raw terror keeping her frozen to the ground. Please don't see him, she begged; please don't see him.

The green dragon stopped his ascent, and gazed down at the lone figure standing amid the smoking and burning buildings of Tsallon Anura. A slight trace of a smile passed over the dragon's lips, and he descended again.

'Colonel Laimos,' the dragon said; 'so kind of you to reveal yourself to me. Before I tear you asunder, I want to hear what complaint you wish to make against our blessed rule of this island.'

Friel lowered his arms. 'I thought you might.' He smiled. 'How long have I got?'

'I shall give you a minute, and then I shall burn the rest of Kaugatz.

The time has come for every ungrateful Zamatan to feel the wrath of my flames and claws. We have nurtured this island, and this is how you treat us? You should be ashamed.'

'I am ashamed, Lord Meer,' said Friel. 'I am ashamed that it has taken so long for us to throw off our chains. You act as though we should be grateful that you have not utterly annihilated us. You treat us like dirt, and then expect us to worship you. But I know a secret.'

'Ha!' said the dragon 'Pray tell – what secret?'

'Hmm,' said Friel. He scratched his chin. 'Are you sure you want to know?'

'Cease wasting my time, human. Talk, or die.'

'Very well. This is the secret – dragons are not gods; they are mortal, and they can die as easily as us.'

At that moment, four yard-long steel bolts were loosed at the dragon from the ground floor of a cloister building. Friel threw himself to the ground as one passed over his head, and then the dragon cried out in agony as a bolt pierced the green scales of his chest. Another two bolts ripped through his wings, leaving long, ragged tears, but the fourth slammed into his right flank. The dragon fell to the ground, and crashed into the smouldering ruins of the tower. His head rose again, and he unleashed a fierce barrage of flames at the building where the ballistae had been hidden. The building exploded into an inferno, its roof collapsing, then, from the other side of the cloister, two huge, weighted nets flew out, launched by small wheeled catapults. The nets struck the dragon, and one entangled itself round Lord Meer's long green neck, while the other enmeshed his left wing.

Friel leapt to his feet. 'Attack!' he screamed.

Armed rebels poured out of the buildings, wielding long pikes and halberds. The dragon tried to turn its head to reach them, but the net had trapped his neck. He unleashed more flames, but they struck the same building he had already incinerated and, within seconds, the rebel fighters were swarming around his great bulk, spearing and piercing his flanks with their steel weapons. Lord Meer lifted a huge forelimb and slashed out with his claws, felling three fighters at once, their bodies ripped apart; but more rebels were inflicting grievous wounds down his flanks with every passing moment. A man loosed a crossbow into the dragon's face, and a bolt struck his right eye. The dragon screamed again, but still would not die. His jaws opened, and he bit off a fighter's head, then a long pike was rammed upwards into the base of his neck. One of the small catapults loosed again, and a boulder the size of a watermelon battered into Lord Meer's head. Someone managed to climb up the net, and he scrambled into position, pulling himself up to the level of the dragon's face. Clinging on with his legs, the man drew back his halberd, then plunged it deep into Lord Meer's left eye with both hands. The dragon wailed out his death scream, a long, chilling, terrible sound that echoed off the ancient walls of the monastery, then he fell silent, and collapsed to the ground in a cloud of dust and ash.

All around the ruins, no one spoke or moved. Leona was still sheltering in the alcove, her hands shaking uncontrollably as she stared at the impossible. Dozens of rebel fighters lay dead or wounded around the corpse of the dragon, but more were on their feet, their weapons frozen in their hands, as if none could believe what they had done.

Friel took a few steps forward, until he was close to the dragon's head. The man who had wielded the fatal halberd was standing there with his mouth open, an expression of utter disbelief on his face. Friel took the man's hand, and raised it into the air.

'Lord Meer is dead!' the colonel cried. 'He came to kill us, but he had not reckoned with the fire that burns within our hearts! Let the chains fall from each of us, for we are free!'

The crowd of fighters erupted in noise, as an almost hysterical fervour swept through the battered and smoking grounds of Tsallon Anura. Men surged forwards, and they lifted Friel and the halberd-wielder onto their shoulders. An old man fell to his knees sobbing, while others were smiling as though every dream they had ever wished for had come true. The only ones not joining in with the celebrations were a dozen or so monks who were standing by the far edge of the cloister. They were staring at the enormous corpse of the dragon with nothing but horror in their eyes, and several were openly weeping, though their tears were being ignored by the massed rebel fighters swarming around Lord Meer.

Leona crawled out of the alcove and stumbled to her feet. She watched as more fighters emerged from where they had taken shelter, then a group took a long, two-handled saw to the dragon's neck. Its steel teeth ripped through scales, flesh and bone, until Lord Meer's huge head had been severed. At this, the monks turned, and then retreated back towards the ancient temple in the heart of the monastery complex.

Bauchlie appeared at the edge of the cloister, and he barged and pushed his way towards the centre of the surging crowds. He pulled at his father's arm, and the men holding the colonel lowered him to the ground. Father and son stared at each other for a long moment, then the crowd erupted in cheers again as they embraced by the corpse of the dragon. Bauchlie's big arms gripped his father, and Leona saw tears on the younger man's face.

Leona turned from the scene, and staggered up the stairs to the top of the curtain wall, stepping over the incinerated bodies of those the dragon had killed when he had first arrived. She reached the battlements, and leaned her arms against them as if a great weight was pressing down upon her. She stared in the direction of Igatz. It looked the same as it always had – its clean, wide streets, and handsome townhouses, and its spires, domes and towers. The buildings were bathed in the light from the rising sun, and the waters of the Cyasarta were glistening.

The Aucterians living in their comfortable homes in Igatz were getting on with their lives, ignorant of what had just taken place in the old monastery in Kaugatz. Most would be waking up, getting ready for work or school, oblivious to the fact that a handful of ragged rebels had just killed one of the mightiest creatures in existence. In the great Temple of the Undying Serpent, the monks would be preparing that morning's devotions, unaware that one of the objects of their daily worship no longer existed, or that his body was being hacked to pieces in a monastery built to honour the serpent gods.

Leona started to cry. She had known the colonel's intentions, and had sat in countless meetings where he and the other rebel leaders had plotted and planned every aspect of the rebellion; and yet the enormity of what she had just witnessed seemed dreamlike and unreal.

They had killed a dragon, and nothing would ever be the same.

CHAPTER 13
REPRIMAND

Kaugatz, Serpent Isle – 3rd Nethinch 1588

Lahnos's eyes snapped open, and he sat up, his forehead covered in sweat, and his breathing ragged.

One of the part-Bullan rebel fighters glanced at him from the end of the filthy alleyway where the small group had been resting.

'Settle down, lad,' the older man said; 'try to get some more sleep.'

Lahnos said nothing, his thoughts consumed by the nightmare that had taken possession of his dreams. He pulled himself to his feet, then nearly tripped over the body of a fighter who had been sleeping next to him in the alleyway.

'Careful, lad,' laughed an old hand.

Lahnos stumbled to the end of the alleyway and out on to the wide street overlooking the harbour of the central ferry terminal. As soon as he was out of sight of the band of fighters he had been with all night, he fell to his knees and threw up into the gutter. His chest convulsed and ached, and his head felt as though it was about to burst. When the last drop had left his lips, he almost fell backwards, then he leaned against the harbour wall and panted.

'You all right, lad?'

Lahnos looked up. Standing in front of him was the rebel leader he had met in the tenement the previous evening – the one who had decided that Lahnos should join them. His grey hair was almost covering the shorn, stumpy horns that were growing from his head, and he was wearing a battered old overcoat.

'Nightmares?' the man said.

Lahnos nodded.

The man crouched down next to him. 'You killed someone last night, lad; and that's not a small thing. Even the toughest fighter can break when they first kill, but you carried on; I was watching you. You put that Bullan down, and then you kept going. That took guts, lad. There's no shame in letting it all come out now.'

Lahnos glanced at the war axe hanging from his belt. There was a notch in the blade from where the axe had struck a Bullan's steel breastplate, but there was no visible sign that it has also killed one of the foreign soldiers.

The older man handed Lahnos a flask. 'Drink.'

Lahnos raised the flask to his lips, and tasted the stale, tepid water. He swallowed, and the taste of bile in his mouth receded.

'Did you kill anyone?' he said.

The older man shook his head. 'No, lad; I did not. I gave a Bullan soldier a knock on the side of the head he won't soon forget, but I didn't kill him. Only two of our little band managed it – and you were one of them. How are you feeling?'

'Like shit.'

'You have the makings of a good soldier, Lahnos. You did what you were told, and you didn't run away.'

'Can I tell you something?'

The older man nodded.

'Fighting the Bullan,' Lahnos said; 'it seemed… wrong. We're part-Bullan. The man I killed was staring at my horns when I cracked his skull open. It felt like we were fighting our own brothers.'

'If only all humans felt that way, then there would be no wars. Look; the way I see it is that the Bullan are doing their job – it's just that their job happens to involve keeping us down. That doesn't mean I hate them. Imagine being one of them, lad. Imagine growing up in that faraway continent where they come from, and then one day the Dominion recruiters come to your village and off you go. You're put on a ship and then you end up here.'

'And now one of them will never go home because of me.'

'That's right. But, if you hadn't killed him, then he would have killed you, and *you* would never be going home. You have the right attitude, lad. Don't let yourself be controlled by hate. Most folk on this island don't see the Bullan as people – but we do. Each one of us part-Bullan has some of their blood coursing through our veins; it gives us a wider perspective.'

Lahnos nodded. 'Thank you. I mean, for your words. They mean a lot.'

The older man smiled. 'I've watched you since you first arrived in the part-Bullan district of Kaugatz nearly five years ago. You walk about as if you're always looking for trouble, but I always knew you were decent at heart. Listen; we have another hour before we have to get moving again. If you can't sleep, then why don't you see if you can find that girl of yours? Only, you must be back here in an hour. Deal?'

'All right; deal.'

'Go on, then; scram.'

Lahnos pulled himself to his feet, then he turned and raced back down the long straight road that connected the harbour to the part-Bullan district of Kaugatz. Hundreds of Zamatans were outside – some were staring at the damage to the ferry terminal, while others were cleaning up the broken glass and pools of blood from the road. The bodies of the fallen had been taken away on carts throughout the night, while the groans of the wounded could be heard coming from an open plaza to the north of the harbour. Lahnos hadn't wanted to admit it to the older man, but his nightmare had been unrelated to the Bullan soldier he had killed. Instead, he had relived the memory of his mother's death, just as he had seen it from the viewpoint of his grandmother.

'Can you hear me?' he whispered to the voice in his mind.

Nothing.

'Grandmother – are you there?'

Silence. Was he going mad? His thoughts went back to the moments before the battle, when he had been almost paralysed with indecision. Had he merely imagined the voice in his mind – the voice that had calmed him and told him to be brave?

He reached the intersection where he and Reyn had been stopped the day before. The old woman was still there, and she glanced up as Lahnos approached.

'Good morning, Granny Lupin,' he said.

'The warrior returns,' the old woman said. 'I heard you killed a Bullan, lad. It seems I was wrong about you.'

'Is Reyn about?'

'She's in the tenement, helping to look after a few of the wounded. Do you have permission to be away from your unit?'

'Yes. I have to be back in... well, fifty minutes now.'

'That means you'll need to leave in forty. I'll send someone up to get you if you're still indoors by then.'

He nodded at the old woman, then carried on. She had looked at him differently, but then, so had the fighters in his little band, as if splitting someone's head open with an axe had earned their respect. He entered the tenement and bounded up the stairs, then he knocked on the apartment door.

A young part-Bullan woman opened the door. She smiled at him, then glanced over her shoulder.

'Reyn,' she called out; 'your lad's here.'

The young woman moved aside as Reyn ran to the door. She threw her arms around Lahnos, and he held her close.

They kissed, and he smiled. 'You aren't wearing your head scarf.'

'None of us are, Lahnos. It's like last night changed everything. Maybe the Zamatans will finally accept us now. But never mind that; how are you? I heard what happened – I heard what you did. My poor baby. Did you get hurt at all?'

'I'm fine,' he said. 'Can you leave for a minute? I need to get back to the others soon, and I want to talk to you alone.'

Reyn pulled herself free from his embrace and hurried back into the room. She re-appeared a few moments later, and came out into the tenement landing, closing the door behind her.

'Are there wounded in there?' Lahnos said.

'Yes, but only the ones who can walk up the stairs on their own. The worst cases are somewhere else. We're supposed to patch the boys up and send them back out to fight as quickly as we can.'

Lahnos nodded. 'I heard the voice in my head again.'

Reyn peered at him. 'When?'

'Just before the battle started. I was having second thoughts, and...'

'Second thoughts? What do you mean?'

'You know I never walk away from a fight, Reyn. It's just, this... rebellion, or whatever it is. I'm not sure I see the point of it all. Does anyone really believe that the Dominion will give up? Even if they did, then the Gunstians will come, and things would be even worse. The Gunstians would kill people like you and me – they would kill every part-Bullan on the island. I'm not saying I like the Dominion – you know I don't, but where will it end? Anyway, these thoughts were going through my head yesterday evening, just as we were getting closer to the harbour; and then the voice came back. I heard it as clearly as I can hear you. The voice told me to be brave – and she told me to fight for the ones I love. Yes, that was it. Fight for the ones I love – and I thought of you. After that, all of my doubts vanished.'

'I don't understand. You heard the voice right after you saw your grandmother's memories – why would you hear it again?'

Lahnos shrugged. 'I was hoping you might know.'

'We need to speak to someone who properly understands the Gifts of Theodora. I can think of one person.'

Lahnos nodded. 'I wonder if he knows we're back in Kaugatz.'

'I heard that he's leading the rebellion from Tsallon Anura.'

'Then he'll know. Shit. I think I'd rather ask Leona. It sounds stupid, but I trust her more than I trust my own uncle.'

Reyn smiled. 'That doesn't sound remotely stupid.' Her smile evaporated. 'You killed someone.'

'Yes. I did my duty.'

'Your duty?'

'Yes, Reyn. No matter how I feel about the rights and wrongs of the situation – I will fight. For you, for the others in my group, and to stay alive.'

'Do you feel any different?'

'I don't know. I've broken plenty of noses before, but I never thought I would ever take someone's life. Everyone looks at me as though I'm different – does that count? I've heard all the platitudes, about how the first time is the hardest; and no one cared that I threw up into the gutter this morning. I will kill again, if I have to. I know that now. Do you still love me, even after my hands are bloody?'

'Of course I love you, Lahnos. I only wish I could have fought by your side. I know that fighting in a battle must have been terrible, but staying here while all the men were away felt like torture. Why can't we fight, too? Zamata belongs to the women of the island as much as it belongs to the men.'

'That sounds like another question for my uncle.'

The sound of boots came from the stairs below them.

'Is Lahnos Laimos up there?' a voice cried.

Lahnos leaned over the railings. 'I've still got twenty minutes.'

'Not any more, lad,' said a rebel fighter, as he hurried up the stairs. 'I have orders to escort you to Tsallon Anura immediately.'

'Oh, come on,' said Lahnos. 'This had better be a joke.'

'No joke, mate. Your uncle wants you.' He glanced at Reyn. 'And he wants you, too, if your name happens to be Reyn.'

'I'm supposed to be back in the harbour soon,' said Lahnos. 'If I leave, then the others will think I've abandoned them.'

'No, they won't. I've just come from the harbour. I relayed my orders, and I was sent here. The boys in your unit know that you have to leave. They weren't too happy about it, but they know.'

'And Colonel Laimos has asked for me?' said Reyn.

'That's what I said, sweetheart.'

'Don't get over-friendly with my girl,' said Lahnos, 'or you'll be limping back to Tsallon Anura.'

'Listen, lad,' said the fighter; 'I have another seven armed men waiting for me at the bottom of the stairs to make sure you two get to the monastery unharmed – that's how valuable your arses are to Colonel Laimos. Now quit complaining, and follow me.'

'I will need to let people know,' said Reyn. 'I'm due back at work in a few minutes.'

'Where do you work?'

Reyn gestured toward the apartment door. The man nodded, then opened the door and walked inside.

'I have orders from Colonel Laimos to take Lahnos and Reyn to Tsallon Anura. Got it? Splendid.'

He emerged from the door, pointed at the stairs, then started to descend. Lahnos and Reyn glanced at each other, then followed him. At the bottom of the stairs an open-topped wagon was waiting. Five men were sitting on the back, while two others were up on the driver's bench.

'Climb aboard,' said the man who had collected them. Lahnos jumped up, then helped pull Reyn onto the back of the wagon. They squeezed in next to the others, and the wagon got underway. Lahnos gazed at the rising smoke as they pulled out of the part-Bullan district, then he noticed a few of the rebel fighters glancing at the horns upon his and Reyn's heads. Reyn's hand moved towards the pocket where she kept her head scarf, but then she stopped herself.

Lahnos smiled as he stared at the others. 'Anything you want to say about me or Reyn? Let's get it all out into the open.'

The man who had collected them shrugged. 'Horns is horns, eh?'

Lahnos raised an eyebrow. 'Horns is horns? I'll have to remember that one.'

'Look, lad,' the man said, 'every fighter on this wagon used to be in the militia, and we've all known your uncle for years. We know how much he wants the Zamatans and the part-Bullan to work together, and we're not about to start drawing attention to our... differences. Now, if you're clever, then you will take this opportunity to get some rest; it might be the last chance you get for a while.'

The wagon joined the main road that bisected Kaugatz, and turned towards the north-east. Lahnos tried to relax, but his eyes were caught by the plumes of smoke rising from the town. Lines of Zamatans were passing buckets of water up from the banks of the Cyasarta, and a few of the fires had already been quelled by the time the wagon had rolled past. The crowds thickened when they were about half a mile from the monastery, and a low roar of noise was reverberating from the network of dense and narrow streets.

'Something's happening,' muttered the fighter holding the reins.

The others glanced up. The wagon began to slow down as it reached a tight press of civilians on the road. Some were laughing, others weeping, while a few looked stunned. Several were glancing upwards as if they expected to see something. Lahnos did the same, but the blue sky was empty.

'Hey! What's going on?' cried one of the fighters from the back of the wagon.

'Lord Meer is dead!' shouted a young woman on the street. 'The colonel brought down a dragon!'

Lahnos stared at the woman, his brain telling him that what she had said was impossible. He turned to the fighters on the back of the wagon – they looked happy, and were slapping each other on the back, but none seemed overly shocked by the news.

'Damn it,' muttered one. 'We missed it.'

'This can't be true,' said Lahnos. 'This is just a stupid rumour.'

One of the fighters shrugged at him, and Lahnos stared down into the jubilant, cheering crowds, his eyes narrowing. Had a night's fighting made the inhabitants of Kaugatz as gullible as children? Reyn nudged him with an elbow, and pointed. He looked up, and saw smoke and flames rising into the sky ahead of them.

'Tsallon Anura is on fire,' she said.

Thick crowds had gathered around the roads surrounding the monastery, and the wagon ground to a halt.

'We'll walk from here,' said the man in charge. 'Form up around the girl and the colonel's nephew, and we'll push our way through.'

The fighters jumped down to the cobbled road, and Reyn and Lahnos followed them. Two fighters went ahead, shoving civilians out of the way, while the others flanked Reyn and Lahnos.

'Clear a path!' one cried, but the civilians ignored them. All were clamouring to get into the monastery, and it took over twenty minutes of pushing for the group to reach one of the ancient site's entrances. Two rows of rebel fighters were keeping the crowds back with shields, but they opened a route when they saw the fighters approach with Lahnos and Reyn.

Lahnos gasped as they entered the grounds of the monastery. Several of the beautiful old buildings were in ruins, and the ground was littered in charred rubble and pools of blood. Two sides of the ancient cloister were burnt-out shells, the old refectory was in flames, and a tower had collapsed. Rebel fighters were carrying bodies on stretchers, while others were tending to the wounded.

'By the gods,' Reyn whispered. She came to an abrupt halt, and started to cry.

Lahnos glanced at her, then turned to see what she was looking at. His eyes widened. No. It was impossible. Was he dreaming? By a wall at the far end of the cloister, an enormous, green-scaled body was lying, its wings and neck entangled in nets, and with dozens of bloody streaks marking its flank. Long, steel ballista bolts were protruding from two places, and its body was studded with pikes. Lahnos broke free of the escort and ran across the courtyard, dodging the dozens of rebel fighters who were there. He skidded to a halt, then saw the dragon's head lying a few yards from its body, its neck severed.

'Lord Meer Mon Adal,' he said, to no one.

Reyn joined him, her cheeks wet with tears. She took his hand.

'King Gahad,' she whispered, 'and now this? How? How could men do this?'

An old rebel fighter glanced at them. 'The bastard killed near thirty men before it went down, girl. That's how we did it, with our own blood and sacrifice.'

Their escort reached them, and they all stood in silence for a few moments, as each took in the sight before them.

'The colonel was right,' muttered one. 'I doubted he could do it, but I was wrong.'

'You're not the only one who doubted it, mate,' said another, wiping a tear from his eye.

'What does it mean?' said Lahnos.

'It means there's one fewer dragon in Igatz, lad,' said the man in charge. 'Come on; your uncle will be waiting for us.'

'Is my uncle still alive?'

'Yes.'

'How do you know? The dragon might have killed him.'

'Look at everyone's faces, lad. Do you think they'd be laughing and smiling if your uncle was dead?'

They turned, and walked away from the vast corpse. The fighters led Lahnos and Reyn to the ancient temple, but they didn't enter through the main doors. Instead, they walked to the rear of the building, and went in via a small side door, passing two guards posted there. The interior of the temple was thick with shadows and the scent of burning candles, and they came to a high-ceilinged chamber with stained glass windows. Two men and a woman were sitting inside, and all three glanced up.

'Here they are, Colonel,' said the man who had led the escort.

Friel got to his feet, then seemed to remember that he was still smiling. His expression changed, and he glared at Lahnos.

'Thank you, lads,' he said; 'leave us.'

The fighters saluted, then filed out of the room and closed the door behind them.

'You killed Lord Meer,' said Lahnos.

'Not personally,' said Friel. 'Many fighters had a hand in the dragon's death; but never mind that – why are you in Kaugatz? I expressly told you...'

'What do you mean, "never mind that"?' Lahnos cried. 'You killed a god.'

'Can this wait?' said the seated man. 'I have places to be.'

Lahnos turned his attention to the two people who were still seated. He recognised Leona, but the man was unfamiliar.

'A god is dead,' Lahnos said.

'No,' said the man. 'A dragon is dead. Colonel – I need a decision. Send the boy and girl out of the room so that we can continue our conversation in private.'

'We can talk in front of Lahnos and Reyn,' Friel said. 'We can trust them.'

'Your trust is too freely given, Colonel,' said the man.

Friel smiled again. 'If that were the case, then I doubt our rebellion would have got very far.' He glanced at his nephew. 'Take a seat. Your reprimand will have to wait.'

Friel gestured to a few chairs, and re-took his own seat opposite the man. Lahnos and Reyn both sat. The man eyed them with suspicion, and Lahnos noticed that he had a long scar down his cheek.

He blinked. 'Are you Bauchlie?'

The man narrowed his eyes. 'How did you know?'

'Your scar. I've heard about it; I've heard about you.'

'And everything you have heard is true. Now, shut up and let the adults talk.'

Lahnos clenched his fists. 'You're a terrorist.'

'That's what the occupation forces call me.'

'That's what everyone calls you.'

'Quiet, nephew,' said Friel. 'Time is pressing. Right now, as of this very moment, we have the initiative, and we must not squander it. Bauchlie, I approve of your plan. I will organise a diversionary attack to clear your path.'

Bauchlie nodded. 'Where and when?'

'Tomorrow morning, just before dawn, I shall send boats and fighters to attack the coastline of Igatz between Handshore and the Fortress of Atzoun. That will draw the Dominion fleet away from your position, and keep the Bullan busy. You will have a short interval in which to act. How many men do you need?'

'Eight for the initial incursion,' Bauchlie said. 'I have already hand-picked them from my own units. I will require a further two hundred for the main assault.'

Friel nodded, his eyes guarded. 'You shall have them. I will ensure the boats are ready to bear them across the Cyasarta at the appointed time.'

'How do I make contact with your agent?'

'His rooms overlook the north-western corner of the palace grounds. He will be watching. Flash a lantern three times before you land, and he will let you in.'

'Can I trust an Aucterian not to betray us?'

'My agent is reliable.'

'Why?'

'He has his reasons.'

'If he betrays me, I will kill him.'

'If he betrays you, Bauchlie, he will deserve it. However, he will not betray you. If this plan works, then the Bullan will abandon the rest of the island and concentrate everything they have in Igatz to oppose you. Will two hundred fighters be enough to repel them?'

'I will be taking a hostage.'

'Ah,' said Friel. 'Yes. Good.'

Friel and Bauchlie stood, and shook hands.

'Good luck,' said Friel.

'Thank you, Colonel.'

Bauchlie's eyes went over the others in the chamber, but he said nothing and strode from the room. Friel sat back down again.

'There were no lies, sir,' said Leona.

The colonel nodded.

'What did he mean by a hostage?' said Reyn. 'What's he going to do?'

'I'm sure you will hear about it at the same time as the rest of the island does,' Friel said.

Reyn nodded. 'So you don't really trust us?'

'I trust you,' he said, 'but the fewer who know the details, the better. I'm sure you understand. Now, I think it is time for that reprimand. Lahnos – I gave you a direct order, and you disobeyed me.'

Lahnos laughed. 'An order? I didn't realise that you were my commanding officer and that I was in the army.'

'I am your legal guardian, and you are obliged to do as I say.'

'Why did you lie to us?' said Reyn. 'There was no exile. The deal you made with the Bullan to have Lahnos released from prison was a lie.'

Friel glanced at Leona.

'I didn't tell them, sir,' she said.

'We worked it out on our own,' Reyn said. 'At least you're not denying it.'

'You are correct,' Friel said. 'I fabricated a story to get you out of the centre of the island because I knew what was coming. Call me foolish, but I had no desire to see my nephew killed in street fighting. I wanted you safely out of the way. My main problem now is that the part-Bullan all know that you disobeyed me. However, in light of your actions last night, the situation is not irredeemable. I am prepared to allow the island to believe that I acted out of selfish interests to protect my family – they will understand that. They won't approve, but they will understand. What I need from you, Lahnos, is a public commitment that you are whole-heartedly devoted to the cause. You disobeyed my orders because of an unquenchable desire to join the rebellion. Youthful high spirits, as it were. The people will also understand that. I am minded to keep you here in Tsallon Anura, at least for a while, so that the rebel fighters can see us working side by side. Are you prepared to comply with my wishes, nephew?'

'Was that really your motivation?' Lahnos said. 'You wanted to keep me safe?'

'Yes.'

'It wasn't because you wanted to use my Gift?'

Leona's eyes widened. 'You have a Gift?'

'I do. I'm a death-reader.'

'He's not lying,' she whispered.

'So much for keeping it a secret,' said Friel. 'I assume you have told Reyn?'

'Of course I did,' said Lahnos.

'Have you mentioned it anyone else?'

Lahnos shook his head.

'That means the knowledge is restricted to the four of us sat in this room,' Friel said. 'Let's keep it that way.'

'You want a death-reader and a truth-finder both working for you, don't you?' said Reyn.

'I would be negligent to ignore the opportunities that arise before me, Reyn.'

'I have another question for you,' said Lahnos. 'Why does my Gift come with a voice?'

A slight flicker of surprise crossed his uncle's features. 'A voice?'

'Yes – the voice in my head. You didn't tell me about that.'

Friel's eyes tightened. 'How many times have you heard it?'

'Twice.'

Friel glanced at Leona, who nodded.

Lahnos laughed. 'I'm not going to lie with her sitting here,' he said. 'Can we assume that she will let you know if anything I say is untrue?'

'Back to the voice,' said Friel. 'What did it say?'

'Comforting, encouraging things,' Lahnos said. 'Is it the voice of my grandmother? Is that a part of being a death-reader?'

'No.'

Lahnos frowned.

'I cannot recall hearing of any Gift that involves a voice in your head, nephew. Is it at all possible that you have been imagining it? You have been through a lot in recent days. My mother's death has hit me hard, and you were also close to her. Then you discover you are Gifted. And last night, I believe you killed a Bullan soldier. Is it beyond the realm of possibility that this has put a strain on your mind?'

Lahnos said nothing for a moment, then he nodded. 'It's possible.'

'You seemed convinced when you told me,' said Reyn.

'I know,' he said, 'but it would be easier to believe that I was going mad.'

A low din of pealing bells began, and the room fell into silence. Lahnos listened to the mournful sound for a few minutes, then the colonel got to his feet.

'It appears,' Friel said, his hands clasped behind his back, 'that the good citizens of Igatz have just learned the fate of Lord Meer.'

CHAPTER 14
UNDER DURESS

Igatz, Serpent Isle – 4th Nethinch 1588

Cisca walked through the dark, silent hallways of the Dragon Palace, her emotions numb. She had barely slept in two nights, and she was shivering despite the close, balmy air that covered Igatz. The previous day had been one of the most traumatic of her life. She had awoken by Lord Kheran's side to be told the news that Lord Meer had fallen, and her body and mind were equally exhausted. The dragon child under her care had wept all day, and then far into the following night, and Cisca had wept with him until, finally, he had fallen into a deep sleep. Major Polarn had then ordered her to rest, but how could she rest when another god had been murdered? Instead, she had chosen to prowl the sombre and lonely marble hallways, as stunned and disorientated as every other occupant of the palace. Even the stolid Bullan seemed shocked, which was the clearest sign in Cisca's mind that the natural order of things had been overturned.

She found herself by one of the arched entrances, and walked outside into the warm air. She glanced to the east, and saw a faint patch of light on the horizon over the waters of the Cyasarta. A tiny sliver of moon was visible over the hills above Chesson to her left, and the stars were out. She walked down to the water's edge, then turned left, and followed the smooth path that skirted the boundary between land and sea. The dark mass of Kaugatz came into view, and she cursed the Zamatans. What manner of people could murder a god? Lord Meer hadn't been perfect, but he had possessed the immortal dragon spirit that protected and ruled Athumia. No, she thought – that didn't make any sense. How could a god be imperfect? How could a god be slain by nets and spears?

She reached the north-western corner of the palace and halted, her eyes on the few lights coming from Kaugatz. Somewhere among the dense warren of streets was Colonel Laimos, the leader of the rebellion – a man who had possessed the shameful audacity to attend the dance in the palace just one night before he had unleashed destruction and violence upon the Serpent Isle. His name was on the lips of every courtier and officer that Cisca had spoken to – the renegade, the traitor. The god-killer.

Cisca turned away from Kaugatz, and her eyes went over the grand façade of the palace. Its tall pillars and columns of white marble, its fine arches and domes, all reduced to a house of despair and mourning. Its balconies were deserted, and... Cisca frowned. Not every balcony was empty. A man was sitting on one, alone, his gaze on the waters of the inlet.

Travers.

Cisca stared up at him, and her heart went out to the man. He looked so lonely, so vulnerable. Just like her, he probably couldn't sleep, and she felt a sudden need for companionship. Perhaps they would be able to comfort each other – not in the way that he had often suggested, but as friends. She walked back into the palace before she could change her mind, and ascended a flight of stairs to the floor where the naval officers had their small apartments. She found the entrance to Travers's quarters and knocked.

A few moments passed before the door opened. Travers peered out at her, then his eyes widened.

'You?' he said.

'Yes. If I am intruding, then please tell me and I shall leave you alone.'

Travers blinked. 'No. Come in.'

He stood aside and Cisca entered his apartment. A solitary lamp was burning by the bedside, but more light was coming in through the open balcony doors.

Travers closed the door.

'Aren't you going to ask me why I'm here?' she said.

Travers nodded. 'Why are you here, Cisca?'

'I know we've had our moments of disagreement,' she said, 'but I saw you on your balcony from the palace gardens, and I thought that you might need a friend.'

'I'm glad you're here,' he said. 'Have you been up all night?'

'Yes. Lord Kheran has been very upset, as have we all. The news about Lord Meer was... I... I don't really have the words to describe it.'

'It was a shock,' he said.

'Yes.'

'Do you want a drink?'

'No, thank you. I'm not sure how long I have to spare. Lord Kheran is sleeping just now, but he might awaken when it gets light.'

Travers gestured towards the balcony doors, and they stepped outside and sat down. His eyes went back to the waters of the Cyasarta.

'How are you feeling?' she said.

'Hmm? Oh. You know. Shocked. You?'

'The world has been turned upside down,' she said. 'Do you know what the worst thing is? The rebels still have Lord Meer's body. Right now, they will be desecrating his corpse. It makes me nauseous.'

'Do you think it was right to send a dragon against humans?'

'No. When I heard the news that Lord Meer had been ordered to quash the rebellion, I disagreed; but I had assumed that Kaugatz would be in smoking ruins by now. I had never imagined that the rebels would have been able to kill him.'

'If they hadn't killed him, how many humans would have died?'

'I'm not comfortable with this line of questioning,' she said. 'A god has been murdered.'

'I'm not debating that, Cisca.'

'Then what are you trying to say – that it was better this way? That it was better for Lord Meer to die rather than thousands of rebelling Zamatans?'

'Think carefully about your words,' he said. 'How many human lives did the rebels save by killing Lord Meer? Put yourself into their shoes, just for a moment. If you had been in Tsallon Anura, and a dragon was soaring down with its jaws open, ready to incinerate not only you, but everyone you loved – would you have just stood there? Would you have thought to yourself – oh, well; Lord Meer is a god, so I shouldn't resist?'

'You are creating a false equivalence,' she said. 'Our lives cannot be weighed against those of the immortal dragon gods.'

'Why not? Isn't every life precious? Or, are some more precious than others?'

Cisca felt her impatience rise. 'The purpose of humans is to serve the dragons.'

Travers shrugged, and gazed back out to the waters of the inlet. 'I tried; I really have tried, Cisca. Still, if that is what you truly believe, then I suppose it makes my job easier in some ways.'

'Your job?'

Travers said nothing.

Infuriated, Cisca stared out from the balcony. How dare Travers compare the lives of mere humans to those of the mighty and ever-living gods? Then she recalled how disturbed she had felt when she had learned that Lord Meer was to be deployed against the rebels, and her thoughts spiralled back into doubt and confusion. Her anger, she realised, had more to do with the fact that Travers had a point. How many people would have been burned or torn to shreds if Lord Meer had not been brought down? Men, women, children; the young and the old – thousands would have perished, and Kaugatz would have been obliterated. She tried to imagine the terror they would have felt at the dragon's approach, and the bravery it had taken for any to stand and fight.

She glanced at Travers, an apology ready on her lips, and noticed a faint light flashing from the waters of the bay.

'What was that?' she said.

Travers turned, and punched her in the face. Cisca's head whipped back, and then Travers was upon her, driving her to the floor of the balcony. He rammed one knee down against her chest, and placed the other on her right wrist, pinning her arm down. Her head spun, her vision blurry, then she felt his hands around her throat.

'This gives me no pleasure,' he said, as he choked her.

Panic flooded her mind, and her left hand clawed uselessly against his strong hands. She felt her consciousness start to recede amid her agony, and then Travers's right hand felt down her clothes, searching through her pockets.

'Shit,' he muttered. 'Where are they, Cisca? Where are the keys?'

He released the pressure on her neck, and her head turned to the side as she gasped and retched.

Travers slapped her across the face. 'The keys, Cisca. Tell me where they are, or I will kill you. You know I will. Do you want to live?'

Cisca didn't respond, not because she wished to die, but because her thoughts seemed as heavy as lead. Travers placed a hand over her mouth, then he grabbed hold of her left thumb and twisted it back, sending bolts of excruciating pain through her body. She writhed, her legs convulsing as agony swept over her.

'Think, Cisca,' he said. 'Where are the keys to Lord Kheran's quarters?' He took his hand from her mouth and lowered his head until she could feel his breath on her cheek. 'Whisper it to me, and the pain will end.'

'They are on a chain around my neck,' she gasped.

'Good girl,' he said, and he released her thumb. He crouched by her, and then dragged her into the apartment and closed the balcony doors. She felt his fingers rip the silver chain from her neck, and then she heard the jangle of keys. He knelt by her again, gripped her hair, then slammed her head against the wooden floor.

. . .

Cisca awoke in darkness and in agony, a gag tied round her mouth. The back of her head was throbbing out a pulse of regular pain, while her throat, nose and left thumb were competing for her attention. She tried to move, but her wrists had been bound behind her back, and her ankles had also been tied together. Her left cheek was resting against the wooden floorboards of Travers's apartment, and she could see the sky start to brighten a little through the balcony windows.

She was alive, she thought; she was still alive.

Then she remembered that she had betrayed Lord Kheran, and her chest tightened in shame and guilt. She had told Travers where the keys were – how could she have done such a terrible thing? It didn't matter that he would have found them anyway if he had conducted a thorough search; she had told him. She had wanted the pain to end, and she hadn't considered the consequences. She was a vile traitor, a disgrace to her family, loathsome, cowardly and weak. She sobbed, her misery complete. Travers was going to kill her, of that she was certain, and she would die a dishonourable death, thousands of miles from home.

She heard a door open behind, her, followed by the sounds of boots entering the apartment. More than one person had returned to Travers's apartment, and she saw the hooded and cloaked figures spread out through the living area. Two men approached Cisca.

'Why is she still alive?' said the taller one, his accent Zamatan.

'I was being careful,' Travers said. 'And I was right. If you want to take Lord Kheran as a hostage, then we will need her.'

'Why?'

'Because the dragon child is besotted with her,' said Travers. 'He would do anything to stop her from being hurt; anything. Whereas, if he learns that we have killed her, then he will be too enraged to cooperate.'

The Zamatan nodded in the shadows, then he crouched by Cisca. His hand went to her face, and his fingers turned her head to face him. She peered up into the shadows, but the man's features were obscured by his hood.

'What is her name?' he said.

'Lieutenant Cisca.'

'Hello, Lieutenant Cisca,' the man said. 'You are now my prisoner. I can't promise that you will survive the next few hours, but if you do as I say, then you might have a chance. Nod if you understand me.'

Cisca nodded.

'What now?' said Travers.

'Why did you beat her?'

'What?'

'You heard me, Travers. Why did you beat Lieutenant Cisca? Won't Kheran be just as angry if he sees that we've hurt his pet human?'

'It was necessary to restrain her.'

The hooded man glanced over his shoulder. 'Untie her ankles and sit her up on the bed.'

Two other men approached. One cut the ropes round Cisca's ankles with a knife, and then they pulled her up by the shoulders and sat her on the bed. She swayed, her eyes wide as she stared at the men crowding the room.

The man in charge crouched by her again. 'Listen to me, Cisca. We are taking you and the keys to Kheran's quarters. It is not our intention to kill the dragon child. If all goes to plan, then you and Kheran will be our hostages, and dead hostages are of very little value. You don't want any harm to come to little Kheran now, do you? Behave yourself, and do as we say.'

Cisca tried to speak, but the gag was tight, and only a low groan escaped her lips.

'We will remove the gag when we are safely inside the dragon's quarters,' the man said. 'Then, it won't matter if anyone hears you scream.' He glanced at Travers. 'The uniforms.'

Travers nodded, then disappeared through a side door. He emerged a moment later, carrying a large wicker basket with both arms. He laid it down onto the floor, and the man by Cisca stood.

'Get changed,' he said to the other men. 'Quickly and quietly.'

Cisca watched as the rebels stripped out of their clothes and donned the uniforms of the Dominion Navy. The man in charge got dressed by the balcony doors, and she saw his broad shoulders and muscular arms silhouetted in the growing light of dawn. He also had a scar that ran down one cheek, and eyes that seemed as dark as his soul.

The men dumped their old clothes into the wicker basket, then the scarred man gestured to the front door of the apartment. Several men picked up large sacks, and waited by the door.

'Let's go,' said the scarred man. 'You two – stay either side of Lieutenant Cisca. If she tries to escape, kill her.'

Travers opened the door and peered out. 'It's clear.'

The rebels followed Travers out into the hallway, then two of them lifted Cisca to her feet and walked her to the entrance. Travers closed and locked the apartment door, then they all strode down the hallway. Cisca stumbled along in their midst, her wrists still bound, and her arms gripped by rebels. Travers avoided the main stairs, and they took a service route instead; following the ways used by the servants of the palace.

Cisca prayed for someone to bump into them – a squad of heavily-armed Bullan soldiers would be ideal – but the corridors and stairs were silent and empty. Travers led the way with practised ease. He knew every quiet staircase and every back corridor, and they arrived outside Lord Kheran's quarters without being seen. Travers took the set of keys from a pocket, and opened the door. Cisca looked back, and saw two servants approaching, but neither were looking up, and the rebels funnelled through the entrance. The scarred rebel smiled.

'Good work, lads. Bring Cisca forward.'

The two rebels pushed Cisca into the middle of the large storage room, and the scarred man raised a knife to her face, and cut through the gag. Cisca wheezed and spluttered, then coughed in pain. Her eyes flashed at Travers.

'You bastard!' she cried. 'You filthy bastard!'

Travers glanced at her and shrugged.

'That's enough,' said the scarred man. 'Cisca, tell me the layout of the dragon's quarters.'

Cisca lowered her eyes.

'I have been honest with you,' the scarred man said, 'now you shall be honest with me. Where are we?'

'This...' Cisca said, her emotions battling with her resolve.

'Yes?'

'This is the storeroom,' she said. 'It contains everything Lord Kheran needs. If you hurt him I will kill you.'

'I'm sure you will try,' said the scarred man. 'Go on.'

'Lord Kheran's sleeping quarters are through the door to your left, and the servants sleep in the room behind you. There is also a wide balcony that overlooks the Cyasarta.'

'Can the dragon fly?'

Cisca stared at him.

'It was a simple question, Cisca. Is the dragon old enough to fly? In other words, is he liable to try to escape from the balcony?'

'He is still learning,' she said. 'Lord Meer was teaching him.'

The man nodded, then he turned to the rebels with the large sacks. 'Prepare the chains and nets.'

Cisca opened her mouth to cry out a warning, and the scarred man lifted a hand to cover her mouth. He moved behind her, his hand gripping her face, as she struggled in vain.

He nodded to two others. 'Kill the servants.'

The two men nodded, raised their crossbows, and crept through the door to the room where the four servants slept. Cisca wept again, and her tears ran down the scarred man's hand as he held her mouth closed. The rebels with the sacks withdrew three nets, a bundle of shackles, and several long lengths of chain, then the scarred man gestured to the door that led to Kheran's sleeping quarters.

Travers eased the door open, and the men listened for a moment, as the gentle sound of the dragon child's breathing reached them. The rebels lifted the nets and chains, then stole through the door, moving silently into the darkness, until only Cisca and the scarred man remained in the storeroom.

'It is futile to struggle,' he whispered in her ear. 'Zamata will be free, and there is nothing you can do to stop that, Lieutenant Cisca.'

The two men returned from the servants' quarters, and nodded. The scarred rebel leader gestured for them to watch the main doors that led to the rest of the palace, and they took up position with their crossbows. Cisca's mind was in turmoil as she stared into the dark entranceway where Kheran lay. She heard sounds of movement and a slight clinking of chains hitting each other, then, finally, one of the rebels emerged.

'It's done, sir. The dragon was sleeping soundly, and we chained him without any problems.'

The scarred man smiled, and released Cisca. 'Go to your dragon, woman.'

Cisca bolted through the door and into the darkness. One of the rebels opened a window shutter, and the sunrise flooded the room. Lying on his great heap of blankets and cushions, Lord Kheran was shackled and chained. Nets bound his wings, and his jaws had been wrapped in chains to keep them closed. His orange eyes were open, and he looked terrified as he gazed around his sleeping chamber. Cisca ran to him, but her wrists were still bound behind her back. She fell to her knees.

'Kheran!' she sobbed.

The dragon's eyes widened at the sight of the blood on her face. He struggled against the chains and nets in his desperation to be free, but the men had done their job well.

The scarred man walked forward, a knife in his hand.

'There is no point in trying to resist, dragon,' he said. 'You are now my hostage. Cooperate, and you and Cisca will be unharmed. Resist, and I will hurt her. You love her, or so I am told. You don't want me to hurt her, do you? Be a good little dragon, and you and she will get to spend many more years together.'

He lifted the knife, then cut the bonds that secured Cisca's wrists. She stood, and slapped him across the face.

The rebels in the room tensed, but the scarred man smiled.

'I'll give you that one,' he said. 'But, if you do it again, I will cut off one of your fingers.'

The dragon struggled again, and Cisca wrapped her arms around his chained face.

'Be brave, Kheran; I'm here. Together, we will get through this.'

'That's right,' said the scarred man. 'Now, I'm going to need some evidence.' He leaned forward and used the knife to hack off the upper two inches of Kheran's scaled left ear. The dragon child tried to scream in pain, but his jaws were clamped shut with chains. His eyes closed, and his head sank down to the blankets.

Cisca wept. 'You said you wouldn't hurt him.'

'I did. Let us all hope that I will have no need to hurt him, or you, again. Now, if you will excuse me, I am going to announce to Lord Rufus that I have his son in captivity.' He glanced at the other rebels. 'If I am not back here in twenty minutes, kill them both. Travers, you are coming with me.'

The rebel and the traitorous naval officer both turned for the door.

'Wait,' Cisca said. 'Who are you?'

The scarred rebel leader halted, and faced her. 'My name is Bauchlie, Lieutenant Cisca. Have you heard of me?'

'No.'

'She's new on the island,' said Travers. 'Your notoriety had not yet reached her attention.'

Bauchlie smiled. 'It doesn't matter if she has never heard of me; she knows who I am now.'

The two men turned and walked from the room. Cisca picked up a blanket, and held it against the bleeding wound in the dragon child's ear.

'I know you're scared,' she whispered. 'I'm scared, too.'

The dragon opened his eyes, and gave Cisca a look that broke her heart.

'I promised I would never leave you,' she whispered, 'and I never break my promises.'

CHAPTER 15
BRAZEN

Kaugatz, Serpent Isle – 5th Nethinch 1588

Colonel Friel Laimos and Leona watched from the battlements of Tsallon Anura as more small boats docked at the little harbour on the far side of the Cyasarta inlet.

'I think my son might well be a genius,' Friel said. 'He anticipated exactly how the Bullan would react to his plan. They don't care about the Aucterian colonists on the island – their loyalty is to the dragons, and the dragons alone. Those boats mean that every single Bullan soldier on the island is now in Igatz, protecting Lord Rufus, and besieging the area of the palace where Bauchlie has Kheran held hostage. With the exception of the naval base and the palace district, Zamata is ours.'

Leona glanced at the colonel. His features were calm, but his green eyes were sparkling with nervous excitement.

'And what happens next, sir?'

Friel smiled. 'We shall see. For now, the rebel fighters in Kaugatz need to rest and recover for a few days, and we need to recruit more Zamatans from the towns and villages beyond the Hansarta, as well as consolidate our positions here. All of that will take time – time that my son has given us.'

Leona frowned.

'I am aware of your feelings towards Bauchlie,' Friel said, 'but you can't deny that he is effective.'

An effective murderer, she thought.

'Were it not for him,' the colonel went on, 'then at this very moment the Bullan would be assaulting us by land and sea, and choking off our supply routes. Instead, Kaugatz is calm and peaceful again, and firmly under our control.'

'Can I ask you something, sir?'

Friel groaned aloud. 'Stop asking for permission to speak, Leona; of course you can ask me something – you can ask me anything.'

'Which murders carried out by Bauchlie did you order?'

'I said you could ask me anything – I didn't say I was under any obligation to provide you with an answer. There are some details that it would better for you not to know, Leona. Do you think the Aucterians are frightened?'

'I would imagine that most are terrified, sir.'

'Good. We need to start moving them from the villages and towns towards Igatz, a job that will be far simpler now that the Bullan have withdrawn from every guard post in the outer island. I will have boats sent to Wayston and Neeton, and the colonists can sail to Igatz from there, while the settlers in Chesson can walk to the ferry terminal in Kaugatz. Yes. Let's get them all gathered into the one spot, where they will be far easier to deal with.'

'Deal with, sir?' said Leona. 'You can't be thinking of...?'

'Of what, slaughtering them?' he said. 'No, Leona, of course not. I am not a monster. I have no desire to wade in the blood of twenty thousand Aucterians. The Gunstians, on the other hand, would have no moral qualms about carrying out a massacre on that scale.' He turned, and glanced over the cloisters of the monastery. 'I wonder if their agent has arrived yet?' He frowned, and narrowed his eyes. 'Is that Lady Sinda I can see? What in all the world is she doing here?'

Leona followed his gaze, and saw the smartly-dressed young Aucterian woman walking through the ruins. She paused by the vast corpse of the dragon, and held a handkerchief to her nose as she regarded it. Around her, several Zamatan rebels were eyeing her with suspicion, but their deference to the settlers had been ingrained in them since birth, and none were insulting or harassing her.

'I think the reason for her visit is obvious, sir,' Leona said.

'Well? Don't keep it to yourself.'

'She will be here to see you, sir. She was one of your favourite mistresses for many months, and she probably hopes that she will be able to come to some sort of arrangement with you – one that spares her family and her wealth, if not her dignity.'

Friel smiled. 'Come; let's see if you are right.'

They went down the steps of the blackened curtain wall, and approached the aristocratic young lady. She noticed them, and took a step away from the corpse of Lord Meer.

Friel bowed with a flourish. 'My good Lady Sinda; what a surprise! I do hope my lads didn't give you any trouble at the monastery gates.'

Sinda kept her expression tranquil. 'Your "lads" acquiesced with my request to enter, as soon as I told them I was here to see the infamous god-killer. I garnered a few ribald remarks, but nothing worse than I had expected.' She glanced at Leona. 'Is this girl your latest paramour, Colonel?'

'She is my assistant,' said Friel, 'and I can assure you that our relationship is strictly professional. One should never mix business with pleasure. So tell me – how can I help you on this beautiful Zamatan afternoon?'

'I wondered if we could have a little chat, Colonel. In private.'

Leona smothered a sigh as Friel and Sinda locked gazes.

'I am sure I can accommodate you, my lady,' the colonel said. He turned to Leona. 'Take a break, and I will catch up with you later.'

'Yes, sir.'

The colonel took Lady Sinda's arm, and they walked through Tsallon Anura as if they were a happy couple out for a summer stroll. Leona overheard a few laughs coming from the rebel fighters down in the courtyard, then she turned away, shaking her head. She wondered what she should do. Being with the colonel amounted to the entirety of her job and, without him, she felt at a loose end. She set off towards the temple, passing a group of rebels in the courtyard who were using a crane to lift Lord Meer's severed head up onto a large post that had been hammered into the ground. Leona had a small room at the rear of the temple, and had raided the monks' library for books the previous evening. Most of the volumes had been on dry religious topics, such as the nature of the divinity of dragons, but she had found several tomes on the history of the island. A few fighters nodded in her direction as she entered the temple, but no one spoke to her. Her presence intimidated them – not because of anything she had said or done, but because everyone knew that she was the colonel's most trusted assistant. If she was like a daughter to him, then he was the overbearing father, scaring off any young men who might have had an interest in getting to know her better. A darker thought occurred to her – what if the rank and file had made the same assumption as Reyn? What if many assumed that Leona was, in fact, Friel's mistress? That would also explain why none wished to approach her. She pushed the thought from her head – it might be true, but it was not something she wished to dwell upon.

She walked to the area of the temple where her room was located, and then, on a whim, she knocked upon the door where Lahnos and Reyn slept. The door opened, and Reyn appeared with her head uncovered.

She glanced over Leona's shoulder, as if wondering where the colonel was.

'It's just me,' Leona said. 'I thought I'd come and see how you were doing.'

'Lahnos isn't here,' Reyn said. 'He's out training with his new rebel unit.'

'Do you... umm, do you want to do something?'

'Together?'

'Yes.'

'Like what?'

'I don't know.'

'Where's the colonel?'

Leona's shoulders sagged a little. 'He's... entertaining a beautiful young Aucterian aristocratic lady.'

Reyn laughed. 'He's what?'

'Do I really have to spell it out for you?'

Reyn said nothing for a moment, then she pushed the door open wider and stepped back into her room. Leona took that as an invitation, and went in after her, then closed the door.

'Sorry about the mess,' said Reyn, clearing away a few piles of clothes. 'Sit.'

Leona glanced around for a chair, then sat on the edge of the bed.

'Does the colonel have a lot of mistresses?' Reyn said.

'A few.'

'At least he doesn't make you stand by his side while he... entertains them.'

'I suppose I should be grateful for that.'

'And she's Aucterian?'

'This one is, yes. Actually, most of them are. I imagine that she is here to eke some sort of concession out of the colonel. Perhaps the rebels have a relative of hers in custody; or perhaps she's just worried about losing her house and her money.'

Reyn pushed some clothes off a chair and sat. 'Does it bother you?'

'Sometimes.'

'Jealous?'

'No, not jealous. Disappointed. Everyone sees him as this brave rebel leader, someone standing up for the Zamatans, when all it takes to distract him is some cleavage and a tight dress.'

'You lead a strange life, Leona.'

'Yours isn't very normal, either. I'm glad you feel free enough not to wear a head scarf, though.'

'I wonder how long it will last,' Reyn said. 'Right now, everyone is too elated about the death of Lord Meer and the success of the rebellion to care about a few horns and tails; but give it time, and I worry that things will go back to the old ways.'

'May I touch your horns?'

Reyn frowned. 'Why?'

'Sorry; did that sound inappropriate?'

'Yes.'

Leona's face flushed.

Reyn rolled her eyes. 'Fine. Make it quick.'

She leaned forward in her chair, and Leona gazed at the two horns. Reyn's brown hair was thick, and Leona couldn't see the join between the horns and her head. The tip of each horn was flat, and covered in tiny straight lines. Leona moved closer, and ran a finger over them, feeling the regular abrasions on their upper surfaces. They were like the marks left by a saw, she realised, and she put her hand to her mouth.

Reyn pulled her head back, her face transformed with anger. 'Disgust you, do I?'

'No!' Leona cried. 'It's... I...'

'Spit it out, Leona,' Reyn snapped. 'There is nothing you can say that I haven't heard before.'

'Those marks on your horns – I know what caused them, and my heart broke for you. I'm sorry.'

Reyn's expression softened. 'Oh. That is something I've never heard before.'

'I remember Lahnos saying that his family wanted to cut off his horns. Is that what happened to you?'

'I don't want to talk about it.'

'All right. I understand.'

'It's time for me to ask you something,' Reyn said. 'What do you think about the voice in Lahnos's head? And before you dismiss it as a symptom of exhaustion or grief, you should know that I believe him. He's told me everything the voice has said. It's not a figment of his imagination, Leona. It's real.'

Leona pondered for a moment. 'Well, the first thing I want to say is that the colonel was right – being a death-reader is not supposed to involve hearing a voice in your mind. I've read a large volume on the Gifts that was smuggled here from Gunst. Do you read Gunstian?'

'I can barely read Zamatan, Leona.'

Leona smiled. 'We don't speak Zamatan, Reyn.'

'No? Then what do we speak?'

'We speak the Divine Tongue. Do you think the settlers would have bothered to learn our language? No, it's the other way around. When the Dominion arrived, they forced everyone to speak like them. That's the real reason they built all of those schools, I think – it wasn't out of benevolence, more convenience. Anyway, the Gunstian book was hard-going and quite technical, but I persisted, and read it cover to cover.'

'So you know everything about the Gifts?'

'Everything that was in the book. It wasn't complete – for some reason, it only contained the first twelve Gifts, rather than the thirteen that are usually associated with Theodora; but there was a chapter on death-reading, and it didn't mention anything about hearing a voice in your head.'

'Never mind the voice for now,' said Reyn; 'tell me more about being a death-reader. What else can Lahnos expect?'

'All right. The first time it happens can be quite unsettling, naturally; but over time, and with lots of practice, a death-reader can pinpoint and draw out specific memories from someone. They can control what they see, rather than being at the mercy of a random series of recollections.'

'Shit. That's what I was worried about.'

Leona raised an eyebrow.

'It means Lahnos will be useful to people I'd rather he avoided – the Gunstians, the Dominion. Colonel Friel Laimos. They will all be wanting to get their claws into him.'

'I see.'

'Don't bullshit me, Leona. You know as well as I do that the colonel didn't send Lahnos away because he cares about him as an uncle should. He sees Lahnos as useful; just as he sees you as useful. You are both assets. Tools to be used to help the cause.'

'Let's go back to the voice,' Leona said. 'If it is real, then it has nothing to do with being Gifted.'

'Then what is it?'

'It could only mean that someone, somewhere, has the power to enter the thoughts of others.'

'Can dragons do that? Powerful ones, I mean?'

'Not that I'm aware of. The mightiest of the dragons, such as King Gahad was, or his children, have powers other than just flames and claws. Some can control the flow of rivers, others can melt stone with a glance; while some can enchant humans with a truth spell.'

'Like your Gift?'

'No. What they can do is this – if they have eye-contact, they can command you to speak only the truth. After that, the victim has no choice – they are physically incapable of uttering a lie; well, for at least as long as the spell lasts. These powers are unrelated to the Gifts of Theodora – they were brought to this world when Gahad arrived with his dragons and settlers.'

Reyn puffed out her cheeks.

'I have another question,' Leona went on. 'If we accept that the voice is real, and we accept my hypothesis that someone on this world can enter the thoughts of others – then why Lahnos? Why not you or me, for example?'

'The voice,' Reyn said; 'she told Lahnos that she was watching over him.'

'It was a woman's voice?'

'That's what he said.'

'Did she sound old or young? Did she have an accent?'

'I don't know. I'll ask him. He also said that she fixed his mind, whatever that means. He told me his mind was lost when he read the memories of his grandmother, and the voice fixed him, and woke him up.'

Leona narrowed her eyes. Nothing Reyn had said had triggered the tingle in the back of her head that denoted a lie.

'Maybe we should ask one of the monks,' said Reyn.

'No,' said Leona, her eyes widening. 'The monks despise the Gifts of Theodora, and they would probably assume that Lahnos has been possessed by a demon. Who knows what they would do to try to force the demon out of him? Something nasty, in all likelihood.' She leaned forward. 'They also don't like the part-Bullan.'

'Fine. Let's not ask the monks. How can we find out more?'

The door swung open, and the colonel strode in. 'Here you are. Do you know how much trouble I've had trying to find you, Leona?'

Leona stood. 'I didn't think you would be free for a while, sir.'

The colonel paced up and down the small room. 'That damned Gunstian agent arrived just as things were getting interesting with Lady Sinda. What a blasted inconvenience.' He took a long slow breath. 'It might be best if I calm myself before I enter negotiations with the Gunstians. Give me a moment.' He took a few more deep breaths, and stopped pacing. 'Right. I'm ready. Follow me, Leona; oh, and hello, Reyn.'

He strode from the room. Leona shared a quick glance with Reyn, then she followed him. They left the temple, and entered a squat building that held a few rooms where the monks lived. Two rebel fighters were standing outside a door, and they saluted as Friel and Leona approached.

'Ensure that we are not disturbed,' the colonel said, then he pushed the door open.

Friel and Leona went into a small, dark room, with only one narrow stained glass window providing any illumination. Seated behind a plain wooden table was a man in a long cloak, his face hidden by a hood.

'I don't like to be kept waiting,' the man said in a thick Gunstian accent.

'We are in the midst of a revolution,' Friel said, as he and Leona sat. 'I'm sure you understand.'

'Before I make my complaints,' the man went on, 'I wish to offer you my congratulations, Colonel. You slew the demon beast known as Meer, and proved to the ignorant citizens of this island that the dragons are not gods. I had the pleasure of seeing the corpse of the vile beast outside in the courtyard, and took a moment to spit upon it – a moment that I will forever treasure within my heart. For this feat, you have the thanks of the Gunstian Empire.'

Friel raised an eyebrow. 'And yet you say that you have complaints?'

'I do. My superiors in Gunst are displeased with your handling of the uprising, and they are angry with me for not ensuring that you kept the promises you made to us.'

'What promises have I broken?'

'The weapons we supplied were meant to be distributed to the ten thousand Gunstians living on this island, and yet I have not seen a single one of my compatriots among the rebel fighters in Kaugatz. Nor have I witnessed any native Gunstians in positions of authority within your leadership. This is not acceptable, Colonel.'

'I am a servant of necessity,' said Friel.

'What is that supposed to mean? Why did you disobey your orders?'

'It's simple. If the weapons had gone to the Gunstians, then the uprising would have failed.'

'And why would it have failed?'

'It would have failed because none of the Zamatans would have joined in. The noble and enlightened government of the great Gunstian Empire must be aware that the native Zamatans of this island do not always hold your people in the highest regard. The last time the Gunstian armed forces were here, they carried out a multitude of atrocities.'

'That was over a century ago.'

'Alas, memories are long. Can you give me any assurances that Gunst will not repeat the horrors of the past if they were to return?'

'The policy of the Gunstian Empire is not for you to decide, Colonel. This island belongs to the Empire; or do you disagree?'

'What I think is surely immaterial.'

'Perhaps, but I would still like to hear your answer. Do you agree that Zamata rightfully belongs to Gunst? Think very carefully before you reply, Colonel; for much depends upon your response.'

Friel stared at the bare surface of the table, then he nodded. 'I agree.'

Leona felt the back of her head tingle, but kept her features frozen.

'Good,' said the Gunstian agent. 'Another shipment of weapons and supplies will be landing tonight, in the same location as before. Please ensure that the Gunstians of Zamata are well-armed this time. I will accept no more excuses if you fail us again in this regard. Now, on to another matter. What is the situation in the Dragon Palace?'

'A small team was able to infiltrate the palace interior at dawn yesterday,' Friel said, keeping his eyes lowered. 'They have taken Lord Kheran hostage, and secured his quarters. A further two hundred rebel fighters then landed overnight to reinforce the position.'

'Two hundred?' said the agent. 'How were they able to pass through the Dominion Fleet unscathed? Did the Bullan not oppose the landing?'

'Neither the fleet nor the Bullan were in a position to do anything,' Friel said. 'If they hadn't allowed the fighters to land by the palace, then my men would have killed Lord Kheran. Lord Rufus and the Bullan are besieging the dragon child's quarters, but they are too afraid to act. Rufus would do anything to preserve his son's life, and the Bullan work for him.'

'And now there are two hundred rebels inside the palace?'

'Yes.'

'That was well done, Colonel. Now, instruct your men to slaughter the dragon child, preferably in full view of his father and the Aucterians in Igatz. I want them to watch as the demon's life is snuffed out. I want them to feel terror and anguish – I want to bathe in their tears.'

'If that were to happen,' Friel said, 'then Rufus and the Bullan would slaughter my two hundred men.'

'What is a mere two hundred next to the life of that foul demon child? Besides, entire legions of Gunstian warriors are currently being assembled in the harbour towns along the coastline of the Empire – a coastline that lies just two hundred and fifty miles west of Zamata. Your losses will be replaced when they arrive here.'

'And when will that be?'

'Do not attempt to divert this conversation, Colonel. Order your men to butcher the demon child.'

'What you ask is impossible,' said Friel, and Leona felt the tingle in her head again. 'The men in the palace are beyond my reach. Nevertheless, I will try to contact them. I cannot guarantee that I shall succeed, but I shall try.'

Leona's head throbbed with the succession of lies spoken by the colonel, but she managed to keep her face still.

The Gunstian agent remained silent, his features hidden by his long hood.

'Now,' said Friel, 'will you answer my question? When will the forces of the Gunstian Empire arrive upon these shores?'

'I will try to find out,' the agent said, his voice rich with irony. 'I cannot guarantee that I shall succeed, but I shall try.'

Friel smiled. 'Do I sense that this meeting is at an end?'

The agent rose to his feet. 'Think long and hard about the promises you have made, Colonel. You have been useful to Gunst, but no one is irreplaceable, not even a demon-slayer.'

The agent opened the door and strode from the room.

'I think that went well,' said Friel.

Leona turned to him. 'You think it went well? It was a disaster.'

'On the contrary, Leona; more weapons and supplies are due to arrive on the island tonight, and that was the only aspect of the conversation that interested me. The rest was just background noise. I assume you saw through my little white lies?'

'But the Gunstians are coming; they're sending soldiers to invade the island.'

'That was always a likely outcome. Did you think the Empire would stand idly by if the Dominion is defeated here? Of course they will be on their way; it would be naïve to believe otherwise.'

She stared at him. 'But...'

'Yes?'

'Are we replacing one set of masters with another, sir? We beat the

Dominion, only for the Gunstians to walk in? I loathe the Dominion, but... the Gunstians? The last time they occupied the island, they demanded that everyone renounce their faith in the serpent gods, and burned anyone who refused. They tore down the ancient pillars, stole the serpent jewels, and turned the surviving monasteries into storage depots and barracks for their soldiers. They dragged the part-Bullan through the streets, and threw their butchered bodies into the Cyasarta. We cannot let them return, sir.'

Friel said nothing, then he looked into her eyes. 'We cannot prevent them from returning.'

Leona's chest ached.

'What we must do,' Friel went on, 'is remain in control. The Gunstians are coming, and there is nothing we can do to stop that. But we are not powerless, Leona. Do you trust me?'

Leona swallowed her immediate response, and then she realised that she didn't know the answer to his question. Did she trust him? The colonel had led the rebellion, and had masterminded the death of Lord Meer, but what did he really want?

'I trust you,' she said, then she wondered why her head never tingled whenever it was she who had uttered a lie.

CHAPTER 16
DREAM CHANGER

Kaugatz, Serpent Isle – 6th Nethinch 1588

The men dragged the woman out of the cottage, and threw her to the ground in the middle of the armed mob.

'Please!' the woman cried. 'I have five children!'

The men stared at her, their hate-filled faces reflecting the light from the burning torches.

'Kill the Gifted bitch,' said one, and it began.

Lahnos watched as the boots and fists descended upon his mother's body. He tried to look away, but the nightmare held him transfixed. He knew he was dreaming, but was powerless to stop the images searing through his mind

'Mother,' he gasped, and the dream began to fade.

He looked around, and saw that he was in the garden of Uncle Friel's cottage near Fidalaimos. Reyn was laughing next to him, her horns showing, and her tail swishing about behind her. She was so beautiful, and her smile made him want to reach out for her and never let go.

Was he still dreaming?

Yes, Lahnos; you are dreaming.

He frowned, feeling violated by the sudden appearance of the voice in his mind. 'Are you watching my dreams?'

You keep having the same nightmare over and over; you keep seeing the death of your mother. It hurts to watch you suffer like this, so I changed your dream.

'You changed my dream? Who are you?'

Does it matter? I am here to help you, Lahnos. The reason I am speaking to you is that I have information – information that you need to give to your uncle.

'What are you talking about?'

I know all about the troubles of the Serpent Isle, or Zamata as you call it. I have witnessed the cruel violence that has swept over the island of your birth in the last few days. On one side you have the Dragon Dominion, and on the other you have the Empire of the Gunstians. I pity you, Lahnos, as I pity all who suffer.

'Why me?' he said. 'I was talking to Reyn, and she asked me why you spoke to me and to no one else.'

I have made mistakes, Lahnos; terrible mistakes. Watching over you is one way I can salve my own conscience. Now, you must listen to everything I am about to tell you. I have read the thoughts of Lord Rufus, and know what he is planning.

'You were in the dragon's mind?'

Yes. Now listen carefully.

Lahnos fell silent, and the voice spoke to him of the plans drawn up by the dragon governor. When she had finished, he opened his eyes, and awoke next to Reyn in their small room in the monastery. He lay still in the dim shadows for a few moments, listening to the sound of Reyn breathing, then he turned, propped himself up on an elbow, and gazed down at the young woman lying under the thin blankets next to him. He leaned over and kissed her, then he nudged her shoulder.

She opened her eyes, stretched, and turned to him.

'Is it morning?' she said, lifting a hand to touch his face.

'Not yet.'

'Then why did you wake me up?' She smiled. 'Or was that a stupid question? I need to go to the bathroom first.'

'I woke you up because I want to speak to you.'

She yawned. 'Oh. What about?'

'The voice came back.'

Her eyes widened.

He told her what had happened in his dreams, and what the voice had said to him.

Reyn sat up and leaned against her pillow. 'What are you going to do?'

'I'll have to tell my uncle,' he said.

'He'll think you've gone mad.'

'What choice do I have? If the voice was right, then I can't keep this information to myself.'

He swung his legs out of bed, then felt around on the table for matches and lit a small lamp.

'He will say that you were dreaming,' Reyn said. 'He can't change his plans because his nephew had a dream.'

'Then I will lie to him. I'll say I got the information from somewhere else. I'll tell him I used my death-reading powers on a dead Aucterian sailor.'

'You can't. Leona will know that you are lying.'

'It's the middle of the night. Leona won't be with him.'

He pulled his clothes on in silence as Reyn sat on the bed with the blanket wrapped round her. He laced up the new boots that the rebels had given him, and got to his feet.

'Please be careful,' Reyn said.

He nodded, then extinguished the lamp and slipped out of their room. He strode through the narrow hallways of the temple, and came to the colonel's private quarters. Two rebel fighters were standing outside a door, and they eyed him as he approached.

'I need to speak to my uncle,' Lahnos said.

'Colonel Laimos is sleeping, lad,' said one.

'I have vital information that he needs to know. It can't wait until morning.'

The fighters glanced at each other, and then another door in the passageway opened, and Leona peered out. She saw Lahnos and emerged from her room, a dressing gown bound at her waist.

'What is it?' she said.

'The lad says he has vital information for the colonel, miss,' said one of the guards.

Leona looked up into Lahnos's eyes. 'Is this true?'

'Yes,' he said.

She nodded. 'I shall awaken the colonel. Wait here.'

Leona eased past the guards and entered the colonel's bedroom. The door closed, and Lahnos leaned back against a wall, cursing his luck. What would he say now that Leona was awake? If he lied to his uncle, then she was duty-bound to tell him.

The door opened again, and Leona gestured for Lahnos to enter. The guards moved to the side, and he walked into the room. Leona had lit two small oil lamps, and the colonel was sitting up in bed rubbing his bleary eyes.

'This had better be good, lad,' he muttered.

'I need a map of Igatz and Kaugatz,' Lahnos said.

Friel frowned, then nodded towards Leona. She crouched down by a chest of drawers, removed a rolled up bundle, and then eased out a large map of the central area of the island.

'Lay it out onto the bed, Leona,' the colonel said.

'How soon is dawn?' Lahnos said.

The colonel shrugged, his irritation with being disturbed evident in the little lines around his eyes.

'Sunrise is in about three hours' time,' Leona said, as she spread out the map on top of the blanket.

'Then we still have time,' said Lahnos.

'Time for what?' said Friel.

Lahnos crouched by the bed and pointed towards the eastern ferry terminal. 'At dawn,' he said, 'ships from the Handshore Naval Base will attack here. They will have landing craft, and warships will strike the coast with catapults and ballistae. However, the landing craft will be empty. This is a diversion, meant to draw our attention away from the main assault.' He moved his finger across the map, to a location of shoreline west of Tsallon Anura where a long beach ran. 'This is where the real assault will take place. Twenty minutes after the warships begin pounding the ferry terminal, two thousand armed sailors from the Naval Base will land along here, and assault the monastery from the south-west.'

Friel scratched his head.

'He's telling the truth, sir,' Leona said.

'Or he believes he is,' said Friel. 'Lahnos, how did you come by this information?'

Lahnos stood and crossed his arms over his chest. 'Is that important?'

'Of course it is. Has it occurred to you that you might have been fed falsehoods? What if the two attacks are genuine, but the first is the real one, and the second is the diversion? I need to be able to trust your source, lad; thousands of lives are at stake.'

Lahnos glanced at Leona.

The colonel sighed. 'Do you know what that little glance told me, nephew? It told me that you are wondering if you can get away with lying to me. You can't, so you can forget about being anything other than completely honest. From whom did you obtain this information?'

'I'm not going to tell you that, uncle.'

'You must.'

Lahnos nodded. 'Do whatever you like with this information. I have done my bit. I'm going back to bed.'

'Stay where you are, nephew,' Friel said, his voice commanding. 'If you leave this room without giving me what I want, the two guards standing outside will lock you in the cells; do you understand? This is a rebellion, not a family get-together. One way or another, Zamatans are going to die because of what you have just told me. You can't walk away as if none of that is your responsibility.'

Lahnos halted by the door.

'Are you protecting someone?' Friel went on. 'I can be discreet, nephew. If your source is worried that their life might be in danger, then I promise you that no harm will come to them – but I need to know.'

Lahnos turned. 'I am not protecting anyone.'

'Then what is it that you fear?' Friel said. 'Did you read the information out of a corpse? Is that it? Am I hearing the first fruits of your Gift?'

Lahnos glanced at Leona again. 'No. It wasn't my Gift. It was the voice.'

Friel stared at him as the bedroom fell into silence.

Lahnos lowered his gaze, his assumptions confirmed. His uncle thought he was mad, or delusional, and Lahnos found it hard to blame him.

'He's telling the truth, sir,' said Leona.

Friel laughed. 'Of course he is. However, his *truth* seems to have little correspondence with reality.'

'The voice came to me in a dream,' said Lahnos, 'and she told me everything about the dawn attacks. She said she had been inside the mind of Lord Rufus.'

'A dream?' said Friel. 'This gets better and better. You woke me up to share the contents of your dream?'

Listen to me, Lahnos, and repeat the following – Uncle, when you were seven, you pushed my father out of a tree. My father broke his leg, but never told anyone the truth about what you had done.

Lahnos blinked.

'Perhaps you should go back to bed,' Friel went on. 'Come and see me in the morning, and we can talk about giving you a break from active duties. I might have been pushing you too hard.'

'Uncle,' Lahnos said, 'when you were seven, you pushed my father out of a tree. My father broke his leg, but never told anyone the truth about what you had done.' He blinked again. 'The voice told me to say that. Is it true?'

Friel's mouth opened.

'Is it true?' Lahnos said again.

The colonel mumbled something inaudible.

'What was that?' said Lahnos.

'I said it was true!' Friel cried, his face creased with rage. 'So? What does that prove? Maybe my brother told our mother about it years after it had happened, and then she told you. What is this, Lahnos? Are your thoughts so twisted that you would stoop to telling tales about my childhood? Who are you working for?'

'I thought I was working for you, uncle.'

'Is someone blackmailing you? Lads! Get in here!'

The door opened, and the two guards appeared by the entrance.

'Sir?' said one.

'Confine my nephew to the cells,' Friel said. 'Don't put him in with any of the other prisoners – make sure he has a room to himself; and don't let him speak to anyone.'

Lahnos clenched his fists as the two guards entered the room.

'Don't make a scene, lad,' said Friel, 'or I'll send fighters to arrest Reyn as well. Don't test me.'

'Leave Reyn alone,' Lahnos spat. 'She has done nothing wrong.'

'Is that so?' said Friel. 'Who knows – perhaps she put you up to this? Go quietly, and I'll let her sleep in peace. Resist, and the rest of her night might turn out to be rather uncomfortable.'

'You bastard.'

'I have been called worse. Go.'

Lahnos unclenched his fists and the two fighters led him out of the room. He considered making a break for it, but the threat the colonel had made against Reyn had been enough to quell his spirits.

You did the right thing, Lahnos.

He ignored the voice, and followed the guards down a flight of stairs and into the dark cellars of the monastery.

His cell had no windows, and only a tiny glimmer of lamplight was entering from under the heavy door that sealed the entrance. There was a rough wooden pallet, but no blankets, and a pail in the corner of the room was giving off a noxious odour. Lahnos lay on the pallet with his hands behind his head, staring up at the dark ceiling, and the hours passed.

'Can you hear me?' he said into the darkness.

Yes.

'I thought you'd gone.'

I was remaining silent. I can feel your anger towards me. I am sorry that things have turned out like this; I was trying to help.

'Who are you?'

You won't have heard of my name.

'Give me something,' he said. 'You owe me that. I am sitting in a cell because of you.'

Very well, she said. *I did not wish to tell you this, but you are right – you are suffering because of me. Lahnos, I am the one the Dominion refers to as the demon witch.*

Lahnos's mouth moved, but no sound came out.

Does that knowledge disturb you?

'You killed King Gahad?'

I did, but not for the reasons that everyone supposes.

'Then why?'

It would be better if you didn't know.

'Why my head? Why not someone else's?'

I never meant for Gahad's death to cause such chaos and violence in this world, Lahnos. I didn't understand how important he was to the stability of Athumia.

'You didn't answer my question. Why me?'

In a few minutes, Leona will be arriving at your cell door. I am going to go now, Lahnos. Perhaps I am causing you nothing but pain. Perhaps this was a mistake.

'Wait!' he cried, but the voice had gone.

Lahnos got to his feet and faced the door. If Leona arrived, then he would know that he wasn't going mad – he would know that the voice was real. He swallowed, his throat parched and dry.

A key sounded in the lock, and the door swung open.

Lahnos stared at the figure of Leona standing in the doorway, the lamplight from the cellar coming over her shoulders.

'Are you here to question me?' he said.

'No, Lahnos,' Leona said; 'I am here to release you. But you must come with me first. The colonel wants to speak to you.'

He walked out of the cell and followed Leona up the flight of stairs. As soon as they had left the cellar, Lahnos noticed the morning sunlight streaming in through the stained glass windows on the ground floor.

'How long was I in the cell for?' he said.

'Five hours, give or take.'

'What happened at dawn, Leona?'

The young woman said nothing. She led him into a large room that was crammed full of celebrating rebel fighters and officers. Everyone was smiling, except for Reyn, who was sitting alone in the corner of the chamber with a sullen expression on her face. Colonel Friel caught sight of Leona and Lahnos, and raised a hand into the air.

'Clear the room if you would, gentlemen,' he said. 'I have a little family matter to take care of, and then I shall join you all outside in the cloister.'

The officers and fighters filed out of the room, many after shaking the colonel's hand first. Reyn got up, and hurried to Lahnos. She took hold of his arm, then turned and shot an angry glance in Friel's direction.

'Close the door, Leona,' the colonel said.

His assistant did so, then the colonel walked forwards until he was standing in front of Lahnos and Reyn.

'This morning's events have cemented my reputation as a tactical genius,' the colonel said. 'It may seem unfair, but I neglected to mention to anyone that I had obtained the information from you, nephew. I put it down to an inspired insight I had into the workings of the enemy's mind. And you know what? I think they believed me.'

Lahnos frowned. 'You followed my advice? I thought you considered it to be a trick, or that I was delusional? You accused me of being blackmailed.'

'Yes. I did, didn't I? And then Leona and I sat and talked it out. I am aware that you have your doubts concerning our cause, nephew, but Leona assured me that you could be trusted and, as you know, I take whatever Leona tells me very seriously. I then questioned Reyn, who also assured me that the so-called voice in your head was genuine.' He clasped his hands behind his back and turned to face a large stained glass window depicting a red serpent entwined around the trunk of a cypress tree.

'And then I did something out of character,' Friel went on. 'I took a risk that, had it failed, it would have meant the deaths of thousands of Zamatans and the end of the rebellion. I decided to listen to what Reyn and Leona were telling me; I decided to trust you, Lahnos.'

Lahnos stared at his uncle's back. 'Did everything happen just as the voice predicted?'

The colonel laughed. 'Why don't we take a little walk, and you will see for yourself?'

Friel began striding towards the door, then Reyn coughed.

'Excuse me,' she said. 'Don't you think you owe Lahnos an apology?'

'For what, miss?' the colonel said. 'Can you fault any aspect of the way I reacted?'

'You stuck him in a cell.'

'Can you blame me? It was a necessary precaution. I needed time and a clear head to calmly evaluate the situation, and no harm came to him.' He glanced at Lahnos. 'Can you forgive me, nephew?'

'I forgive you for putting me in the cells,' Lahnos said, 'but not for threatening Reyn.'

'Alas; that, too, was necessary, to prevent you from starting a fight with my two guards. I didn't mean any of it. Come – let us gaze upon the fruits of our combined labour.'

Friel opened the door, and the others followed him out. They remained within the temple, and took stairs that led up onto its flat roof. Lahnos blinked from the glaring sunlight as they emerged into the open air, then he walked with his uncle and the two women towards the edge of the roof. Friel gestured down, and Lahnos gazed into the large courtyard that sat by the monastery cloisters. Sitting on the ground, surrounded by dozens of armed rebel fighters, were hundreds of Dominion sailors, their heads bowed, and their uniforms unkempt.

'We captured over a thousand naval personnel this morning,' Friel said. 'This amounts to around half of them, and the rest are being held close to the central ferry terminal. Hundreds more drowned in their ill-judged assault upon the beach. I had every ballista in my possession lined up to oppose their landing, and hundreds of rebel fighters with crossbows did the rest. The sands are soaked with Aucterian blood. The ships of the mighty Northern Fleet could do nothing but watch and weep. They had expended their entire arsenal upon the diversionary attack, and the eastern harbour is now in ruins, but not a single rebel fighter lost their lives there. Look out across the Cyasarta, Lahnos, and tell me what you see.'

Lahnos shielded his eyes from the sun and peered over the clear waters of the inlet.

'I see ships,' he said. 'What does it mean?'

'It means that the Northern Fleet is preparing to evacuate; that's what it means, lad. Naval personnel have begun boarding transports, and packing away their possessions. With no landing craft, no munitions, and no ground attack forces, the navy is powerless to prevent us moving into Igatz. And what are the Bullan doing? Nothing. Nothing but sitting uselessly outside the Dragon Palace. Lord Rufus and his son mean more to them than the occupation of this island. This is the greatest victory I could have ever imagined. I have toiled for years to find a way to neutralise the power of the Northern Fleet, but it was a puzzle that I was never able to solve. That is the real reason I took the risk of trusting you – I knew that, if your words were true, then I was being afforded an opportunity that might never arise again. Lahnos, you have saved the rebellion.'

'I did nothing,' Lahnos said. 'It was the voice in my head that told me what to do.'

'Whatever you say, nephew. I look forward to hearing more from this voice of yours. What else has it told you? Has it spoken to you since?'

Lahnos chewed his lip.

'I will take that as a yes,' Friel said; 'however, something about your expression disquietens me.'

'Did you hear her again, Lahnos?' said Reyn. 'What did she say?'

'She was upset that I was being punished for trying to do the right thing,' he said.

His uncle's face fell.

'And then she left,' Lahnos went on. 'She said that she didn't want to cause me any more pain.'

Reyn's eyes flashed with anger, and she turned to the colonel. 'Do you see what you've done? You've scared her away!'

Friel swallowed. 'Do you think that she will come back?'

Lahnos shrugged. 'I have no idea. I asked why me, but she wouldn't tell me. I asked her what her name was, but...'

'Yes?' said Leona. 'What did she say?'

Lahnos looked down at the three faces staring at him, each hanging on to his every word.

'She told me that I wouldn't know her name,' he said.

'That's unfortunate,' said Friel. 'Leona told me about her theory – that the voice belongs to a very powerful individual; someone with the ability to see into the minds of others. Did she have an accent?'

'Yes,' said Lahnos, 'but not one I recognised.'

'Then she isn't Gunstian?' said Leona.

Lahnos shook his head. 'To be honest, I feel a little sad that she's gone.'

'You are not the only one,' said Friel. He gazed up at the sky. 'Great lady,' he said; 'if you can hear me, then I apologise for doubting Lahnos, and I am truly sorry that I locked him up. Thank you for helping us. Zamata owes you its gratitude.'

Reyn rolled her eyes. 'So he can apologise to her, but not to Lahnos?'

'The colonel has explained his reasons,' said Leona. 'He only did what he thought was right.'

'Do you always stick up for him?' said Reyn.

Lahnos lowered his gaze as the others bickered, then he stared out over Igatz. He had never meant to join the rebellion in the first place, and yet he had done as much to ensure its success as his uncle had. Except, of course, for the fact that his uncle was taking the credit. That didn't bother him, he decided. Let his uncle bask in the glory.

'I want Reyn and I to move to a better room,' he said, cutting through the words of the others.

His uncle glanced at him. 'Go on.'

'I want a room with more privacy, and one that has a balcony overlooking the Cyasarta.'

'And its own bathroom,' said Reyn.

'Are you trying to extort concessions out of me, nephew?' said Friel.

'No. I'm not asking for much. You said I saved the rebellion. A better room hardly amounts to extortion.'

'And you will keep the voice a secret from all but those standing here?'

'Of course I will. You don't need to worry on that account.'

'Then I would be delighted to have you relocated to a more comfortable apartment. Pack your things; I will see to it today. Do I have your assurance that you will inform me if the voice reappears?'

Lahnos nodded. 'I will, but she's not who you think she is, uncle.'

'No? I thought she refused to tell you her name.'

'She didn't tell me her name – she told me what others call her.'

'By all that is holy, Lahnos,' said Friel, 'spit it out.'

Lahnos turned back to gaze at the view of the ships in the inlet. 'She is the demon witch who slew Gahad.'

CHAPTER 17
PROOF OF LIFE

Igatz, Serpent Isle – 6th Nethinch 1588

The roar of anger shook the walls of the marble palace, and dozens of rebel fighters glanced up as dust fell from the ceiling of the domed chamber. Cisca put her hands over her ears, as Kheran whimpered on the heap of cushions next to her.

'Rufus isn't happy about something,' said one of the fighters, as the noise faded away.

'We have four ballistae pointed at his son's head,' said another. 'It might have something to do with that.'

Cisca shuddered. One of the ballistae was sitting only two yards to her left and if it were loosed, then the yard-long steel bolt would pass through her body on its way to striking the dragon child. The four ballistae were positioned in a circle surrounding the young dragon, and each had three rebels standing or sitting next to the levers that controlled the weapons. Cisca turned her eyes to the floor, unable to bear having to look at the barbed ends of the razor-sharp bolts.

Kheran whimpered again, and she tried to smile.

'Are you thirsty?' she said. 'Do you want some water?'

The dragon child inclined his head a fraction, and the chains enclosing him clanked. For two days, Kheran had been unable to move his wings or his limbs, or open his mouth more than a couple of inches, and the sight of him filled Cisca with pity and despair. She filled a jug with water from a pail that sat next to her, then she lifted the jug to Kheran's mouth. Trying to give the dragon food or water had become a laborious task, and much of the jug's contents spilled down his chin and onto the filthy cushions as she poured. The area around the dragon was also starting to smell. No allowances had been made by the rebels for the passing of waste, and many of the blankets were soiled and wet. Cisca, on the other hand, was permitted to visit the same bathroom that the rebel fighters used, but the young men had left it in a terrible state, and she had to hold her nose every time she entered.

Dozens of armed Zamatans were loitering throughout the child dragon's living quarters, guarding the entrances, manning the ballistae, or just sitting and waiting for something to happen. Outside the doors, thousands of Bullan soldiers had taken up position, surrounding Kheran's large apartment within the white, marble palace. They, too, were waiting, but for what, Cisca did not know.

Cisca saw Bauchlie and Travers walk across the sleeping chamber, and her eyes narrowed with anger at the sight of the traitor and the rebel commander together. She still felt pain from the punch that Travers had given her, and she had large bruises under her eyes and around her nose where his fist had struck her face. The two men went through the door that led to the balcony, and Cisca went back to work, clearing up the spilt water with a cloth.

Kheran groaned, and Cisca wondered how much pain he was feeling. As a grandchild of the mighty King Gahad, there was a reasonable chance that Kheran had inherited some of his grandfather's healing abilities. It was well known that Gahad had possessed the power to heal his own injuries, and some of his twenty-one children could do the same. Among his grandchildren, however, the proportion of those who could heal themselves had fallen further. Cisca got to her feet and examined the wound along the dragon child's left ear. It had stopped bleeding, but it hadn't healed itself. What did that mean? Did it mean that he was suffering?

Bauchlie and Travers walked back into the sleeping chamber and approached the pile of cushions and blankets where Kheran and Cisca were sitting.

Bauchlie nodded to a rebel fighter. 'Unshackle the woman.'

Cisca said nothing as a young man hurried forward. He slung his crossbow over a shoulder, then he knelt by the wall and unhooked the chain that led to the shackle around Cisca's left ankle. It was a procedure she was familiar with, but it normally only occurred when she needed to go to the bathroom. The young fighter picked up the end of the chain, and handed it to Bauchlie.

'Follow me,' Bauchlie said, then he set off again, returning the way he had come.

'I'll be back soon,' Cisca whispered to Lord Kheran, then she started walking before the chain could go taut.

The chain rattled on the marble floor as she moved after Bauchlie and Travers, and they slowed a little to allow her to catch up.

'We want your evaluation of something,' Travers said.

Cisca said nothing, keeping her eyes lowered. She had been trying to suppress her own sense of dignity, and had struggled to quell all thoughts of defiance. Her main goal – no, her only goal – was to try to ensure the survival of the dragon child. Her own feelings were irrelevant.

Bauchlie, Travers and Cisca went through the arched doorway, and Cisca caught her first glimpse of sea and sun since the palace had been infiltrated. Ahead of her, at the far end of another large chamber, was Lord Kheran's wide balcony. It was empty, but over fifty rebel fighters were sitting or resting within the large room, while keeping away from the balcony windows. Cisca stared at the view, then frowned. Sailing south-east, towards the narrow channel that led to the ocean, was a long double line of large ships. She could see frigates, cruisers, and two large battleships, along with a multitude of supply vessels.

'I assume you can see the fleet, Lieutenant Cisca,' Travers said. 'They started passing the palace over twenty minutes ago, heading out from the Handshore Naval Base to the west of here. At first, we thought that they might attempt to attack our positions, but they have done nothing but sail past. What do you think they are doing?'

'You're the damned sailor,' Cisca said. 'You tell me.'

Travers glared at her, and she immediately regretted her words. She had to think of Lord Kheran, and bury her defiance.

'They're leaving,' said Bauchlie, his dark eyes on the inlet. 'Why?'

'Are you asking me?' said Cisca.

'Yes.'

Cisca narrowed her eyes at the endless procession of ships sailing past the headland of Igatz. She tried to take a step towards the balcony doors to get a better view, but Bauchlie put an arm out to stop her.

'Move any closer,' he said, 'and the Bullan are likely to put a bolt through your skull.'

'The Bullan are outside the balcony?' she said.

'We are completely surrounded,' said Travers. 'As soon as the two hundred rebel fighters arrived in the palace, the Bullan sealed off every entrance.'

'Then your position here is hopeless,' Cisca said. 'How much food do you have?'

'Enough for ten days,' said Travers.

'It was a mistake to have brought so many men,' Cisca said; 'surely you must realise that.'

'I didn't ask for your opinion on our supply situation,' said Bauchlie, his heavy gaze piercing her. 'I asked why the fleet is leaving Zamata.'

'They can't have been recalled,' she said, 'so they must have made a judgement that their position here was untenable. Perhaps the rebels cut off their supplies of fresh water. It could be any number of reasons.'

'What will their orders be?' Bauchlie said.

'I am not privy to the thinking of the commanders of the Northern Fleet.'

'Your best guess will do. Will they return to Aucteran, or will they stay in the area?'

'If they are short of fresh water, then they won't make it across the ocean,' she said. 'Did you really need me for this? Lieutenant Travers is, or was, a member of the Northern Fleet. I am Dragon Corps.'

'I've already heard Travers's opinion,' Bauchlie said. 'I wanted to see what you thought.'

'Also,' said Travers, 'we felt that you needed to see this. The fleet is abandoning the island, and all of the Aucterian settlers. History is being made. How does it make you feel, Lieutenant Cisca?'

'Five thousand Bullan remain in Igatz,' she said.

'True,' said Travers, 'but those Bullan are now stranded. Their loyalties lie with the dragons. If both die, then perhaps the Bullan will be prepared to come to an arrangement.'

'We are not going to slay Kheran,' said Bauchlie; 'not unless it becomes absolutely necessary.'

'The fleet won't have left without Lord Rufus's permission,' said Cisca.

'They might have mutinied,' said Travers.

Cisca smiled. 'If that were the case, then Lord Rufus would be airborne by now, burning any ship that refused to return to their post. Also, if they were truly fleeing the Serpent Isle, then they would have packed the ships with settlers. No, Lord Rufus has merely ordered them to retire to a position of safety. That means two things – firstly, the settlers and the Handshore Naval Base are only being temporarily abandoned and, secondly, the fleet could return at any moment.' She glanced at Bauchlie. 'For the sake of the Serpent Isle, you had better hope those ships return soon; otherwise the Imperial Gunstian Fleet will be here the moment they learn what has occurred. You may hate the Dominion, but would you really prefer the Gunstians to be in charge of the island?'

Bauchlie said nothing, but Cisca saw the faintest trace of a smile crease Travers's lips.

'Why are you smiling?' she said. 'Do you think it's amusing? I may be new here, but even I have heard of the terrible things the Gunstians did the last time they occupied the island.'

'I am amused by the look of panic on your face,' Travers said.

Cisca stared at him. 'You're lying. Do you... do you actually want the Gunstians to get here?'

'What I want is absolutely none of your concern,' Travers said. 'You are our prisoner, not the other way around.'

Cisca's eyes narrowed. 'Are you working for Gunst, Lieutenant Travers?' she said. She turned to Bauchlie. 'Is he working for Gunst?'

The tall Zamatan rebel leader said nothing, but a flicker of unease crept over his features.

'Don't be ridiculous,' said Travers.

'Then why did you betray the Dominion?' said Cisca.

'That is none of your business.'

'Do you know?' she said to Bauchlie.

The rebel leader shook his head.

'Let me get this straight,' said Cisca; 'you are in charge, but you have no idea why this traitor is helping you?'

'I was told to trust him,' Bauchlie said. 'Sometimes, it's better not to ask too many questions.'

'He will betray you, too,' she said; 'just wait and see. You think you're leading a fight for freedom, but what if Travers is delivering you into the hands of the Gunstian Empire?'

'Shut up,' said Travers. 'I've heard enough of this nonsense. Bauchlie, this silly girl would say anything to attempt to divide us. Don't believe a word she says.'

Bauchlie said nothing, then he pulled on Cisca's chain and nodded towards Kheran's living chamber. Cisca glared at him but moved her feet, and the two men led her away from the balcony. They escorted her back to the great heap of blankets and cushions, and a fighter reconnected her chain to the wall.

Bauchlie turned to Travers. 'Don't go near her again without my permission.'

The naval officer snorted. 'Why? Do you believe the lies that came from her mouth?'

Bauchlie shrugged. 'You heard what I said.'

The rebel leader turned and strode away, and Travers stared at Cisca.

'You won't survive this,' he whispered to her. 'No matter what happens, I will make sure of that.'

Cisca sat down on the cushions as Travers walked away. Kheran bumped her with his nose, and she smiled at him.

'Don't worry,' she said to the young dragon. 'Everything is going to be fine.'

The hours of the afternoon dragged by, and Cisca passed the time by watching the ballista crews. Only three of the four machines pointing at them were primed to loose at any one time, she realised. The rebel fighters said nothing about what they were doing, but every hour or so one team would release the tension in the twisted cords that sat behind the yard-long bolts, allowing them to unwind, while another team would re-tighten theirs by turning a wheel. Cisca knew little about the workings of the devices, but she doubted that they had been designed to sit in a state of constant readiness for days on end. Would the cords lose their tension over time, she wondered; and if so, what would happen if the order came to loose at the dragon? She turned to gaze at Kheran, but the dragon child's eyes were closed, and she hoped that he had managed to fall asleep.

A rebel fighter entered the chamber at a run, his crossbow clutched in both hands. He looked around, then saw Bauchlie and sprinted towards him. The two men talked together, then Bauchlie nodded, and the fighter ran back across the dragon's sleeping chamber. Bauchlie spoke to a few more fighters, and they grabbed their weapons and took up positions by the walls. Within seconds, everyone inside the chamber was on the move, and Bauchlie strode over to where Cisca was sitting.

'We have visitors,' he said.

Cisca sat up. 'Who?'

'A delegation of Bullan officers. They are demanding proof that Kheran is alive, and so I will allow them to enter.'

'Are you going to gag me?'

Bauchlie shook his head. 'I want you to answer their questions.'

'You want me to lie?'

'Did I say that?' He chewed his lip. 'What if I had asked you to lie?'

'I would have refused.'

He nodded. 'Good.'

He walked away, and Cisca narrowed her eyes. The sound of boots on marble attracted her attention, and she glanced at the archway that led to the storage room. Four Bullan soldiers appeared in the entranceway, and the rebel fighters by the walls tensed, their bows up and aiming at the new arrivals. The Bullan were wearing leather armour, but none had weapons, and their thickset eyes took in the scene. One of them nodded to the others, and they approached the heap of blankets and cushions where Kheran and Cisca were sitting.

They halted when they were five yards away, and bowed.

'Lord Kheran,' said one, 'can you hear us?'

The dragon child didn't respond.

'He's sleeping,' said Cisca.

The four Bullan turned their attention to her.

'Are you Lieutenant Cisca of the Dragon Corps?' said the one who had addressed Kheran.

'I am.'

'Has Lord Kheran been tortured or abused?'

'The top of his left ear was cut off,' she said.

'We know that,' said the Bullan officer; 'we saw it. Have the rebels been feeding him and providing him with fresh water to drink?'

Cisca nodded.

'Have they beaten him?'

'No, but the chains must be painful.'

'Awaken him.'

'I... don't know if I should. He hasn't slept much, and I want him to rest.'

'I will not ask again, Lieutenant. Lord Rufus will expect us to have spoken to his son directly.'

Cisca placed a hand onto the side of the dragon's face. 'Kheran,' she said. 'Wake up, my darling.'

The dragon child groaned and struggled against the chains and nets that were binding him. His eyes opened, and he stared at Cisca.

'I'm sorry,' she said. 'Listen; some Bullan soldiers are here to speak to you.'

The dragon groaned again, and closed his eyes.

'Lord Kheran,' said the Bullan officer; 'please acknowledge that you can hear me.'

The young dragon opened his eyes again with an effort, and turned his head to gaze at the four soldiers. He tried to open his mouth, but the chains were too tight.

The Bullan glanced at each other.

'Your father has a message for you, my lord,' said the officer. 'Stay resolute, and remember your bloodline. Do not shame your father or your mother in front of humans who are beneath your contempt. Your father wants you to live, but if you must die, then die well; for it is better to die with honour than to live in shame. Give your captors nothing, and your father will always be proud of you. Nod if you have understood these words, my lord.'

Kheran gave the slightest of nods, then he closed his eyes, and his head sank back down to the cushions.

'Why has the fleet left the isle?' said Cisca.

The Bullan ignored her.

'Do you have a message for me from my superior officers?' Cisca went on.

The Bullan nodded to the rebel fighters positioned by the walls, then they turned and walked from the chamber. A dozen fighters followed them out, and then Cisca heard the sound of doors opening and closing. The rebel fighters came back into the chamber, and Bauchlie spoke to them all in a hushed tone as they gathered around him.

Cisca turned back to Kheran. 'Your father loves you very much.'

The dragon child didn't respond.

'Don't lie to him,' hissed a voice.

Cisca frowned, and noticed Travers lingering to her left.

'Dragons are incapable of love,' Travers went on. 'Rufus cares more about honour than he does about the fate of his own son. The only reason he hasn't attacked us is that he is afraid to face the wrath of his mate if he allows Kheran to be butchered by rebels. These are the gods you serve, Cisca. These are the beasts you worship.'

Bauchlie began to approach the great heap of cushions, and Travers disappeared into the shadows. The rebel commander looked down at Cisca, his scarred face impassive.

'Thank you,' he said.

'I didn't do it for you,' she spat.

'You're doing well,' he said. 'Sit tight, and you and your dragon have a good chance of walking out of here alive.'

Her features tightened. 'Don't lie to me!'

Bauchlie said nothing, then he turned and walked away.

Cisca remained frozen upon the cushions as her anger surged within her, then she put her head in her hands. Don't despair, she told herself; Lord Rufus was wise and noble – he would know what was best. She glanced at the dragon child. His eyes were still closed, and she wondered if the visit from the Bullan had comforted him, or if it had made him feel more alone and frightened.

'I wish I knew what to do,' she whispered to him. 'I wish I knew how to help you, Kheran.'

She rested her head against his scales, so that none of the rebels would see her tears.

CHAPTER 18
INTO IGATZ

Igatz, Serpent Isle – 8th Nethinch 1588

The ferry tacked into the breeze, its wide prow churning through the waters of the Cyasarta inlet. A heavy spring shower had inundated the island overnight, but the morning wind had cleared the skies, and the water was glistening as the sun rose in the east. Leona's eyes picked out the buildings and streets of Igatz as the vessel neared the coastline. On their left was the huge naval base of Handshore, its quays and docksides deserted and quiet, and its basin empty of ships.

Leona felt her nerves rise as the ferry sailed ever closer to the jetty. Kaugatz had been in rebel hands for six days, but Igatz seemed almost like a foreign land – a colonised enclave in the heart of the island.

'Are you anxious?' said the colonel.

She glanced at him. 'How did you know?'

'Because it would be strange to imagine otherwise,' he said. 'It may look different from the rest of the island, but never forget that Igatz is as much a part of Zamata as anywhere else. The Aucterian settlers just borrowed it from us for a short while.'

Leona smiled. 'Twelve thousand of them still live in Igatz, sir.'

'Oh, there will be more of them there by now, I would think. Settlers have been arriving from all over the island since the Bullan were reassigned to the siege of the Dragon Palace, leaving their farms and villages for the safety of Igatz.'

'And is it safe, sir? For them, I mean?'

'That depends upon how willing they are to adjust to the new reality,' he said, as he leaned on the railings by the ship's bow. 'For almost a century, native Zamatans have had to live under their rule, obeying their laws, and paying taxes to the Dominion. If the Aucterian colonists are as well behaved as we were, then they will be fine.'

He turned and gazed at the deck of the vessel. Over a hundred rebel fighters were on board, all armed and carrying large packs as they stared at the approaching coastline. A dozen other ferries had already set sail that morning, transporting over a thousand Zamatans to Igatz.

Leona swallowed. 'So much could go wrong, sir,' she said. 'Kaugatz was ours, even before the rebellion began; it felt as though it belonged to us. There were a few Aucterians, but we vastly outnumbered them; but in Igatz...'

'It will be fine,' he said. 'The fleet has gone, the Bullan are distracted, and the Aucterians are completely surrounded. They have nowhere else to go, Leona. Unless they want a bloodbath, they will do the sensible thing.'

Sailors began taking down the sails as the craft approached the long jetty. Rebel fighters were stationed around the ferry terminal, guarding its perimeter, and standing in the shade of the palm trees that lined the stone quayside. A few of them began to cheer as they caught sight of the colonel standing by the bow, and he raised an arm to greet them. The ferry bumped against the side of the jetty, and sailors threw ropes to the waiting fighters, who looped them around the iron cleats. A gangway was put into place, and the colonel strode towards it, while the others on board waited their turn.

The colonel stepped onto dry land to the sound of another loud cheer from the rebels, and someone placed a long chain of flowers around his neck. The colonel smiled, and waved to his men. Leona followed him onto the jetty, and a chain of flowers was also offered to her. She bowed her head, and the rebel fighter put them round her neck.

'Wave to them,' the colonel whispered.

Leona raised her hand, and the fighters let out another cheer.

An officer approached. 'Welcome to Igatz, sir.'

The colonel smiled. 'My home is in Igatz, Captain, but thank you for the sentiment. It is marvellous to be back.' They strode along the jetty, as the colonel waved to more people. 'Do you have the latest situation report for me?'

'Yes, sir,' said the rebel captain. 'Central and southern Igatz is under our control.'

'Where have the Bullan set up their defensive lines?'

'Just to the west of the Merchants' Harbour, sir. They have blockaded the streets between there and the northern ferry terminal and are letting no one pass.'

'And the Aucterians?'

'The majority have fled, sir.'

'Fled? Where?'

'To the Fortress of Atzoun, sir, on the southern tip of Igatz. It was lying empty after the Bullan withdrew to the Palace and Temple Districts, and thousands of Aucterian civilians are now crammed in behind its walls. The few that remain in the area under our control have given us no problems.'

The colonel kept smiling at the crowds. 'Why did you allow this to happen, Captain? I am gravely disappointed.'

'The Aucterian locked themselves in the fortress before we arrived this morning, sir. Their homes and possessions have been abandoned.'

'But the Fortress of Atzoun has only one well, Captain; or am I mistaken?'

'No, sir – you are not mistaken.'

'And there are thousands of civilians trapped inside?'

'They are not trapped, sir. A delegation of rebel officers approached the main gates of the fortress not long after our arrival; and we announced that it was safe for the Aucterians to return to their homes.'

'How did they react?'

'Settlers loosed their crossbows at us from the walls, sir. It appears that the Bullan may have left behind considerable stocks of weapons and other military supplies.'

The colonel turned to Leona. 'Cancel my schedule,' he said. 'It seems that we shall have to pay a visit to Atzoun before we approach the Bullan defences.' He resumed his broad smile and gazed at the fighters gathered by the quayside. He saw a cart, climbed up onto its back, and raised his arms. 'Soldiers of Zamata!' he cried. 'I congratulate each and every one of you! What you have achieved in the last few days has been nothing short of a miracle. First, we took Kaugatz; then we slew a mighty dragon!' He paused as the crowd roared out in jubilation. 'Then we destroyed the Dominion Navy's counter-attack and sent their fleet scurrying away in shame and disgrace. The settlers and Bullan have evacuated the outer island, and now cling on to two small outposts – the Fortress of Atzoun, and the Temple and Palace Districts of Igatz. Soon, the entire island will be ours! But – we must not be complacent. Four and a half thousand Bullan still stand against us, barricaded into the eastern tip of Igatz; while thousands of Aucterian civilians and vigilantes are holed up in Atzoun. With the departure of the fleet, they have nowhere to run!' He stood back as the crowd of rebels cheered again, then his demeanour changed. His smile dropped, and his eyes glinted with determination. 'Now for the rules. There will be no looting, no harassment of civilians, no theft, and no disorder. We are not savages – nor are we a brutal occupying force. We are Zamatans, not Gunstians. Many of you might long for revenge against those who have oppressed us – to you I say this: revel in your victory, but bloody not your hands with cruel vengeance. Justice is not the same as revenge; the settlers are not our prey, and we are not predators. For centuries, the Dominion has looked down on us, thinking us ignorant or simple; let us prove to them that we are civilised people, that we follow the rule of law, and that we respect the right of others to live in peace. For centuries, this island of ours has been locked in a cycle of violence and occupation; let us today pledge to break that cycle forever; let us dream of a new dawn for

Zamata – a dawn of tolerance and prosperity, where all men and women live as equals. The old laws will be torn up, but that does not mean we should usher in an era of violence and anarchy. You brave fighters have liberated Zamata; now you must also liberate your hearts!'

The crowd cheered, but it was more muted than before, and a few rebels glanced away. The colonel waved again, then stepped down from the cart.

'Fetch my carriage from the ferry, Captain,' he said, 'and fetch it now.'

It was little over a mile from the ferry terminal to the gates of Atzoun Fortress, and the streets were quiet and deserted. A few fighters were posted by the major junctions, but were standing idle under the glare of the morning sun.

'I liked your speech,' Leona said, taking off the necklace of flowers as the carriage wheels bumped over the cobblestones.

Friel raised an eyebrow. 'I fear it will make as much difference as a drop of water poured into the ocean. Still, it had to be said. At this very moment, hundreds of Aucterian mansions and townhouses are lying empty and unguarded; it would take an unprecedented amount of will and forbearance for the rebel rank and file to be able to resist the temptation to go on a looting spree. At least they now know that I disapprove, for all the good it will do. By tonight, entire areas of Igatz will be laid waste.' He drummed his fingers off his knee. 'What possessed the Aucterians to hide in the damn fortress? Have I carried out massacres, Leona? Have I unleashed barbarism upon civilians?'

His eyes widened as they reached the main road, and Leona followed his gaze. Strung up from lampposts were the naked and mutilated bodies of over a dozen men and women.

'Stop the carriage!' Friel cried.

The driver tugged the reins, and the horses pulling the vehicle slowed and then halted by the roadside. Friel opened the side door and jumped down to the ground, then he strode towards the grisly scene. Leona held on to her skirt and clambered down after him, while eight wagons full of rebel fighters also came to a halt on the road behind them. The colonel reached the foot of the lampposts, and gazed up, his eyes filled with a rage that Leona had never seen before. A few rebel officers dismounted from the wagons, and joined Leona and the colonel. For a moment, Friel seemed too angry to speak, and Leona stared up at the bodies. Nine men and four women were hanging from the lampposts, some upside down and suspended by their ankles, others with nooses around their necks. Pools of blood had collected under each corpse, and flies were buzzing around the open wounds.

The captain from the ferry terminal coughed. 'Sir?'

The colonel brought his composure under control. 'Were you aware of this display, Captain?'

'No, sir. This is the first I have seen of it.'

'But you have heard of other... outrages? I saw your face during my speech. I saw the reaction to my words on the faces of many.'

'There have been three murders that I know of, sir; and several assaults upon the Aucterian civilians, but I was unaware of anything of this scale.'

'Cut them down.'

The captain gestured to a wagon. 'Get these bodies down!'

'Which officer was in charge of this area?' the colonel said.

Another captain stepped forward. 'This area is under my authority, sir.'

Friel's anger exploded and he grabbed the officer by the throat. 'Your men did this? Where were you when it was happening? Sunning yourself under a palm tree with a girl in one hand and a glass of wine in the other?'

The captain tried to respond, but only a choked gasp came from his lips. The colonel released him, and the officer fell to his knees, his hands on his throat, as the other officers shared nervous glances with each other.

'Sir?' said a lieutenant. 'It has been hard to rein the men in, sir. Many hate the Aucterian settlers with a passion, and some feel that a blood price has to be paid. Perhaps it would be wise to allow them to let off a little steam?'

Friel punched the lieutenant in the face, sending him sprawling to the cobbles. Friel stepped forward to kick the officer, and the others lunged in, pulling the colonel back, as eight wagon-loads of rebel fighters watched from the backs of the wagons. Amid the fray, a stray arm went swinging, and Leona was knocked to the ground. She landed on her back in one of the pools of blood under the swinging body of a naked and gutted Aucterian. She lifted her hands, and they were red. She began to shake, her breath coming in gasps, then a drop of blood fell from the body and splashed down her cheek. It was still warm, and she rolled onto her knees and vomited across the cobbles.

A hand touched her shoulder. 'Miss?'

She looked up, and saw that the men had stopped fighting. The lieutenant punched by Friel was crouching on the cobbles, a handkerchief covering his bloody nose, while Friel and the others were gazing down at her. The captain from the ferry terminal offered her his hand, and she took it.

'I am sorry, Leona,' said the colonel, as the captain helped her stand. 'I lost my temper. Are you all right?'

She glanced down at the blood and vomit smearing her dress.

'Captain,' Friel went on, 'have a wagon remain here to cut down the bodies. I want them delivered to the Aucterian cemetery before noon. Launch an investigation into this incident, and stop at nothing to bring those responsible into custody. Send me a report by sunset. The rest of you shall follow me.'

He took Leona's arm and escorted her back to the carriage. She took his hand and allowed him to help her up into her seat, then the driver closed the door. As soon as the carriage was underway, the colonel lowered his head.

'I would cry bitter tears of disappointment, but to what end?' he said.

Leona said nothing, her hands still shaking.

'If you hadn't fallen,' he went on, 'I might have killed that lieutenant. Perhaps I should have.' He reached under the seat and opened a cupboard. He withdrew a fresh set of clothes and a towel, and set them down on the seat next to Leona. 'Get changed.'

'I...'

'Get changed, Leona. This day has only begun. There will be further trials ahead, and I need you by my side.'

She gazed at the clean dress, confused as to why the colonel would keep spare women's clothes under the seat of his carriage. Of all the things to be thinking about, why had her thoughts gone to that? The image of the body swinging above her flashed through her mind, and she touched the patch of blood on her cheek.

'You're making it worse,' he said. 'Clean your hands before you do anything else.'

'I don't know if I can do this, sir.'

He rubbed his bruised fist. 'I don't want to hear it. You have ten minutes to get ready to face the Aucterians in the Fortress of Atzoun. After that, we can go to the beach and you can wash in the Cyasarta. Ten minutes, Leona.'

She nodded, her mouth dry, and began to wipe the blood from her hands. She peeled off the vomit- and blood-soaked dress while the colonel looked away, then she pulled on the clean clothes. They were a little loose around the hips, but anything was better than what she had been wearing. When she was dressed, the colonel leaned forward and cleaned the blood from her face, then he smiled at her, though his eyes remained grim.

'Be strong,' he said. 'You are stronger than you think you are. That day when I first found you, you were lost; a beggar on the streets. But even then I could sense your inner strength. I need you to look inside yourself and find it for me. Can you do that?'

She nodded.

'Take a deep breath, and push what you saw into a dark corner of your mind.'

'Will that work?'

'In the long run – no; but it might suffice for the next hour or so.'

The carriage drew to a halt, and the driver leaned down to the little window.

'We're here, sir. I have parked out of crossbow range of the fortress.'

'Good man,' said Friel.

The driver dismounted and opened the side door. The colonel stepped down, and then helped Leona to the ground. The driver caught her glance, and he gave her a sad smile. She looked away, and steeled her heart. To their rear, the other seven wagons had arrived, and the rebel fighters began to line up in the street.

Friel turned, and gazed at the walls of the huge fortress. Atzoun was the largest fortification on the entire island, larger even than the Fort of Hortz in the Temple District, and its high curtain wall cut off the cape at the end of the peninsula, running from coast to coast. Up on the battlements, Leona could see dozens of people watching the rebel fighters down on the street, and several were aiming bows in their direction.

Friel took a few steps forward, and raised an arm into the air.

'People of Igatz!' he cried. 'I am Colonel Friel Laimos.'

The moment the words had left his lips, crossbow bolts began raining down onto the cobbles of the road. They landed several feet in front of where the colonel was standing, and skittered away. Friel folded his arms over his chest and waited for the barrage to cease, his features calm. Leona watched him, and then did the same. Her insides might be in turmoil, but she couldn't afford to show it, not in front of the Aucterians, and not in front of Friel.

The colonel smiled when the last bolt ricocheted off the road ahead of him.

'I am here to talk,' he said, his raised voice carrying up to the battlements. 'I wish no harm upon any civilian of this island – not on the Zamatans, or those Gunstians who dwell here, and not on the Aucterians. Is there anyone in Atzoun who wishes to speak to me?'

'We have nothing to say to you, traitor!' cried a voice from the walls.

'Then what do you intend to do?' Friel said. 'You have weapons, I hear – enough to defend yourselves, while we have no siege equipment, and besides, I have no wish to spill any of your blood.'

'Our blood has already been spilled, Laimos!' cried the voice. 'We have seen what your rabble has done to our people. Go back to Kaugatz, and leave us in peace.'

'I will leave you in peace,' Friel said, 'but I shall not be returning to Kaugatz. Igatz is my home. It is your home, too. Come out. Open the gates and return to your homes.'

'We will open the gates when the fleet returns,' the voice shouted back. 'Until then, if you want us, come and get us!'

'And how is your food situation? And your water supplies? You have children in there, I believe – hundreds of children. Will you let them die of thirst?'

'We have plenty of food and water, Laimos.'

'They're lying,' whispered Leona.

'Can we not negotiate?' Friel cried. 'This entire district can be yours, from the fortress to the ferry terminal. I will keep my fighters out if you pledge to remain in this district and, together, we can keep the peace.'

'You are a renegade and a liar, Laimos, and you will hang when the fleet returns.'

'The fleet could be gone for months, and you know it,' said Friel. 'Handshore Naval Base is under the authority of the Zamatans, and the Bullan soldiers have shown how little they care about your fate. Let us come together, and we can sit down like civilised people and talk. There will be no going back to the old days, but there must be a path upon which we can both agree.'

'Spare us your lies, Laimos,' cried the voice. 'You have one minute to depart, or we shall loose the catapults that the Bullan left here.'

'That wasn't a lie, sir,' whispered Leona.

'Very well,' said Friel. 'We shall go. If you change your minds, send out a messenger under a flag of truce. And please, consider what a few days of no water will feel like. Your children are your future – do not let them perish due to your pride.'

Friel turned, and signalled for the rebel fighters to board the wagons.

'The biggest catapults within the fortress have a range of a quarter of a mile,' the colonel said to his officers, as they strode away from the fortress. 'Keep all fighters that far away from the walls, and have patrols watch the streets. If they send a messenger out, escort them to me immediately.'

The officers saluted, and re-boarded their wagons. The horses turned in the street, and the rebels pulled back. Leona and the colonel got into their carriage, and then the driver pulled on the reins, and they followed the wagons down the main road.

The colonel sat in silence as the wheels juddered over the cobblestones. They passed the area where the bodies had been strung up, and Leona averted her eyes from the lampposts. She caught a glimpse of corpses stacked onto the back of a wagon, while rebel fighters toiled in the sun, and lowered her gaze.

'I wonder why they didn't hit us with their catapults as soon as we arrived,' she said.

The colonel glanced at her. 'I don't know, but it's a good sign. There will be some within the fortress desperate for a fight, but perhaps others are restraining them. One well isn't nearly enough to provide the water they need. Let's say they give it all to the children, then the adults will be stricken with thirst in about two to three days from now. Some of those inside must realise that.'

'I think you might be misjudging the Aucterians, sir,' she said. 'Imagine that it was Zamatans besieged inside the fortress, with Bullan soldiers or Gunstians waiting outside. How many would be willing to open the gates and put their lives into the hands of others? Some would rather die.'

He looked at her for a long moment. 'Do you want to go to the beach before we see the Bullan?'

'No, sir. I did what you said, and pushed what happened to the corner of my mind.'

'And will it remain there?'

'For now, I think. Perhaps tonight, when I get to my room, then it will all come out.'

'Right now,' he said, 'I hate the men who carried out those murders more than I hate the Aucterians, Bullan and Gunstians combined. If we catch them, I will hang them in front of the entire island, and then throw their bodies to the dogs.'

'Please don't,' she said. 'The dogs, I mean. Think about the words of your speech. We are trying to show that we are civilised.'

She looked out of the window and noticed that they were passing the Handshore Naval Base. Rebel fighters were guarding the entrances, but the yards beyond were empty.

Friel saw where she was glancing. 'I might move our headquarters from Tsallon Anura to the naval base. I have been inside the commander's quarters – you'd like them. He would have had an excellent view from which to observe the destruction of the navy's counter-attack. Besides, the old monastery is full of captured sailors and disgruntled monks, not to mention the decomposing body of Lord Meer. Tonight, I shall order that the dragon be burned; I think enough people have had a chance to view it.'

The road eased to the right, and the carriage followed it, trailed by the seven wagons of fighters. They began to slow as they neared the main square of Igatz, a vast, open plaza between the Merchants' Harbour and the northern ferry terminal, lined with ornate buildings, including the island's only theatre. The entrance to the square was blocked with a large barricade, and the side streets stretching across the isthmus had also been closed.

'Here we are,' said the colonel, as the carriage came to a halt.

The driver opened the door, and they dismounted from the carriage, while the fighters from the seven wagons did the same.

'Remain here,' the colonel said to his officers. 'I shall approach the Bullan alone.'

The officers nodded, and Friel set off. By *alone*, Leona knew that the colonel had included her, and she walked by his side as they approached the high barricade. A line of wagons had been turned on to their sides across the street, and the Bullan had erected sharpened stakes that protruded over the tops of them. Friel raised his arms as he walked closer, then stopped fifty yards from the blockade.

'I wish to talk with an officer of the Bullan,' he said. 'May I approach in peace?'

'Who are you?' cried a Bullan.

'I am Colonel Friel Laimos.'

'And the woman?'

'Her name is Leona and she is my assistant,' Friel said.

'Approach.'

Friel took a breath and resumed his course towards the barricade, while Leona kept pace by his side.

'Halt,' cried a Bullan when they were twenty feet from the blockade. 'That's far enough. What do you want?'

Friel lowered his arms. 'I wish to come to an arrangement with the Bullan,' he said. 'We are in control of the entire island, with the exception of the Fortress of Atzoun and the area under your control. I want to reopen the markets of Igatz tomorrow morning, and I wish to know if I can do so without any interference.'

A Bullan officer climbed up onto the top of a wagon, then leapt down to the other side.

'You are a traitor, Colonel Laimos,' he said.

'I am a Zamatan,' Friel replied, 'and this is Zamata. How goes the siege of the Dragon Palace, Major Zinetu?'

A faint smile brushed the lips of the Bullan. 'I admire your audacity, Colonel,' he said. 'It was you who ordered the capture of the son of Lord Rufus, was it not? It was you who planned this insurrection against the legitimate authority of the Dragon Dominion, was it not? Can you give me a reason not to strike you down where you stand?'

'Yes,' Friel said. 'The Bullan are honourable people. I asked if I could speak, and you agreed.'

'We shall grant you unhindered access to the rest of the island if you promise the following, Colonel – that you will not lend any more assistance to those holding the son of Lord Rufus hostage.'

Friel nodded. 'You have my word.'

'Can it be trusted, Colonel?'

'Have I ever lied to the Bullan, Major?'

'Not to my knowledge. You should know that Lord Rufus has sworn to eviscerate you.'

Friel smiled. 'I would be disappointed if he hadn't.'

'We shall rescue the acting Governor's son, and kill every one of the rebels inside the palace,' the Bullan major went on. 'Once that has been accomplished, we will crush your rebellion.'

'But until then?'

'Until then, Colonel, we shall not interfere with your occupation of the island. You have my word.'

'And you have my gratitude. Good day, Major Zinetu.'

The Bullan tilted his head an inch. 'Good day, Colonel Laimos.'

The colonel turned, then he and Leona walked back to the carriage.

'I sensed no lies,' she said.

The colonel smiled, but said nothing.

CHAPTER 19
THE DRAGON PYRE

K**augatz, Serpent Isle – 8th Nethinch 1588**

Lahnos cried out, then awoke in the darkness of the bedroom. He sat up, panting and sweating, his fists clutching on to the sheets. He felt a hand touch his arm, and he almost lashed out.

'It's me,' said Reyn.

He lay back on the bed, his breathing sore and ragged. A match flickered into life, and Reyn lit a lamp. He saw her gaze down at him, her eyes lined with tiredness.

'Was it the same nightmare?' she said. 'Your mother?'

He nodded.

'You have the same dream every night.'

'You say that like it's my fault.'

'It happened twelve years ago, Lahnos. I know it was terrible, but you have to put it behind you.'

'Do you think I want to relive her death every night?' he snapped. 'I thought I had put it behind me. What a stupid thing to say.'

'Don't shout at me.'

'Then don't act as though I can control my dreams.'

She rubbed her face. 'I'm not getting enough sleep.'

'Are you blaming me for that as well?'

'That's not what I meant,' she said. 'Lack of sleep is making me irritable.'

'Then maybe you should sleep somewhere else.'

She narrowed her eyes at him, then got out of bed. She pulled on a dressing gown, slid the balcony door open, and stepped outside. Lahnos glared at the door, then cursed under his breath. Was it too much to expect a little support from her? Every time he managed to drift off to sleep, his dreams focussed on the scene he had witnessed through his grandmother's eyes, yet all Reyn seemed to care about was the quality of her own sleep. He went over the argument in his mind, the words going round and round his head. Maybe he would be better off alone. How dare she tell him to put it behind him? Did she believe that he wanted to see his mother beaten to death every night?

You were angry, too, Lahnos.

He groaned and closed his eyes. 'You again? Get out of my head.'

Reyn was trying to apologise, but you wouldn't listen.

'Why do you care?' He felt despair roll through him. 'Leave me alone.'

Do you truly want me to leave you? Forever?

'I... No. It's just... you don't speak to me for days, and then you appear while I'm in bed with Reyn. Are you watching us?'

I felt bad about how we parted, after you were locked in a cell for telling your uncle what I told you. I thought I would check on you, and I found you like this. I will leave you now. Think about what I said.

He felt the voice vanish from his mind, and he opened his eyes and stared at the ceiling. He took a breath and got out of bed. He found a pair of shorts lying on the floor and pulled them on, then he walked to the balcony door. He slid it open, then saw the flames rise from the courtyard of the monastery forty yards to his right. Reyn was leaning against the railing, her eyes on the huge fire.

'I'm sorry,' he said.

Reyn turned. 'I'm sorry, too. I shouldn't have said that about putting it behind you. It's not your fault you have nightmares.'

He put his arms round her waist. 'I don't want you to sleep anywhere else.'

They kissed, then they both turned to watch the flames.

'Is that the dragon?' he said.

'Yes. They are finally burning it. At last.'

'I'm going to talk to my uncle about my father,' he said. 'I can remember Uncle Friel telling my grandmother that he might have been put on board a slave ship and taken to the Dominion. I might be able to move on if I can find out the truth about what happened.'

'Would it help to know that he was put on to a slave ship?'

'I don't know. Yes, I think. Maybe I could go across the ocean to look for him.'

'Have you heard anything from the voice?' Reyn said.

Lahnos kept his gaze on the flames. 'No.'

'That's a pity. You could have asked the Demon Witch to help you find him; or at least to tell you if he's still alive. She could read Uncle's Friel's thoughts and discover the truth.'

'You don't think he would tell me the truth?'

'No, not if he suspects that you might sail across the ocean.'

'You think it's a stupid idea, don't you?'

'I think it's very brave,' she said. 'Don't you think you might stand out a little in the Dominion with those horns?'

'But imagine if my father is alive – all this time, he will have been in chains, thinking that none of his family cares about what happened to him. He fathered five children, and not one of us tries to help? It's so unfair.'

'I know.'

'Would you come with me?'

'Across the ocean?'

'Yes.'

Reyn looked away. 'We would be arrested as soon as we landed in the Dominion, and put into a dungeon; or maybe even executed. But, if you went, then how could I stay here on my own, knowing where you were? Yes, Lahnos – I would come with you.'

'Why would we be arrested? Being part-Bullan isn't a crime.'

She smiled. 'We are rebels, or had you forgotten? You, in particular, are related to the leader of the rebellion. It has nothing to do with us being part-Bullan.'

'Damn this rebellion,' Lahnos muttered. 'It's turned me into a murderer, and now people are dancing around the burning body of a dragon.'

Reyn raised a clenched fist. 'But Zamata is free!' she said in a low voice, mimicking the colonel.

Lahnos laughed.

'Do you want to go down and watch?' he said.

'Watch what? The dragon?'

'Yes.'

'We can see it from up here.'

'I know,' he said, 'but I want a better view – not of the dragon, but of the people. I want to see what they're doing. Besides, I won't be able to go back to sleep now. I don't want to go back to sleep.'

'I suppose so,' she said.

'Come on; let's get dressed.'

They went back into their bedroom. The lamp Reyn had lit was still burning, and they changed into their day clothes. Reyn was quiet as she pulled on a long dress, and Lahnos suspected that she wasn't too keen to go. It would be fun, he thought.

Reyn reached for her head scarf as he was lacing up his boots.

'What are you doing?' he said.

'There will be a lot of drunk people down there,' she said.

'So? My horns will be visible. And aren't we Zamatans all supposed to be one big happy family now? We did our bit for the stupid rebellion.'

'All the same, I...'

'Don't be ashamed of who you are, Reyn.'

'You are confusing shame with taking simple precautions.'

'We'll be fine. As you said, my uncle is the leader of the rebellion – no one will touch us.'

Reyn frowned, then she shoved the head scarf into a pocket of her dress. They left their new apartment and locked the door, then descended the stairs to the ground floor. The alleyways around the apartment block were quiet, but Lahnos could hear the growing roar of noise coming from the main courtyard in the centre of the monastery complex, while the smoke and flames from the dragon pyre were visible over the rooftops. Lahnos and Reyn came to a wider street, and joined the crowds of singing and cheering Zamatans. Hundreds of people had gathered round the large pyre, and many were drinking from wine jugs as they jostled to get a better view. Lahnos took Reyn's hand, and they pushed through the crowds. A few people glanced at their horns, but no one said a thing about them, and Lahnos smiled. They reached the edge of the cloister, and came into full sight of the pyre. Even at that distance, the heat was intense, as the flames tore through the flesh and scales of the slain dragon. A few workers on duty were feeding the flames with wood, and glowing embers were floating and spiralling upwards into the warm night sky. Lahnos and Reyn took cover under an arch along the side of the cloister.

'It's true, isn't it?' Reyn whispered. 'The dragons aren't gods. They are mortal beings, just like us.'

Next to the fire stood a huge cauldron that was also being heated by the flames, and steam was rising from it in thick clouds, while men stirred the contents with long poles.

'They're boiling Lord Meer's head,' Lahnos said.

'Your uncle probably wants the skull as a souvenir,' whispered Reyn.

The pyre crackled and spat as a section of the dragon's burning flank split open, and the crowd cheered. On one side of the pyre, a dozen yards to Lahnos's right, a group of black-robed men had appeared. They were pointing at the dragon corpse, while a few were on their knees, their arms raised as if in prayer.

'Damn Gunstians,' Lahnos muttered. 'There's no party that they can't ruin.'

'Death to the demons!' cried one of the robed Gunstians, and the others took up the chant.

A few Zamatans started laughing at the praying and chanting Gunstians, and someone threw a jug of wine at them. The jug smashed into the flagstones of the courtyard, showering the Gunstians in red wine and fragments of pottery.

One of the Gunstians pointed into the crowd. 'Death to all unbelievers!'

'Go back to Gunst, you freak!' someone cried.

Another jug was thrown, a punch flew and, within seconds, a whole section of the courtyard was brawling. The Gunstians were outnumbered, but they held closely together, while the Zamatans surged around their perimeter. One of the Zamatans was pulled into the mob of Gunstians, and they surrounded him, their feet and fists lashing out and the crowd erupted in anger. A flaming brand of wood was flung and one of the Gunstian's black robes ignited, his scream mingling with the cries of pain and rage. The crowd surged back and forth, and five Gunstians were swept towards the side of the cloister where Lahnos and Reyn were standing.

One of them pointed at their horns. 'Demons! Death to...!'

Lahnos swung his fist and cracked the man in the jaw, then two others leapt at him, pushing him back against the wall of the alcove. Another grabbed Reyn's hair and brought down a wine jug over her head. The jug cracked but didn't break, and Reyn slumped to the ground. Lahnos punched another Gunstian, then kicked one in the shins as he tried to reach Reyn. A fist connected with Lahnos's cheek, and he put his head down, and barrelled his way towards Reyn, as more blows struck his shoulders and back. One of the Gunstians kicked Reyn in the stomach, and Lahnos reached out to grab the man's throat, but was pulled back by two others who were hanging on to his arms.

'Demon Witch,' Lahnos called out in his mind; 'help us!'

A whistle blast pierced the night air, and dozens of armed rebel fighters wearing the uniform of the town militia charged into the crowd. They were wielding clubs, and seemed to be targeting the Gunstians, as the Zamatans began to clear that area of the courtyard. The two men next to Lahnos were pushed to the ground and clubbed. The one who had been kicking Reyn raised his hands in the air, but the militiamen ignored his pleas and battered him across the back of the head with an iron bar, cracking his skull. The crowd of Zamatans calmed and pulled back as they watched the militia at work. No one intervened to plead for the Gunstians, and the militiamen gave no quarter until every one of the black-robed men was lying on the ground, some in pools of their own blood. Lahnos went to Reyn's side. His own head was hurting, but Reyn was unconscious, her hair matted with red wine and blood.

'Reyn,' he gasped, taking her hand.

One of the militiamen crouched down by his side. 'Get her to the monastery infirmary, lad. The monks will take care of her. Do you require an escort, young Laimos?'

'What?'

'An escort, lad – to the infirmary?'

Lahnos said nothing, unable to take his eyes from Reyn.

The militiaman nodded to one of his colleagues. 'Give the Laimos boy a hand taking the girl to the infirmary. The rest of you – drag these Gunstian bastards out of here and dump them on the street.'

One of the men strapped his club to his belt, and nodded. He knelt down next to Reyn and took hold of her feet, while Lahnos picked up her shoulders, and they lifted her from the ground. They carried her past the groaning bodies of the beaten Gunstians, while dozens of Zamatans watched in silence. To their side, the vast pyre was still burning, but all attention was on the aftermath of the brawl.

The militiaman holding Reyn's feet shook his head at the bodies of the black-robed men on the flagstones.

'Stupid bastards,' he muttered. 'What did they expect, eh? Coming down here and screaming like that? They should have stayed in their slums. And no offence, lad, but showing your horns in front of these zealots is asking for trouble.'

The crowd parted for them, and they carried Reyn away from the main courtyard. They walked to the infirmary building, which was always open, and entered its cool and shadow-wreathed interior. A monk in long brown robes hurried over to them, then halted, his eyes on the horns atop Lahnos's head.

'The girl got injured in the fight, brother,' the militiaman said.

The monk glanced down at Reyn, as if noticing her for the first time, and his eyes narrowed.

'She was hit by a wine jug, brother,' the militiaman said. 'Can you see to her?'

'It is the middle of the night,' said the monk, 'and this infirmary is not the place to be tending to alcohol-induced injuries.'

'She wasn't drinking,' said Lahnos, his temper rising. 'Are you...?'

The militiaman raised a finger to silence Lahnos. 'Do you know who this lad is, brother? This is Colonel Laimos's nephew. Am I going to have to report to Colonel Laimos that you refused to tend to his nephew's girlfriend? What do think he will say when he finds out?'

The monk's lips curled in distaste, then he gave the briefest of nods. 'Follow me.'

The two men carried Reyn down a hallway, following the monk through the dark building. They came to a chamber occupied by sleeping patients, and the monk gestured to an empty bed. Lahnos and the militiaman placed Reyn onto the bed, and the monk lit a lamp and brought it close to her head. He leaned down to examine the wound, but kept his hands away from her.

'There is bleeding,' he said, 'but I don't think her skull has been fractured.'

'How about you do a proper check?' Lahnos said. 'She could be dying.'

'Many have died in this... insurrection against the rule of the Dragon Dominion,' the monk said. 'This infirmary cannot save them all. If this girl dies, then it will be the will of the dragon spirits, and nothing I do will make any difference.'

'Is this because she has horns?' said the militiaman.

'Her blood is tainted,' said the monk. 'She is not of true human stock, and therefore she has no soul. Again, there is little I can do about that.'

Lahnos lunged at the monk, his fists swinging, but the militiaman was ready, and grabbed him by the arms, pulling him back.

'Settle down, lad!' the militiaman cried. 'And you!' he said to the cowering monk. 'Soul or no soul, you will do your damn job and examine this girl properly. Clean the wound, and make sure her skull is in one piece. If you refuse, then this building will be full of rebel fighters in the next five minutes, and every one of them will be demanding to know why you're disrespecting the colonel.'

The monk swallowed. 'I will do so, for the sake of Colonel Laimos. However, you must remove this young... man from my presence. I cannot work if I am being threatened.'

'If you touch her horns,' said Lahnos, 'I will kill you.'

'Believe me,' the monk said, 'I will do everything in my power to avoid having to make my hands unclean.' He glanced at two other monks who had appeared by the entrance to the chamber. 'Get me a basin of warm water, dressings, scissors and bandages. Now, if you please, brothers.'

The two monks bowed and hurried away.

'Come on, lad,' said the militiaman, releasing his grip on Lahnos's arms. 'Let's leave the monks to work in peace.'

'I don't trust him alone with Reyn.'

'There are hundreds of rebel fighters in Tsallon Anura, lad,' the militiaman said. 'The monk will behave himself, if he values his life.'

Lahnos gave the monk a long stare, then the militiaman pulled his arm and led him away. They went back out into the open air, and Lahnos gazed at the pillar of smoke and flames arising from the dragon's funeral pyre.

'I knew there was going to be trouble,' muttered the militiaman, as he leaned against the wall. 'You can't burn a damn dragon god in public without consequences.'

'The Gunstians and the monks hate each other,' Lahnos said. 'The monks believe in the dragon gods, while the Gunstians think every dragon is a demon.'

'Do you have a point?'

'There's only one thing that unites them.'

The militiaman nodded. 'Yeah – they both hate folk like you. I get it, lad; I do. Life isn't fair. If it was, there would have been no need for a damned rebellion, eh?'

'And is the rebellion going to help folk like me and Reyn? At least the Bullan soldiers didn't discriminate against us.'

'That's because you make them feel guilty. They look at you, see the horns, and wonder if you're a long lost or distant relation.'

'Are there any part-Bullan in the rest of the Dominion?'

'I would seriously doubt it. As far as I know, the Bullan are only used for two things – to protect the dragons in Inopei, and to garrison the overseas colonies. There are none of them stationed on Aucteran, for example. Therefore, why would there be any part-Bullan over in the East?'

'So there might be some in Irlan and Elso?'

'It's possible, but I've never heard of any. I think the Bullan regiments are more tightly controlled down there.' The man hesitated for a second. 'Do you... uh, know the circumstances of...?'

'No,' said Lahnos.

'Was your father...?'

'My grandfather.'

'I see. It's terrible luck.'

'Why? I don't care that I'm a quarter Bullan; why should anyone else?'

'You get your stubbornness from them,' the militiaman said. 'Everyone who knows the slightest thing about you, Lahnos, knows that you walk about as if you're proud of those horns.'

'I am proud of them.'

'And Reyn? You need to be more careful, lad.'

Lahnos lowered his head, as an image of Reyn being struck by the wine jug burned its way into his thoughts. The militiaman was right – what had happened was his fault. He had cajoled Reyn into leaving her head uncovered, and a demented Gunstian had almost cracked her skull open.

'I'm sure she's going to be all right,' said the militiaman. 'Most of what was on her hair was wine.'

A roar of cheers and laughter arose from the courtyard where the dragon was burning.

'Seems like the party is restarting,' the militiaman said.

'Are you not going back?' said Lahnos.

'No. I'll stay here until the monks give us news, in case they try to fob you off again. And to make sure you don't beat up any of them.'

'He said she has no soul. What does that even mean?'

'He means that when she dies, she won't be joining the dragon spirits.'

'Do you believe that?'

The militiaman shrugged. 'I used to. And then your uncle killed one of the ever-living dragon gods. I don't know what to believe any more.'

'The monks must hate him.'

'Who, your uncle? Yes. They loathe him. It was bad enough when he led the uprising against the Dominion, but now he's also a god-killer in their eyes. Luckily for us, they fear him more.'

Lahnos fell into silence, his insides tight with worry over Reyn. Her injuries were bad enough, but what kind of future awaited them? If the militiaman was right, and there were no part-Bullan in the Dominion, then maybe people like Lahnos and Reyn were found only upon Zamata, which made the island their sole home. How could that be right? He felt like a stranger and an outsider on the island, surrounded by people who mistrusted and despised the part-Bullan – people who shouted *demon* in their faces, and people who refused to touch their horns lest they rendered themselves unclean.

After a long wait, a different monk emerged from the building and bowed his head.

'The girl has had her wound attended to,' he said. 'Do you wish to see her?'

'Where's the other monk, brother?' said the militiaman.

'He is taking a ritual bath.'

'Take me to Reyn,' said Lahnos, his anger replaced by a sullen bitterness.

The monk bowed, and they followed him into the building. Reyn had been moved to a room of her own, though whether it had been done for the sake of her privacy, or because the monks wished to isolate her from the others, was unclear to Lahnos. She was lying in bed, her face reflecting the light from a solitary lamp. A clean bandage had been wrapped round her head, and her chest was rising and falling beneath the thin blanket.

'The girl's skull is intact,' said the monk, 'and the wound has been cleaned and stitched. We had to cut the hair on the right side of her scalp, but no scar should be visible once it has grown back. She was lucky.'

Lahnos ignored the monk's last comment and approached the bed. He glanced down at Reyn, his eyes going to her horns to make sure that none of the monks had tried to interfere with them.

'When will she wake up?' said Lahnos.

'After injuries of this nature,' the monk said, 'the patient usually regains consciousness within a few hours. When she does awaken, she will be in pain.' He held out a small clay vial. 'This contains a remedy of crushed bark from the white willow tree mixed with wine. It will ease her discomfort.'

'Thank you,' said Lahnos.

The monk bowed. 'I shall leave you in peace. You may remain here while she recovers.'

Lahnos put the vial into a pocket as the monk left the room.

'See?' said the militiaman. 'The monks aren't all bad. I'm going back to work. Look after yourself, Lahnos, and try to stay out of trouble.'

The militiaman walked out of the room and closed the door. Lahnos dragged a seat over to the side of the bed and sat, then he took Reyn's hand.

'I'm sorry,' he said. 'I should have listened to you.'

. . .

It was almost dawn by the time Reyn opened her eyes. Lahnos had remained in the seat for the entire time, his heart weighed down by guilt and anger.

She groaned. 'My head.'

'Try not to move,' Lahnos said, squeezing her hand.

She turned her eyes to look at him.

'You're in the infirmary,' he said.

'The monks hate...'

'I know, Reyn, but there was nowhere else to take you.'

She reached up and touched her horns, then her fingers brushed over the bandage.

'You're in one piece,' he said.

'My hair,' she said.

'They had to cut it off down one side. It will grow back, Reyn.'

A tear spilled down her cheek. 'Will we ever be safe, Lahnos?'

He gazed at her. He wanted to say that he would protect her, and make sure nothing bad would ever happen to her, but the previous night had proved how powerless he was to stop the hatred of others. He wondered what would have happened if he hadn't been the colonel's nephew. Would he and Reyn have been thrown out into the street along with the Gunstians, and left bleeding in the gutter?

And the voice – where had the Demon Witch been when he had needed her? She had spied on their quarrel, but had been missing when the fight had begun. He had called on her, and had heard nothing but silence.

Reyn turned to him. 'I want to go home, Lahnos,' she said. 'Take me home.'

CHAPTER 20
CHAINS

Igatz, Serpent Isle – 10th Nethinch 1588

Cisca frowned at her reflection in the warped and mottled mirror. Her hair was unkempt and her clothes stank from where she had been sleeping upon the soiled blankets next to Kheran. She washed her hands and face in the basin of cold water, but there was no soap, and she looked just as dirty when she had finished as she had before she had begun.

'Get a move on,' said a rebel fighter, who was leaning against the bathroom wall watching her.

'You may enjoy living in filth and squalor,' Cisca said, 'but some of us on this island are civilised.'

'What's that supposed to mean?' said the young rebel. 'Are you saying that Zamatans are uncivilised? Are you calling us savages?'

'Read into my words whatever meaning you prefer,' she said.

She picked up a grimy towel, and dabbed her face dry.

'I don't like you,' said the rebel. 'You think you're so clever, but you're just another Aucterian bitch. Like one of these well-dressed sows who expect us to step into the gutter whenever they walk past.'

'Would your mother be proud if she heard you talk to a woman like that?'

The rebel laughed. 'My mother hates you lot more than I do. You're lucky she isn't here.'

'Why isn't she here?' Cisca said. 'Why are there no women among the rebel fighters?'

The young man narrowed his eyes. 'Eh?'

'You heard me. In the Dominion, women are allowed to join the navy, army, and any other branch of the armed forces. All they have to do is pass the admissions test; if they are good enough, they are accepted – just like the men. Why isn't it the same on the Serpent Isle?'

'Where? There's no such place. This is Zamata.'

'Don't divert the subject. Answer my question.'

'No,' he said. 'I don't have to answer any of your stupid questions.'

'You mean you don't know how to answer it.'

'We're freeing the entire island,' he said, 'and that includes the women.'

'But you won't allow them to take part? Interesting.'

'Shut up,' he muttered. 'Come on; you've had long enough to get cleaned up for the day.'

'Why is there no hot water?'

'The Bullan have cut off the water supply, and there's no fuel to warm what's left.'

Cisca's eyes widened. 'The water supply has been cut off?'

'As of yesterday,' the young rebel said. 'The pipes from the cisterns have all run dry. So you can forget about having a bath any time soon; in fact, today might be the last day we let you wash.'

He gestured towards the bathroom door and picked up the end of her chain. Cisca folded the towel and draped it over the side of the basin, then followed the rebel out of the bathroom. The smell arising from the dragon child's sleeping chamber had worsened, but she was getting used to it. Every blanket and cushion from the storage room had been used, and some of the worst-soiled ones had been thrown over the balcony, but still the rebels would not loosen any of Kheran's chains to allow him to relieve himself with a modicum of privacy and hygiene. Dozens of rebel fighters were lounging on the marble flooring, playing with dice or talking about what they were going to do as soon as they got home. Even the teams by the ballistae seemed relaxed and bored, and their discipline regarding the regular loosening and tightening of the tension cords had begun to slip. Cisca was led back to the great heap of stinking cushions, and her chain was re-attached to the wall. Kheran was watching her, and she sat down by his head.

'The rebels are running out of water,' she whispered. 'I can't imagine this lasting more than a few days. You have been very brave, Kheran, and I am so proud of you. Your father will rescue you soon; I am sure of it.'

'Why are you talking to that lizard?' said a fighter standing by one of the ballistae. 'He doesn't care what you have to say – none of them care what we mere humans say.'

Cisca gave the man a cool stare. 'Do not refer to the grandson of King Gahad as a lizard. He is a prince of the Dragon Dominion.'

'Is that right? You're one of those people who actually believes that the dragons are better than us; that we should all be their slaves. Do you think Kheran is a god? If he is, then he's the first god I've met who stinks like an open sewer.'

'You deliberately degraded him,' Cisca said, 'and now you are complaining about the consequences of his degradation? Tell me – how would you smell if you had been chained up for six days, and forced to lie in your own waste?'

'You have some mouth on you, woman,' the fighter said. 'I think I preferred you when you were first captured – you were much quieter back then.'

'Is that how you like your women – quiet? Obedient? I am an officer in the Dominion armed forces, and I am not afraid of you. I was, when I was first chained to the wall, but I have come to see that there is nothing special about any of you. You are thugs who pretend to be freedom fighters; boys who think they are men.'

A few of the fighters laughed.

'She doesn't think you're a man, mate,' said one. 'Maybe you should show her.'

Kheran groaned, and nudged Cisca's shoulder, and she wondered if she had gone too far. One part of her desired to remain quiet and hidden, so that the rebels would almost forget that she was there, but she had been battling a growing sense of defiance that she was finding harder to suppress as the days went by. She should be more frightened, she told herself. She turned away from the fighters and stroked the side of the dragon child's head, her fingers brushing against his scales.

'That's right, Dominion bitch,' said the rebel, 'go back to comforting your lizard god.'

Cisca took a breath and ignored them.

'Any time you want me to prove that I'm a man,' the rebel went on, 'just let me know.'

Something inside Cisca snapped.

'You think you're a man?' she cried. 'What kind of man leaves a woman and a child chained up day and night with ballistae pointing at their heads? You are a coward, a weak little coward. If you were a man you would be standing up to your commanders, and telling them that what they are doing is wrong. If you were a man you would be helping this child instead of hurting him. Shame on you; shame on you all!'

The fighters stared at her in silence, then they burst into laughter. The man she had insulted, however, glared at her in silence, his eyes darkening and his fists clenched. He took a step forward.

'You will pay for that,' he spat.

'Get back to your post,' muttered a corporal. 'Don't let her get to you.'

'She called me a coward.'

'I heard what she said. You have been assigned to that ballista – get back to your post.'

The rebel fighter remained where he was, his eyes never leaving Cisca.

'I'm not going to tell you again,' said the corporal, as the laughter stopped.

'Bauchlie isn't here,' the fighter said, taking another step closer to

Cisca. 'Just give me five minutes with her, corporal, and he need never know. What use is she, anyway? She's just another mouth to feed.'

The corporal moved forward, and stood between the fighter and the great mound of cushions.

'If you return to your post,' he said, 'then I will forget I heard that. We've been here six days, and we've done our jobs. Do you want to ruin all that now? Think very carefully about what you do next.'

'Get out of my way,' the fighter said; 'the bitch needs to be taught a lesson.'

The corporal turned his head to look for more officers, and the fighter punched him on the ear. Three other fighters jumped down from the nearest ballista and charged into the melee, while another ran in the other direction, heading towards the chamber from where the balcony was accessed. The corporal and the three others brought the rogue fighter down, but he was lashing out, and a fist clipped one in the eye. The fighters held the man down, each gripping one of his limbs as he struggled. They rolled him on to his front, and the corporal bound his wrists with a cord.

'Get off me!' the fighter yelled.

'You should have listened, you stupid bastard,' the corporal said, as he placed a knee onto his back.

The other fighter returned from the balcony chamber, bringing Bauchlie and Travers with him.

Bauchlie surveyed the scene.

'This man disobeyed a direct order, Commander,' said the corporal. 'The prisoner was insulting him, and he lost his self-control.'

'Lock him in a storage cupboard until he calms down,' Bauchlie said.

'Yes, sir,' said corporal. 'You three – help me.'

The four men stood, and dragged the struggling fighter away. He was yelling abuse and curses at the top of his voice, and everyone in the chamber was watching. He was dragged out of sight, and, a few moments later, the sound of his cries faded away.

Bauchlie glanced down at Cisca. 'Did you insult him, Lieutenant?'

'Of course I did,' she said.

'She called him a coward, sir,' said another fighter.

'You are all cowards,' said Cisca.

Bauchlie turned to face his men. 'Just words. That's all. Meaningless. Here are some more – if anyone harms the woman or the dragon child without my permission, I will kill you. They are the only reason we are still alive. If there comes a time when they have to die, then I will do it myself. Travers, unfasten the prisoner's chain and bring her to the balcony chamber.'

The crowd of fighters said nothing as Bauchlie strode away. Travers shrugged at them, then walked to the wall and loosened Cisca's chain.

'On your feet,' he said.

Cisca stood.

Travers pulled on the chain, and she stumbled after him. They passed through the gathered fighters, and Cisca felt every eye upon her. Some looked conflicted, while others were making the contempt they felt for her obvious. Cisca kept her head held high. She was an officer; she had deserved her commission, and had been trained to face adversity. Travers led her into the large chamber overlooking the balcony. It was full of resting rebel fighters, none of whom seemed interested in staring at her. There was a small side door that she hadn't noticed before, and Travers pushed her through and into a small room with a vertical window. There was a mattress on the floor, and two seats next to a small table. Sitting in one was Bauchlie. He gestured to the other. Cisca frowned, then sat.

'We need to talk,' Bauchlie said.

'Do we?' said Cisca. 'That's one thing you don't seem to do very much of – talk. I've watched days go by without you so much as opening your mouth.'

'The men are tense,' he said. 'Stop provoking them to anger.'

Cisca laughed. She hadn't meant to, but once she had started, she found it hard to stop. Bauchlie watched her in silence, while Travers muttered something incomprehensible from the doorway.

Bauchlie waited until she had stopped, then he leaned back in his seat. 'Do you want to live?'

'I want Lord Kheran to be released.'

'That's not what I asked.'

'I am in the service of Lord Kheran.'

'You don't care about your own life?'

'I've told you,' said Travers. 'Cisca is a dragon fanatic. She thinks our sole purpose is to serve those beasts. That's all humans are worth to her.'

Bauchlie nodded. 'Is that true?'

Cisca hesitated, unsure how she felt about the place of humans and dragons any more. She knew what she had been taught, but the contradictions in her faith could no longer be ignored. Furthermore, she was unwilling to enter into a theological discussion with her captors.

'See?' said Travers. 'She knows that her response will anger us.'

'What are the dragons to you?' she said to Bauchlie.

'They are sentient creatures like us,' the commander said. 'I neither adore nor hate them for who or what they are. They are not gods, but neither are they demons. I do not believe in demons, and I am unsure if any gods exist. What concerns me about the dragons is their rule and occupation of this island. They came to Zamata as colonial overlords and found, much to their satisfaction, that the natives here already worshipped serpent gods. It was easy for them to insinuate that they were the physical manifestations of the gods we followed. For this island to be free, we must break that connection in the minds of the people who dwell here. The death of Lord Meer was a first step. You may mourn his passing, but he was on his way to incinerate thousands of my people, and I will not weep for him. Does that answer your question?'

Cisca raised an eyebrow. 'I think that's the most you have ever said to me.'

'Return me the favour. What are the dragons to you?'

'I... I don't know. Travers accurately summarised my previous convictions, but... Lord Kheran is dear to me; I will say that. He is a child, and I wish to protect him from the barbarity of your men. I'm not calling all Zamatans barbarians, but after six days of being trapped in here, I can see how good men can fall.'

'Stick to the point at hand,' said Bauchlie.

'I'm trying to, but the truth is that I don't know any more. That connection you mentioned – perhaps it has been broken in my own mind. But, I swore oaths to the Dragon Dominion, so do not mistake my doubts for disloyalty.'

'Do you think they are gods?'

'I don't know what that means.'

'Are they all-powerful? Are they all-knowing? Infallible?'

'Clearly, Lord Meer was not infallible.'

A faint smile traced its way over Bauchlie's lips.

'What is your plan?' said Cisca. 'Not once has anyone mentioned to me how you intend to walk out of this palace alive. At some point you will run out of food and water, and your men will likely mutiny after a few days of thirst. I assume that you do have a plan?'

'You are more at risk from my men than I,' he said. 'Will you stop provoking them?'

'You are their commander; their actions are your responsibility.'

A rebel fighter opened the door. 'Sorry, Commander,' he said. 'Some lads are fighting over the water supply. Can you come and sort it out, sir?'

Bauchlie got to his feet. 'Stay here,' he said to Cisca and Travers. 'I will be back soon.'

Cisca watched Bauchlie leave, then she noticed a glimmer of something in Travers's eyes.

'You don't respect him, do you?' she said.

Travers turned to her. 'What did you say?'

'I said you don't respect Bauchlie. You think he is weak.'

'What I think is none of your business. And what about you? I was watching you and Bauchlie speak, and I think you are starting to admire him. It's a little pathetic, don't you agree?'

'I don't admire him. Bauchlie is a criminal.'

'You got that part right. Do you have any idea of the things he's done? He's a brutal murderer.'

'I'm sure he is.'

Travers laughed. 'You say that, but I don't think you quite understand. Did you know that he once broke into the townhouse of a rich Aucterian aristocrat? He crept into her bedroom in the middle of the night and slit her throat while she slept. What was her crime, you might ask? What terrible thing had she done to warrant such an end? She had bought up a parcel of land on the island. For that, Bauchlie ripped out her throat. Her children found her the next morning – can you imagine?'

Cisca felt her insides tighten. 'Why are you telling me this?'

'So that you know the kind of man you are dealing with.'

'Does he know that you are secretly working for the Gunstians?'

'Back to that again, are you?' he said. 'He didn't believe you. I talked to him about what you had said. We agreed that you would say anything to drive a wedge between us.'

'But it's true though, isn't it, Lieutenant Travers? For some unfathomable reason, you have sold out your country to a foreign power. Do you think the Gunstians will spare you if they arrive? To them, you will just be another Dominion officer.'

Travers sat down in the seat where Bauchlie had been. 'What do you know about the Gunstian religion?'

'Not much,' she said. 'I know that they believe in one god, and no others. This has led them to the conclusion that the dragons are demons.' Her eyes narrowed. 'Is that why you are helping them? Have you converted to their faith?'

Travers said nothing.

'Bauchlie will kill you if he discovers this, Travers.'

Travers took a knife from his belt. 'Not if I kill you first. Bauchlie's ideas are... incompatible with my objectives. He truly believes that he will be able to negotiate our way out of this. He doesn't realise that our fate was sealed the moment we walked into the palace. He isn't weak, but he lacks the determination required to do what is necessary.'

'And killing me is necessary?'

'Yes. You and the demon-child. You will be aware of the concept of martyrdom?'

Cisca said nothing, her eyes on the four-inch steel blade in Travers's right hand.

'Kheran is the spawn of a demon,' Travers went on, 'and I will be rewarded for taking his life. The only thing standing between me and eternal paradise is Bauchlie. If he gets his way, we will die of thirst in this miserable cesspit, and Kheran might well survive. I would rather die in glory than die of thirst.'

His hand lunged out, and Cisca pushed herself backwards. She fell off the chair as the knife blade cleaved through the air, then Travers came after her. He lashed out again, and she swung the free end of her chain, and the steel links struck him across the face. She tangled the chain over his wrist, and kicked him in the stomach; then she crawled backwards. She pulled on the chain with all her weight, and Travers cried out as the chain tightened round his wrist. He dropped the knife and Cisca hauled herself to her feet and ran from the room. She got three yards then toppled to the hard marble floor, as Travers jerked on the chain. He pulled it towards him, reeling her in, and she was dragged by the ankle back towards the room.

'Help!' she cried, as the rebel fighters in the balcony chamber stared at what was happening.

'Nobody panic,' Travers cried. 'The prisoner was trying to make a run for it.'

'He's working for the Gunstians!' Cisca yelled, then a boot stamped down onto her stomach and she doubled over on the floor, wheezing and gasping in pain.

Travers hauled her back into the room, and slammed the door shut.

'You stupid little bitch,' he muttered, as he examined the blood on his wrist from where the chains had been wrapped. 'Look what you did.'

Cisca tried to speak, but the pain in her stomach was taking up most of her attention.

The door opened again and Bauchlie entered. He frowned at Travers.

'She tried to escape,' Travers said. 'I had to drag her back in here.'

'Escape?' said Bauchlie, closing the door. 'Where?'

'I don't know,' Travers said.

'Why is there a knife on the floor?'

'I dropped it,' said Travers.

He leaned over and picked it up, as Bauchlie crouched next to Cisca.

'Why did you run?' Bauchlie said to her. 'There is nowhere to go.'

Cisca gazed upwards, her arms wrapped round her stomach. Behind Bauchlie, Travers still had the knife in his hand. He glanced at the blade, then at Bauchlie, and raised his arm to strike.

'Bauchlie, look out!' Cisca cried.

Bauchlie moved to the side, and the knife blade ripped through the clothes and flesh on his upper right shoulder, missing the back of his neck by inches. Travers swung the blade again, and Bauchlie barrelled into him, knocking them both to the floor. Travers held the knife pointing upwards, and tried to drive it into Bauchlie's chest, but the Zamatan was stronger. He turned the blade round, forcing Travers's hands until the knife was aiming at his own throat, then Bauchlie pushed down. The blade entered Travers's throat, and Cisca looked away. She heard a strange gasping, gurgling sound, then Travers's limbs flailed and went still.

'Why?' Bauchlie mumbled. 'Why would you do that, Travers?'

Cisca turned her head, and saw Bauchlie sitting on the floor with his back against the door, his hands covered in blood. Lying next to him was Travers, his lifeless eyes staring up at the ceiling, and the knife still embedded in his ripped-out throat. She remembered what Travers had told her about the woman Bauchlie had murdered in her own bed, and Cisca shuddered.

'And you,' Bauchlie said; 'why would you warn me?'

'Travers was going to kill me,' she said; 'that's why I ran.'

'No,' said Bauchlie. 'That doesn't make any sense.'

'He was working for the Gunstians, Bauchlie. He wanted to be a martyr and you were in his way.'

Bauchlie stared at the body of Travers, then at the blood on his hands.

'I owe you my life,' he said.

'You owe me nothing,' Cisca cried. 'You are a murdering criminal, and the only reason I warned you is because Travers was even worse. You both disgust me.'

Bauchlie said nothing, his dark eyes like bottomless pits of pain and regret.

'Travers told me that you slit the throat of a woman while she slept in her own bed,' Cisca went on. 'Was it true?'

Bauchlie nodded.

'Please take me back to Lord Kheran. I can't bear to look at you any longer.'

Bauchlie stood, and extended his hand to her.

'Do you think I would take anything you offered?' Cisca said.

She put one hand on a chair and struggled to her feet. The pain in her stomach was peaking, but she was determined to walk unaided. She picked up the chain attached to her ankle, and opened the door. Several rebel fighters got to their feet as soon as they saw the body lying on the floor of Bauchlie's room.

'Take Lieutenant Cisca back to Kheran,' Bauchlie said, 'then help me clear up the mess. Throw Travers off the balcony. The Bullan can have him.'

One of the rebels approached, and grabbed hold of Cisca's arm.

'Treat her with care,' Bauchlie said. 'She saved my life.'

The fighter stared at Cisca as he led her away.

'What happened in there?' he whispered, as they entered Kheran's main living chamber. 'Did you really save the commander's life?' He glanced up as dozens of other fighters saw them. 'Travers is dead,' he announced to the room. 'The commander killed him, and he said that this woman saved his life.'

The fighters stared at her as she was escorted back to Kheran's side, and then several ran off into the balcony chamber amid a hubbub of chatter. Cisca's chain was refastened to the wall, and she sat down on the soiled cushions next to the dragon child.

'Stop staring at me,' she said to the fighters manning the ballistae.

'Is it true?' said one. 'Did you save Commander Bauchlie?'

Cisca returned their stares. 'It would have been dishonourable to have allowed Travers to stab him in the back.' She lowered her gaze. 'It means nothing.'

'You heard her, lads,' said the corporal. 'Get back to work.'

CHAPTER 21
DETECTED

Kaugatz, Serpent Isle – 11th Nethinch 1588

The colonel smiled as he and Leona entered the room.

'How are you, Reyn?' he said. 'Leona, put the fruit basket and wine onto the table.' He took a seat by the bed. 'I'm sorry I haven't been able to see you since that awful incident a few nights ago. How are you feeling?'

'A little better,' said Reyn, from where she lay on the bed.

'Good,' said Friel; 'that makes me glad.'

Lahnos cleared some dishes and plates from the bedside table, and Leona placed the fruit and wine down. She glanced up at Reyn, and saw the bandage covering her head.

'And did the monks treat you well?' the colonel went on.

Lahnos rolled his eyes. 'I have a few things to say about them, uncle.'

'I'm sure you do,' said Friel, 'but I was asking Reyn.'

'I didn't see any monks,' Reyn said. 'I was unconscious when I arrived at the infirmary, and then I sneaked out with Lahnos as soon as I woke up.' She smiled, but Leona could tell it was forced. 'They didn't cut my horns or tail off.'

'If they had,' said the colonel, 'their bodies would currently be floating down the Cyasarta.'

'The monks don't like you much,' said Lahnos.

'Yes,' said Friel. 'I am aware of that. However, the monastery of Tsallon Anura was built over one and a half thousand years ago, and it holds a special place in the hearts of many Zamatans. I would rather not get into a public fight with the monks if it can be helped.' He glanced back at Reyn. 'I hope my nephew has been taking good care of you.'

'He has,' she said. 'How are things in Igatz?'

'Tense,' he said. 'The Aucterians are still refusing to leave the Fortress of Atzoun, and the siege of the Dragon Palace goes on. I seem to spend most of my time chasing down looters and criminals from among our own forces – a dispiriting experience. I try to love all Zamatans, but these past few days have tested my resolve. I am glad to get away from it all, even if it's just for a few hours to come and visit you.'

'Is that the only reason you crossed over to Kaugatz?' said Lahnos.

'It's the main reason,' he said, 'but I also wanted a quick word with you, nephew. Balcony?'

Lahnos frowned. 'Will Leona be standing next to us while we talk?'

'Of course,' said Friel.

'Then we can talk here,' said Lahnos. 'I'm not leaving Reyn lying on her own while we discuss matters. Anything we say can be said in front of her.'

Friel raised his palms. 'I have absolutely no problem with that. Should I begin? I wanted to ask if you have heard anything more from our friend the Demon Witch – have you?'

'No.'

Leona felt a faint tingle in the back of her head.

'That is disappointing,' the colonel said. 'Not any indication, however slight, that she might return to offer us more sound advice?'

Leona coughed. 'That, uh, wasn't entirely true, was it, Lahnos?'

Lahnos's shoulders sagged. 'Shit.'

'I see,' said Friel. 'What are you keeping from me, Lahnos?'

'He wasn't just keeping it from you,' said Reyn. 'He told me the same; that she hadn't been in contact.'

'Oh dear, nephew,' said the colonel. 'It appears you have been caught out. Let me ask you again – have you heard from the Demon Witch since the last time we spoke?'

Lahnos sat by the bed. 'Yes.'

'Why did you lie to me?' Reyn cried.

'Because... because I was too embarrassed to tell you the truth,' Lahnos said. 'Do you remember that argument we had – just before we went down to watch the dragon pyre? It was then. She came into my head and gave me a telling off for the way I had treated you.'

'Is that why you apologised to me?'

'I would have apologised to you, anyway,' he said; 'but the voice might have... speeded up the process.'

Reyn glared at him.

Friel glanced at Leona. 'It seems that we have intruded into a personal matter.'

'I'm sorry, Lahnos,' Leona said. 'I hated doing that.'

'It's not your fault,' Lahnos said. 'I can't believe that I forgot you were sitting there. No; I forgot about your Gift.'

'So,' said Friel, 'apart from trying to mend your relationship with Reyn, what else did she say to you?'

'Not much,' he said. 'I was angry, and I accused her of spying on me while Reyn and I were sleeping.'

'She was watching us?' said Reyn, her mouth twisting into a scowl.

'She said she felt bad about how we parted the last time, and wanted to check up on me. She also offered to leave me alone forever.'

Friel swallowed. 'And how did you respond?'

'I told her I didn't want that.'

'Praise all that is holy,' said Friel.

'I'm going to ask you something now,' said Lahnos; 'but before I do, I want to know if Leona will tell us if you lie to me.'

'Her job is to tell me if others lie, nephew.'

'Why?' said Lahnos. He stared at Leona, and she squirmed in her chair. 'Will you tell me?'

'I, uh... it depends.'

'On what?' said Lahnos.

'Yes, on what?' said Friel.

'Well,' Leona said, 'if it's about a political matter, or the rebellion, or something that should remain a secret, then I won't say anything. But, if it's personal then... it depends.'

Lahnos smiled. 'It's a personal question about the Laimos family. It has nothing to do with the rebellion.'

Friel groaned, and put his head in his hands.

'Uncle,' said Lahnos, 'do you know what happened to my father when he disappeared?'

'Not for certain,' he said.

'But you suspect something?'

'I might.'

Lahnos's eyes narrowed. 'Give me straight answers, uncle. Do you know what happened to him? I don't care that you kept it secret from the family for all these years; you presumably had your reasons, but I need to know.'

'Why?' said Friel. 'What good could it possibly do?'

'This is my father we're talking about – your brother. Is he alive?'

'I don't know. Twelve years have passed since he vanished.'

'Then tell me what you do know.'

'Tell him,' said Reyn.

'I agree,' said Leona. 'What harm could it do, sir?'

Friel glanced at the others in the room. 'Has it come to this – I am being bullied by three teenagers? Fine. I will tell you what I know, but be warned – it is a mixture of guesswork, rumour and supposition.' He leaned forward. 'I was in Igatz when your father left Fidalaimos. The first I learned of his disappearance was when my mother, your grandmother, sent me a note. I went to Wayston, and asked around. My list of contacts was not as extensive in those days, and I had trouble finding anyone willing to talk to me.'

'Why did you go to Wayston?' said Reyn.

'Because that was where he was last seen. May I continue? Thank you. I was eventually put in touch with a man who worked in the harbour, who claimed that he had seen someone fitting my brother's description being bundled onto a small boat. I tracked down the boat, after many days of fruitless enquiry, and discovered that it had been rounding up convicted criminals from the jails of the island. They were being taken to an ocean-going vessel anchored in the Cyasarta, but by the time I learned that fact, the vessel had already sailed for the Dominion. Its destination was Inopei, and its human cargo was destined to live the rest of their lives serving the dragons upon that continent. I checked the records, and found a list of every criminal who had been placed on board. Needless to say, your father's name did not appear on that list. But why would it? If a few Aucterians had decided to get rid of your father, they would have been unlikely to have left any evidence behind, not when I know for a fact that a small bribe would have been sufficient to have added a single extra passenger onto that ship. I found the man who took the bribes. He claimed that he had illegally placed on board the ship half a dozen Zamatan men not officially on the list – people that someone, somewhere, wanted off the island. However, he also claimed that he didn't ask any questions about their identities. I had him tortured, and...'

'What?' said Leona. 'You tortured him?'

'Leona, he was responsible for the abduction of six innocent Zamatans, and took money to ship them into slavery. Yes, I tortured the bastard. Unfortunately, he revealed nothing new. It appears that he really didn't ask any questions. He remembered seeing a man that may have been Lahnos's father, but the ocean-going ship had departed several months before I found him and his memory was a little hazy. I went back to Wayston, but the Aucterian settlers there had closed ranks, and no one would talk to me.' He paused. 'If I had to guess, then yes – your father was on that ship, Lahnos. However, I have no proof. And that, my nephew, is the whole truth.'

He glanced at Leona.

'There were no lies,' she said.

'Inopei?' said Lahnos.

'Nom Karta, one would assume,' said Friel; 'the great dragon capital city of the Dominion. The Dominion had a habit of shipping large numbers of Gunstian prisoners of war there during the last conflict. There is no slavery upon Aucteran, or so I believe, but the dragons, in their hypocrisy, allow human slaves on their continent of Inopei.'

'But Gunstians would never serve dragons,' said Reyn.

'There are rumours of vast mines on Inopei,' Friel said. 'I would imagine the prisoners were sent there. No one seems to know for sure because no one ever returns alive from these places.'

'Thank you, uncle,' said Lahnos.

Friel nodded. 'You now know all that I know, nephew. The question is – what will you do with such knowledge? Your father, my brother, is probably dead. The man who abducted him and placed him onto the ship is also dead.'

'You killed the man you tortured?' said Leona.

'He died from his wounds, yes. In a sense, I got some justice for what he had done.'

'There must still be Aucterians in Wayston who conspired to give Lahnos's father to this man,' said Reyn.

'They won't be in Wayston any more,' said Friel. 'The settlers evacuated when the Bullan pulled out. If any of those responsible for what happened to my brother still live, they will be in Igatz – either closed up inside the Fortress of Atzoun, or sheltering in the area controlled by the Bullan. The two men convicted of murdering Lahnos's mother are still in prison, if you remember.'

'Which prison?' said Lahnos.

Friel narrowed his eyes. 'And why would I give you this information?'

'So that I can kill them.'

'No, nephew. Those two men are among a very small number of Aucterians who were ever convicted for committing crimes against a Zamatan. The Bullan investigators had to push hard against a wall of opposition from the settlers to secure a guilty verdict, and the case remains one of the few triumphs of the rule of law under the Dominion. Those two men are a symbol of justice. Let them rot in jail for what they did.'

'I watch my mother's death every night when I sleep,' said Lahnos. 'There were more than two men involved.'

'I know. Your father also knew that, and this is what drove him to keep asking questions. His bloody-minded persistence then led to his abduction, or perhaps his death.'

'What you are saying, uncle, is that somewhere in Igatz there could be men who killed my mother and enslaved my father – and they got away with it? Am I wrong?'

The colonel said nothing for a long while, his eyes lowered; then he nodded. 'You are not wrong.'

'I'm going to ask the Demon Witch about it,' Lahnos said. 'The next time she appears in my head, I will ask her to help.'

'You are free to do that,' Friel said. 'Personally, I would rather she helped keep the island safe.'

'You don't actually care about justice, do you?' Lahnos said, his features betraying his anger. 'Those bastards killed my parents.'

'I care about the island, nephew. I am the leader of the uprising – should I allow my personal feelings of anger, guilt and bitterness to sway the decisions I must take? Decisions that could lead to more bloodshed? I am trying to break the cycle of violence, not endlessly repeat it. Leadership is a burden, Lahnos; it is not a tool to be used to settle old scores.'

Lahnos looked away, and Leona could feel the anger radiate from him.

'Perhaps it is time we left,' the colonel said. 'Reyn – I am relieved and pleased to see how well you are doing, and I hope you are up and about on your feet soon. Lahnos – bury your rage, if you can. Maybe, once the island has settled down, we can discuss this again, but for now we must focus on what is at hand.' He stood. 'It was a pleasure to see you both. Come, Leona.'

Leona got to her feet. She shared a glance with Reyn, then she and the colonel left the room.

'That was unfortunate,' Friel muttered, as they descended the stairs to the ground floor of the apartment block.

Leona said nothing.

They emerged into the tight alleyways of the monastery complex. A few rebel fighters were waiting for them, and they moved into a flanking position as they walked towards the ancient cloisters.

'Nothing to add?' Friel said.

'I don't know what to say,' said Leona. 'I understand why Lahnos was so angry.'

'And that is why I would have preferred not to have had the discussion in the first place. I knew he would be angry. I am angry. To think that my brother and his wife were so mistreated by people who might still be free to walk the streets fills me with rage. But what is the alternative? Round up every Aucterian and have them questioned? I am trying to build bridges, not burn them.'

'But...'

'Did you not hear me, Leona? Once the crisis is over and we are in full control of the island, then I might reopen the case. If I do, then you can help with the investigation; but until then my hands are tied.'

They reached the large courtyard where the body of Lord Meer had been burned. The ashes and bones had been swept away and thrown into the waters of the Cyasarta, but a scorched circle of discoloured ground remained in the centre of the courtyard. Next to it, a wooden frame had been erected, and the bare skull of the dragon was on display, its great fangs glistening in the morning sunshine. A few dozen captured Dominion sailors were taking some exercise on the far side of the yard, surrounded by crossbow-wielding rebels, and many were staring up at the enormous skull as they shuffled past.

The colonel strode towards the curtain wall that enclosed Tsallon Anura, and they passed through an open gate which led down to a small stone jetty. The waves of the Cyasarta were brushing against the coast where the monastery walls stood, and Leona gazed across the inlet towards Igatz. In the distance she thought she heard a noise, and she halted.

Friel gestured towards the small vessel tied up by the jetty. 'Don't linger, Leona. We have a boat to catch.'

Leona frowned. 'I thought I heard something, sir.'

'What?' said Friel.

'Bells,' said one of the rebel fighters, his eyes straining towards Igatz. 'I heard them, too, sir.'

The colonel turned, and they all stared at Igatz. The sound came again, unmistakable.

'I hear them,' said Friel. 'Everyone – into the boat. Let us make haste.'

They stepped down into the small vessel, and its single sail was raised. The rebel fighters in the colonel's personal guard all had sailing experience, and the craft was on its way within a few moments, its bow rising as it sped across the inlet in the strong breeze. Leona took a seat on a bench near the bow, her hands clinging on to the wooden railings as the boat bucked up and down on the waves. Ahead of them and to their right loomed the massive naval base of Handshore, while the Bullan-occupied northern ferry terminal of Igatz was on the left. The small craft was aiming for a point halfway between the two landmarks, where another small jetty lay. When they were two hundred yards from their destination, one of the rebel fighters raised his arm towards the west.

'Ships, sir! Ships!'

Leona turned, and her spirits seemed to drain away. Sailing round the headland where the Dragon Palace was situated were over a dozen large vessels, each flying the green and black standard of the Gunstian Empire.

'How did they get past the chains?' gasped one of the fighters.

'The Chain Castles were manned by Bullan,' Friel said, 'and the Dominion Fleet left them lowered when they evacuated. Keep your eyes on the jetty, men; the sooner we land, the better.'

Leona continued to stare at the new ships as their small craft sailed closer to the shore.

'I thought the Imperial Gunstian Fleet was chasing pirates a thousand miles to the south,' she said.

'These ships are not part of their main fleet,' Friel said in a low voice. 'They must have been rustled up from the coastal garrisons. They are troop-carriers. Each will hold around a thousand Gunstian soldiers. They must know that the Dominion Navy has fled; otherwise they would never have risked such a bold move.'

'Twelve thousand soldiers?' Leona said.

'The main fleet will be on its way,' Friel said. 'Presumably, the Gunstians are hoping to occupy the island before the rest of their ships get here.'

The ships disappeared from view as the craft reached the small jetty. Friel clambered off the boat, then turned to the rebel fighters still on board.

'Sail back to Tsallon Anura immediately,' he said to them. 'Order all fighters in Kaugatz to defend themselves. The Gunstians will strike Igatz first, but then they will turn their attention to the rest of the island.'

'What about you, sir?' said one of the fighters.

'I will attempt to buy us some time,' Friel said. 'The longer the Gunstians are delayed in Igatz, the better chance Kaugatz will have to hold out.' He helped Leona climb up to the jetty. 'Go,' he said to the fighters; 'and good luck.'

Leona and Friel watched as the men raised the sail again. The small craft edged away from the jetty, turned into the wind, and began to sail back towards Tsallon Anura.

'What do we do now?' said Leona.

Friel sat down on the jetty with his legs dangling over the water.

'Sir?'

'Be quiet, Leona; I need to think. This has... caught me off guard. I expected the Gunstians to arrive once their fleet had returned from chasing pirates, and that would have given me time to train Zamatans how to operate the chains across the Cyasarta straits; but this? Twelve thousand soldiers won't be enough to occupy and subdue the entire island, not when four and a half thousand Bullan are still in Igatz. This is a risk I didn't believe the Gunstians would take. I had assumed that they would act rationally and strike only when their chances of success were all but assured. If the Dominion Fleet had caught the troop-carriers in the open sea, every Gunstian vessel would be at the bottom of the ocean by now.' He shook his head. 'I have to salute their courage, if nothing else.'

The twelve vessels came into view again as they sailed past the Palace District of Igatz. They were moving slowly, their wide and ungainly hulls finding it awkward to manoeuvre within the tight narrows of the Cyasarta inlet. Leona glanced down at the colonel and saw that he had his eyes closed. She turned back to watch the fleet, then noticed a form rise up into the sky over Igatz.

'Lord Rufus!' she cried. 'I never thought I would be so happy to see a dragon!'

Friel's eyes snapped open. 'He is making a mistake.'

Leona kept her eyes on the huge dragon as he circled high over the Palace District, his great wings extended.

'Go back to the palace, Rufus,' Friel hissed.

'Why?' said Leona. 'He could burn those ships; he could save us from the Gunstians.'

'You don't know what you're talking about,' said Friel. 'The Gunstians have Gifted on board.'

'Gifted?' she said. 'How do you know that, sir? What Gifts do they have?'

'One of them has the Gift of Pain,' said Friel, as he got to his feet, his eyes on the dragon. 'Go back, Rufus; think of your son.'

The huge dragon circled one last time, then turned and soared down towards the Gunstian troop-carriers. He opened his jaws, ready to unleash a barrage of flames upon the ship, then a terrible cry pierced the air. Rufus reared up, his wings drooping as he screamed in agony above the waters of the Cyasarta. His scream rose in intensity, a roar of pain that echoed over the inlet; and flocks of startled birds wheeled up into the sky all over Igatz as his cry rang out. Leona put her hands to her ears as the dragon began to fall from the sky. For a moment, she was sure he would crash into the clear waters of the Cyasarta, but Rufus managed to extend a wing, and he veered to the south as he lost altitude, then he smashed into the side of the Dragon Palace, sending a rumble through the ground. The scream stilled, and the air fell deathly silent.

'Is he dead?' Leona whispered.

'I don't know,' said Friel. 'Let's go.'

'Where?'

The colonel didn't respond as he walked away from the jetty. Leona followed him as he entered the neat and wide streets of Igatz. They were in the Handshore District, and rows of empty housing blocks lay to either side. They hurried through the quiet streets, until they reached the fortified headquarters of the militia. A few fighters were gathered in little groups, all talking in low and anxious whispers.

'Summon every officer in the building,' Friel cried, 'then make your way to the eastern ferry terminal. I am ordering every rebel fighter to evacuate to Kaugatz. Move!'

The fighters scattered, and Friel walked into the main building.

'Everyone out!' he cried. He grabbed a sergeant by the shoulder. 'Get your men to the ferry terminal, and collect anyone you see on the way. We're leaving Igatz – go!'

A few officers ran down the hallway towards him.

'The Gunstians have been spotted, sir!' one cried. 'Troop-carriers, and...'

'I know,' Friel said. 'We're pulling out. The Gunstians are making for Handshore Naval Base, which gives us less than an hour before they will be flooding the streets of Igatz. I intend to get as many fighters as we can over to Kaugatz before that happens.'

'Are we abandoning Igatz, sir?'

'We are. Take every available boat, and leave none behind. Send runners to the Bullan and to Atzoun Fortress to warn our foes that our mutual enemy has arrived. There's going to be a bloodbath as soon as the Gunstian soldiers reach the Bullan barricades. The Gunstians have brought Gifted with them.'

'An hour won't be long enough to evacuate every fighter, sir.'

The colonel paused, then his eyes darkened. 'Leave me fifty volunteers. The Gunstians will be coming here to the militia headquarters to arrest me. Perhaps I can hold them off for long enough for most of our lads to flee.'

The officers stared at him.

'Every second is precious, gentlemen,' said Friel. 'Get to work. I shall be in my office.'

He strode away, and Leona hurried after him.

'We're staying?' she said, as they walked.

'Yes. Sorry about that. Do you wish to leave with the others? I won't force you to stay here with me.'

'I am not abandoning you, sir.'

They reached the area where the legal department was situated, and Friel unlocked the door to his old office and strode inside. He gazed around at the room from where he had overseen so many legal cases over the years, and sat behind his desk.

'Pour me a glass of wine,' he said. 'Pour one for yourself, too.'

Leona opened a cabinet and took out a bottle of wine and two glasses. Her hands weren't shaking, she noticed. Despite the raw terror inside her, she felt calm. She half-filled the two glasses, then a young lieutenant appeared at the door.

'Sir,' he said. 'The fifty volunteers you requested are being assembled. What are our orders?'

Friel looked up at him. 'Did you volunteer, lad?'

'I did, sir.'

'Good man. Help the others to evacuate. Hurry them along. As soon as the last of them have left the headquarters, close and lock every gate and entrance, then set guards by each. When the Gunstians arrive, we shall not be letting them in without a fight. However, once they have breached the interior, you and the others will lay down your arms and surrender to them. Our purpose here is to delay the Gunstians, not to throw our lives away. Have you got all that?'

The young officer swallowed. 'Yes, sir.'

'Take a couple of bottles of brandy from the cabinet and share them out with the other volunteers.'

Leona returned to the cabinet, and handed two bottles to the young lieutenant.

'If the Gunstians ask where I am,' Friel said; 'direct them here. I shall be waiting.'

'Yes, sir.'

The officer hurried from the room.

'Close the door, Leona,' Friel said. He put his boots up onto the desk and took a sip of wine. 'This is a fine vintage, from the vineyards above Chesson, if I am not mistaken.'

Leona closed the office door and sat on the other side of the desk from the colonel.

'Take a drink,' he said. 'Don't waste such an excellent wine.'

'Are they going to kill us, sir?'

'Me – probably. You? I don't know. You are my secretary and assistant, so there is a good chance they will let you go.' He smiled. 'As long you tell them that you are most definitely not a dragon-worshipper.'

'What about my... my Gift?'

'They haven't brought anyone with the Gift of Truth, Leona, so your secret should be safe. No, the Gifted accompanying them have been selected for their more... aggressive qualities. Pain, Immolation, Withering... these are the Gifts they have brought to Zamata. Perhaps the truth doesn't interest them.'

Leona's gaze fell. 'Why did you never tell me you had the Gift of Kenning, sir; that you were able to sense the Gifts of others?'

He smiled again. 'We all have our little secrets, Leona. Surely you must have suspected? I always thought that you might have known all these years. How did you think I found you in the first place? Did you imagine that it was a coincidence that the girl I rescued from the streets just happened to have a Gift?'

'And you sensed that Lahnos was Gifted, too, even before he did?'

'Yes. Kenning has allowed me to detect every other person on this island who is in possession of a Gift. You would be surprised, I think, by just how many people walk about in complete ignorance that they are Gifted. Some have several Gifts, and yet they remain oblivious to that fact. I have known that Lahnos was a death-reader for years. But what could I do about it? I could hardly arrange for him to touch a dead body, could I? I only wish the body in question hadn't belonged to my mother.'

They fell into silence, and waited. For over half an hour, the rebel Zamatans fled from the militia headquarters, and then a long, painful silence had followed. The Gunstians arrived twenty minutes later, battering at the gates of the compound. There was a brief struggle of noise and then more silence.

Friel refilled his glass as the sound of boots approached his office, then six burly soldiers in dark green uniforms burst through the door and aimed their bows at Friel and Leona.

'Good afternoon,' the colonel said in Gunstian. 'Welcome to Zamata.'

'Colonel Friel Laimos?' said one.

Friel smiled, and nodded.

'For the crime of treason against the Empire of Gunst,' said the soldier, 'you are under arrest.'

CHAPTER 22
SOMETHING WORTHY

Kaugatz, Serpent Isle – 11th Nethinch 1588

'Give me the damn crossbow, Lahnos!' Reyn cried from the bed.

Lahnos glanced up from where he was pulling on his boots. 'No.'

'Why are you allowed to fight, but I can't?' she said. 'I can shoot Gunstians from the balcony.'

'And what will happen when they notice bolts raining down on them from up here? Stay in bed, Reyn – you are still injured. Besides, you wouldn't hit anyone – you haven't been trained.'

'If you walk out of that door without leaving me a weapon,' she cried, 'then I will hunt you down, Lahnos Laimos – do you hear me? You know what the Gunstians will do to me if they find me.'

Lahnos hesitated. 'I should stay here.'

'You can't,' she said. 'You are part of a rebel squad, and you need to go to your post. Defend Tsallon Anura, Lahnos; that's your job.'

He stood, and gazed down at her.

'The crossbow, Lahnos?' she said.

He pulled the strap from his shoulder, and handed her the weapon.

'Remember to turn the safety lever before you loose,' he said, 'and you load it by...'

'I know how to load a crossbow, Lahnos. I might never have received any formal training, but I know how to point and loose.'

He sat on the bed. 'We should have stayed in Fidalaimos.'

'Maybe, but we didn't.' She put the crossbow down and took his hand. 'Defend the walls of the monastery. The Gunstians used Tsallon Anura as a fortress for hundreds of years when they were last here. Use their own fortifications against them.'

'If they breach the defences then I'm coming back here,' he said. 'I'll carry you on my shoulders, and we'll fight our way out.' He smiled. 'You can shoot them from my back.'

'I love you,' she said.

'I love you, too, Reyn.'

'Go, before you get into trouble.'

He stood again, his mind conflicted, then he walked to the door. 'If...'

'Go, Lahnos.'

He opened the door and left the apartment. He stared at the closed door for a moment, then hurried down the stairs. The interior of the monastery had been a hive of activity since the Gunstian ships had been seen several hours earlier. The monks had locked themselves inside their quarters, while the rebel fighters had prepared to defend the compound. Lahnos ran through the crowds, until he reached the section of curtain wall where his squad of Zamatan fighters had been ordered to assemble. His sergeant strode across to him as soon as he arrived under the shade of the high wall.

'You took your time, Laimos,' the sergeant said. 'Where's your crossbow?'

'I gave it to Reyn,' he said.

The sergeant scowled, opened his mouth, then closed it again. 'Fine,' he mumbled. 'Collect another one from the stores, then meet us up on the battlements. Quickly, now.'

Lahnos turned, and ran back the way he had come. He joined a queue of fighters by the entrance to a large hall, from where weapons, armour, water and uniforms were being distributed by the quarter-master and his team.

He nudged the man in front of him. 'Do you know what's happening?'

The man turned. His gaze went to Lahnos's horns, then he shrugged. 'The Gunstians have docked in Handshore, and now they're ferrying troops across the Cyasarta. That's about as much as I know, lad.'

'Are we just going to stay here in the monastery?' Lahnos said. 'Won't the Gunstians rampage through Kaugatz?'

'It's the dragons, Bullan and Aucterians they'll be after first,' the man said; 'in that order. And then the part-Bullan; and then the rest of the Zamatans. It's not too late to knock those horns off, lad. If you file them down hard enough then you might pass for Zamatan.'

'I'd rather die.'

'Then you probably will. Your uncle has made a right mess of things. Give it a month, and I'd be amazed if any part-Bullan are still alive on the island.'

'We can beat them,' said Lahnos. 'We can beat the Gunstians.'

'It was a dream,' the man said. 'Our freedom – it was only a dream. It's time to wake up, young Laimos. The dream is over.'

They reached the front of the queue, and Lahnos was handed a fresh crossbow and a wrapped bundle of steel bolts. He raced back through the cloisters and ran up the stairs leading to the battlements along the curtain wall. He reached the parapet at the top, and found the rest of his squad there. He joined them, and gazed out at the view. Their section of wall faced east, and overlooked the old Aucterian enclave that had clustered around the eastern ferry terminal. Much of the harbour had been destroyed in the diversionary attack carried out by the Dominion Fleet five days previously, but enough of the quayside remained to allow a single Gunstian troop-carrier to dock. Soldiers were streaming down the gangways, while another two troop-carriers sat anchored out in the middle of the inlet, awaiting their turn to disgorge their human cargo into Kaugatz.

On the other side of the Cyasarta, the remainder of the Gunstian ships were hidden out of view behind the huge breakwaters protecting Handshore Naval Base. No sounds of battle were drifting over the waters from Igatz, but Lahnos knew it was only a matter of time before the Gunstians engaged the Bullan defences around the palace.

Lahnos's eyes went back to the ferry terminal where the Gunstians were disembarking.

'We should attack them while they land,' he said. 'Why are we giving them time to organise themselves?'

'We have been ordered to defend Tsallon Anura, lad,' said the sergeant.

'But why? They could easily bypass the entire monastery and cut us off. We should strike now, before those two other ships have a chance to dock.'

'Orders are orders,' said the sergeant. 'Do you think every fighter should get to decide what they should be doing? That's not how it works.'

'But...'

'That's enough, Laimos. I need to know that you will obey orders, or we might have a problem, you and I.'

'Where's your uncle?' cried out another member of the squad.

'I don't know,' said Lahnos. 'I saw him this morning, but then he went back to Igatz.'

'Did he know the Gunstians were coming?'

'If he did then he didn't say anything to me about it.'

'Quiet, lads,' said the sergeant.

They settled down and watched as the first troop-carrier began to edge away from shore, the last of its soldiers having disembarked into Kaugatz. The second troop-carrier raised its sails, and prepared to dock.

'Maybe Lahnos is right,' said a fighter. 'Why are we standing here and allowing those bastards all the time in the world to land?'

'Because we obey orders,' snapped the sergeant.

'But what if the colonel has been captured or killed? Maybe our orders no longer make any sense, but there's no one around to change them.'

The sergeant's eyes darkened.

'This is bullshit,' muttered another fighter.

'That's enough!' cried the sergeant. 'The next man I hear questioning our orders will be joining the Dominion sailors in the prison cells – is that understood?'

The squad seethed, but no one spoke. Lahnos felt his anger rise as the second troop-carrier began to manoeuvre alongside the harbour quayside.

Losing your temper will help no one, Lahnos.

'Are you here to help?' he said in his mind.

I am.

'Where have you been? I called on you a few nights ago, but you weren't there.'

I cannot always be with you, Lahnos. I have other responsibilities. But, I am here now.

'Do you know where my uncle is?'

Yes. Friel Laimos is being questioned by Gunstian officials. They are using the Gift of Pain on him.

'The what? There is a Gift that causes pain?'

There is. Now, listen carefully; there is a task I wish you to carry out. It will be dangerous, but you can do it, Lahnos. Politely ask the sergeant if you have permission to lead a small detachment out of the monastery on a raid.

'He will refuse.'

He will not. He will agree, because I shall compel him to agree.

Lahnos raised an eyebrow, then he turned to the sergeant. 'May I please have your permission to lead a detachment beyond the walls on a raid?'

A few of the fighters in the squad stared at Lahnos, and the sergeant's eyes narrowed.

'I, uh...' said the sergeant, as his features softened. 'Yes. Yes, Lahnos. Take half the squad.'

'Thank you, sergeant,' said Lahnos. He glanced at the others. 'Any volunteers?'

'A raid?' said one.

Lahnos nodded. 'I'll lead. It shouldn't take too long, and then we'll come back to the monastery.'

'Have you ever led a detachment before, lad?' said an older fighter.

'No,' said Lahnos. 'This will be my first.'

'Is this a good idea, sergeant?'

'I have given my permission,' said the sergeant. 'Get going, before the sun sets. That's an order.'

'You heard the sergeant,' said Lahnos. 'I'll take eight men with me. Let's go.'

He turned towards the stairs, and there was a flurry of movement behind him as the other fighters either stood back, or hastened to join him. Among those volunteering was the older fighter, along with one other experienced man; while the others looked as though they were in their teens. Lahnos hurried down the stairs, and led his detachment towards a barred gate in the wall that faced east. Six fighters were stationed there, guarding the position.

'Voice?' Lahnos said in his head. 'What now?'

You will see. Keep walking.

Lahnos strode towards the gates, and the six fighters pulled down the bars, and opened it for him.

Tell them you will return soon, Lahnos. Tell them to be ready to let you back into the monastery.

Lahnos paused by the open gate. 'Stay alert, lads,' he said. 'When we come back, we might be running. Bar the gate behind us, but be ready to let us in.'

'No problem,' said one.

Lahnos led the detachment through the gate, and the fighters inside closed it as soon as they were out on the street.

'How are you doing this, lad?' said the older fighter. 'Did your uncle give you authority over the rest of us? If he did, then I never heard anything about it.'

'What now, Lahnos?' said another.

Towards the ferry terminal.

'We're going to the ferry terminal,' he said. 'Follow me.'

He set off, and the others formed a column behind him on the street and hurried after him.

The Gunstians have thirty Bullan soldiers in their custody, the voice said in his head. *You are going to free them, Lahnos.*

'Why?'

Because the Gunstians will butcher them if you don't.

'I thought every Bullan soldier was in Igatz.'

Almost all of them are. These thirty were cut off, and have been hiding in the ruined harbour buildings of the ferry terminal, trying to find a boat that will take them to Igatz. The Gunstians found them as soon as they had landed, and subdued them with the Gift of Pain. The Gunstians intend to torture and slaughter the Bullan at dawn, in front of the Dragon Palace. You will prevent this, Lahnos.

'I killed a Bullan soldier at the start of the uprising.'

I know you did.

'And now you want me to save them?'

Trust me, Lahnos. I am going to place a mental image of their location into your mind, along with a route through the back streets that will take you there. You will be swift; you will be ruthless, and you will bring the Bullan back to Tsallon Anura alive.

Lahnos felt a strange sensation in his head as various images appeared. He saw the thirty Bullan soldiers crowded together in a cellar close to the ferry terminal. They had been beaten, and were hooded with their wrists bound behind their backs. He then saw the streets surrounding the building, and the positions of the Gunstian patrols.

'How did you make the sergeant agree?' he said to her.

I can be persuasive.

'Then why don't you persuade the Gunstians to let the Bullan go?'

Because I cannot read their thoughts, Lahnos. Their language is unintelligible to me.

'If you can't understand them, how do you know what they are going to do to the Bullan?'

The Gunstians announced it to them in the Divine Tongue. Turn left.

Lahnos raced up a narrow side street, and heard the boots of the others following him. He raised a hand, and they came to a halt.

'We are going to rescue some trapped prisoners,' he said to the eight fighters. 'They are being held in the cellar of one of the harbour buildings. We're going to break inside, free them, and then get back to Tsallon Anura.'

'Hold on,' said the older fighter, raising a hand. 'And how would you know all that, lad?'

'I saw it from the battlements.'

'You must have bloody good eyesight.'

'I do. Thanks.'

'Eyesight that can see through walls?'

'You volunteered to come, didn't you? You agreed to serve under my command?'

'I came along to stop you doing anything crazy, lad. This certainly counts as crazy.'

Lahnos shrugged. 'Then go back to the monastery; it makes no difference to me. I only want willing volunteers. I'll do it myself if I have to.'

'You're going to get these young lads killed, Laimos.'

'We'll make it back if you all do exactly as I say. Let's move.'

Lahnos set off again, and followed the twisting route that had been imprinted into his mind. They ran down narrow alleyways, then crossed through the empty back yards of a row of large housing blocks. The sun was setting over the hills to the west, and it grew darker as they approached the harbour.

There are two Gunstians round the next turn, on your left.

Lahnos raised a hand and came to a halt. He placed a finger to his lips for silence, then beckoned for the older fighter to join him.

'Two Gunstians are on duty around that corner,' he whispered, pointing. 'Can you deal with them?'

The older fighter stared at him, then nodded. He gestured to the other experienced fighter, and they crept forwards. The older man crawled the last yard, peered round the corner, then nodded to his colleague. The two men drew knives and disappeared into the gloom. There was a low, muffled cry, and then the two fighters returned, each dragging a dead Gunstian soldier by the boots. They dropped them into the alleyway, then the older fighter prodded a finger into Lahnos's chest.

'Why didn't you tell us you were Gifted, Laimos? That's the only explanation.'

'Can a Gift make him see round walls?' said a younger fighter.

'I don't know all the Gifts, lad,' said the older man; 'but what else could it be?'

Lahnos said nothing, then he leaned over and took a war axe from a dead Gunstian's belt. He hefted it in his right hand, then handed his crossbow to another fighter.

'Absolute quiet from now on,' he said. 'The building with the cellar is close. Stay in line, and follow me.'

Lahnos led them to the junction, and took another narrow lane to their right. They skirted by a large open yard where dozens of Gunstians were being assembled, and stole along in the shadows as the dusk deepened into evening. Very few streetlamps in the old Aucterian enclave had been lit, but the moon was out, and was just a few nights away from being full.

Two soldiers are approaching, Lahnos; ahead of you! Move!

Lahnos raced forward, and almost collided with the two Gunstians as they were patrolling through the back lanes. Without thinking, Lahnos brought his axe down, and it struck the first soldier in the face, its blade cleaving through the man's nose and mouth. Behind him, the two older fighters loosed their crossbows, and the other Gunstian fell to the cobbles. Lahnos ripped the axe free, and the man he had killed slumped down, a pool of blood forming around his head.

Be brave. You are fearless, Lahnos; fearless and ruthless.

His heart swelled, and he glanced at his men. The younger ones were looking at him differently, while the two older men nodded.

Lahnos gestured, and they followed him. They crept like ghosts along the dark lanes, until Lahnos stopped them opposite a large harbour building. Its roof and upper floor had been hit by the Dominion Navy's barrage, but the lower levels had remained intact. Four Gunstian soldiers were standing guard by a door, and it took an effort for Lahnos not to charge them single-handed. He had never felt so liberated from fear, so focussed on the task at hand. He gestured to the six younger members of his team, signalling that they should get down to one knee and form a line. They did as he commanded, while the two older fighters shouldered their crossbows and drew their knives.

'Loose upon my command,' Lahnos whispered to the six, 'then follow us into the building. Shoot any Gunstian you see. The soldiers we are rescuing are Bullan.'

Some of the fighters stared at him.

'Loose!'

Six crossbow bolts flew out from the shadows, and Lahnos charged. All four Gunstians had been hit, but two had received only light wounds and Lahnos raised his axe as he neared them. One cried out, a bolt in his left wrist, and Lahnos almost decapitated him, the axe blade hacking through his neck. The two older fighters dispatched the other wounded soldier, then Lahnos pulled the door open and entered the building. An unarmed Gunstian official glanced up, and Lahnos lunged at him, pulling him round the neck with his free arm. The older fighter sunk his knife blade into the official's chest, and they moved on, racing through the dark building. Lahnos followed the route in his mind, and they came to a set of deserted stairs. He charged down them fearing nothing, his heart singing with nervous exhilaration. They came to another guarded door, and a volley of four crossbow bolts struck the two Gunstians on duty.

'Demon!' one of them cried as he fell, his eyes on Lahnos's horns.

Lahnos brought a boot down and stamped on the soldier's head, ending his cries. He pointed at the door, and two of his fighters hauled it open. Inside were the thirty Bullan. It was exactly as he had pictured it – each Bullan was hooded, and all had their wrists bound behind their backs.

'Cut them free,' said Lahnos.

His team ran into the room. It was being lit by a solitary wall lamp, and the fighters began to cut the cords that bound the Bullan's wrists. Some were in a bad state, their tails hacked off, and their bodies beaten. The first to have their hoods removed tried to lash out at their rescuers, their eyes seeing nothing but more humans, and Lahnos stepped forward.

'My name is Lahnos Laimos, nephew of Colonel Laimos,' he cried. 'We are here to free you from the Gunstians.'

The Bullan stared at him in disbelief. Many gazed at his horns, and a few muttered words in their own language. Lahnos picked up an axe and a crossbow from one of the slain Gunstians, and handed the weapons to two Bullan.

'Will you fight with us?' he said.

The Bullan looked at the axe he had been given. 'You are our enemy, Laimos.'

'Would an enemy rescue you, and arm you?' Lahnos said. 'The Gunstians are our enemy. They hate you, and they hate me. Fight with us.'

More Bullan started to get to their feet as their hoods were removed and their wrists freed. Several of them were glancing at one Bullan in particular, and Lahnos approached him.

'Are you the senior officer here?'

'I am a sergeant,' said the Bullan. 'There are no officers.'

'We have to hurry,' said Lahnos. 'The Gunstians will discover what we have done soon enough. We are taking you to Tsallon Anura.'

'Why would we wish to become prisoners of the rebels?' the sergeant said.

'You will not be prisoners,' said Lahnos. 'Our quarrel ended the moment the Gunstians arrived. The only way we can defeat them is together.'

The Bullan glanced at each other.

'Do you wish to stay here?' said Lahnos. 'The Gunstians intend to have you all executed in boats in full view of your comrades besieging the Dragon Palace. If that is the fate you desire, then stay. I cannot force you to accept our help.'

The sergeant turned to face the other Bullan, and began to speak in their own tongue. Others spoke up, and the room was filled with a low hubbub of their voices.

'We need to get out of here, Laimos,' whispered one of the older fighters.

'We shall come with you,' said the Bullan sergeant; 'but if this is a trick, and you betray us, the dishonour shall never leave your name.'

Lahnos tilted his head, then he gestured to his team. 'Collect the weapons from the dead,' he said, 'and hand them to any Bullan able to fight. Let's go.'

Lahnos led the way, and soon discovered the presence of the Bullan sergeant by his side. They ascended the stairs as three Gunstians were hurrying down them, and the Bullan sergeant roared out and charged. He leapt up the stairs, his axe ripping through the torso of a Gunstian. Lahnos was a pace behind him. He fended off a wild lunge from a Gunstian, then three Bullan brought the soldier down, using their bare hands to break his neck. The last Gunstian turned and ran, and was struck in the back of the head with a crossbow bolt.

Lead them, Lahnos; lead them to safety. You are fearless.

Lahnos smiled, and ran up the stairs. The corridor at the top of the steps was empty, and Lahnos gestured for his team to keep going.

'Straight for the door, lads,' he said, as the Bullan crowded the passageway. Several were being helped along by their colleagues, and Lahnos put his arm round one who was carrying an injury to his side. 'Keep moving,' he cried; 'we're leaving no one behind.'

The door opened ahead of them, and Lahnos saw the street outside, bathed in pale moonlight. Lahnos helped the injured Bullan to the doorway, and they ran and staggered across the street.

Here is your route back, Lahnos. The bodies of those you killed on the way have been discovered, and you must return to the monastery by a different path.

'This way!' Lahnos cried, as he supported the injured Bullan. 'Take the left-hand lane.'

The journey back should have been one of most terrifying experiences of Lahnos's life. The Gunstians had raised the alarm, and patrols were out in large numbers, combing through the back streets and alleyways of the old Aucterian enclave. They were almost discovered on several occasions, but the voice kept issuing fresh guidance on their route, and they were always able to get away unseen. It should have been terrifying, but Lahnos was utterly without fear. He had never felt so alive, so liberated, so sure of himself.

Some of the rebel fighters were shaking with fear and relief as they approached the gates of Tsallon Anura. The gates swung open without Lahnos having to call out, and the fighters and rescued Bullan stumbled into the grounds of the monastery. A few of the younger fighters fell to their knees, panting and almost weeping, and one threw up onto the dry ground, as a Bullan soldier patted his shoulder. The gates closed, and the Bullan surrounded their rescuers.

'No matter what happens now, young Laimos,' said the Bullan sergeant, 'we are in your debt. What you did for us this night will never be forgotten. Are we now your prisoners?'

'No,' said Lahnos. 'This was no trick.'

The Bullan sergeant smiled. 'I am not sure your superior officers will agree.'

Lahnos turned, and saw a wall of armed rebel fighters blocking the way from the gate into the rest of the compound. Each was aiming a crossbow at the Bullan. Behind the line of fighters, many more had gathered in the torchlight to see what was happening.

Lahnos stepped forward, until he was standing halfway between the rebels and the Bullan.

'That's far enough!' cried a rebel captain.

'This night,' Lahnos said, 'we have freed thirty Bullan whom the Gunstians were going to execute in the morning. I know how you feel about the Bullan, and I know how the Bullan feel about us, but if we don't unite, the Gunstians will destroy us both.'

'You had no right to lead a raid, Laimos!' said the captain. 'You disobeyed the orders handed down to you.'

'No,' said Lahnos. 'My sergeant gave me permission to leave.'

The sergeant from the curtain wall took a step forward. 'This is true, sir. I take full responsibility for Lahnos's actions. I ordered him to go out on the raid.'

The rebel officer stared at the sergeant, then at the Bullan.

The Bullan sergeant raised his hands. 'May I speak?'

The captain looked lost for words for a moment, then he nodded.

'We didn't ask to be rescued by rebels,' the Bullan sergeant said, taking a few steps forward, 'and I don't know why the Laimos boy risked his life to save us. If you wish to take us into captivity, then that is your right, but know this – no one here will fight the Gunstians any better than we will. They tortured, humiliated and abused us for hours before Laimos arrived. They cut off the tails of five men, and laughed. They think we are demons. They also think Laimos is a demon. If they had caught him, they would have tortured and abused him in the same manner. And yet... and yet he came for us. I swear to you all that if you allow us to fight by your side, we will reserve our anger for the Gunstians alone. If we defeat them, then we can resume our old quarrel; but until then, I ask that you let us fight our common enemy.'

The rebel captain said nothing for a moment, then he lowered his gaze. 'I will have to await orders from Colonel Laimos regarding this.'

'My uncle has been arrested by the Gunstians,' said Lahnos, 'and is currently being tortured with the Gift of Pain. He will not be able to issue you with any fresh orders. You, Captain, are in charge of Tsallon Anura – you are the senior officer here. You must make the decision.'

Every eye turned to the rebel captain. He swallowed. 'Do I have your solemn vow, Bullan, that you will only fight the Gunstians?'

The sergeant placed a hand onto his chest. 'I swear it by the blood of my people.'

'Then I am not opposed to a truce,' the captain said. He nodded to the line of armed Zamatans. 'Stand down. Someone find me the quartermaster; we have a lot to do.'

The captain stepped forward. He took a breath, then extended his hand towards the Bullan sergeant, who took it. The other Bullan approached, and embraced the fighters who had freed them, then they surrounded Lahnos and the rebel captain.

'Amid all the evil, Laimos,' said the Bullan sergeant, 'you have done something good; something worthy of your horns.'

'He's done something, all right,' said the rebel captain, shaking his head. 'I can't imagine what his uncle will say.'

The Bullan sergeant smiled. 'I can.'

CHAPTER 23
MOONLIGHT

Igatz, Serpent Isle – 12th Nethinch 1588

The midnight bell of the palace tolled, and Cisca opened her eyes. She hadn't meant to doze off, but it had been an exhausting and miserable day.

'If I know the Gunstians,' Bauchlie was saying to his men, as he strode through the dark living chamber, 'then they will attack the Bullan positions at dawn. Their first target will be Lord Rufus, if he still lives. Their second will be Kheran. Get some rest, if you can.'

Cisca sat up, and yawned. The rebels had run out of fuel to light their lamps, but moonlight was entering through the shafts in the domed ceiling, and more was spilling through from the balcony chamber. Kheran's scales were glimmering in the pale, silvery light, but he looked drained and weak. Everyone in the palace had heard the scream that had come from Lord Rufus's jaws on the previous morning, and Kheran had become almost hysterical, writhing and struggling against the chains, and weeping until he was gasping for breath. He had finally gone to sleep just before Cisca had nodded off, and she checked him for signs of movement.

'How is he?'

She turned, and saw Bauchlie gazing down at her, his features cloaked in shadows.

'You chained him up,' she said; 'why don't you tell me how he looks?'

Bauchlie nodded and turned away.

'Wait,' she said.

He halted.

'What have you to lose by freeing him?' she said. 'His father might be dead – if he isn't, then he is grievously wounded; and the Gunstians have landed. Free Kheran, and you have a chance to escape while the Gunstians are fighting the Bullan.'

'No.'

'You brute,' she cried. 'Your heart is rotten.'

'The Gunstians outnumber the Bullan two-to-one, Lieutenant,' Bauchlie said, 'and they have brought Gifted warriors with them. If we flee, they will tear Kheran to pieces. Is that what you want?'

'You're guessing,' she said. 'You don't know that the Gunstians have brought Gifted with them.'

'I'm not guessing. What do you think caused Rufus to scream like that? Those troop-carriers have no catapults or ballistae on board. How else could they have brought a dragon down?'

She stared at him.

He went down to one knee next to her. 'What Gifts do you know of?'

'None,' she said. 'I know that the Demon Witch was probably Gifted, and she killed King Gahad. Perhaps the Gunstians have brought the Demon Witch with them.'

'The Demon Witch is nothing but a rumour. The Gifts are not. There is the Gift of Pain, which is the one I suspect was used against Rufus. There is the Gift of Vitrification, which can destroy a human with a single touch. The Gift of Immolation, which can cause a human to burst into flames with a glance. The Gift of Famine, which can kill entire fields of crops. None of these are rumours, Lieutenant.'

She shuddered, then she remembered the woman whose throat had been slit while she had been sleeping.

'Why did you murder that Aucterian aristocrat?'

Bauchlie said nothing.

'Are you ashamed?' she said. 'You should be. What kind of animal could kill someone in their own bed? Her children were in the house at the same time. It's evil – there's no other word for it.'

'I agree.'

'You agree that you are evil?'

'I agree that it was an evil thing to do. My soul will never be rid of the shame that murder has brought me. I will never be free of it, nor do I deserve to be.'

'Then why did you do it?'

'I am not going to make excuses for my behaviour, Lieutenant. I was young, yes, but not naïve. I was under strict orders, but I could have walked away. I didn't. I was too weak and too anxious to please a certain person. I walked away from that person afterwards, but I should have done so before I broke into the house.'

'What person? Who are you talking about?'

'The person who gave me the order. Their identity is irrelevant. In truth, I don't know why that person wanted me to kill the Aucterian woman. I don't know because I didn't ask. I didn't care. I thought of myself as a soldier, and I was determined to obey the orders that had been given to me. It was only after I had walked away that I realised how wrong I had been.'

'But you have murdered people since then.'

'I have. Soldiers, sailors, corrupt magistrates and officials working for the Dominion government – I have killed over two dozen people, Lieutenant, but I have never killed anyone else while they slept.'

'Do you think that makes you a good person?'

'No.'

'Then why are you telling me this?'

'Because you asked. Get some sleep.'

'I can't sleep,' she said. 'Are the Gunstians going to attack in the morning?'

'I don't know. If it's not at dawn, then it will be soon.' He paused for a moment. 'Would you like to see the moon? You may never see it again after tomorrow.'

'I... I am not your friend, Bauchlie.'

'Did I say you were?' He stood. 'Good night, Lieutenant.'

'Wait,' she said, then she cursed herself.

He halted again.

'I would like to see the moon.'

He nodded, then walked between the nearest ballistae and unfastened her chain from the wall. The fighters on duty nodded to him as he passed, but no one spoke. Bauchlie returned to the great heap of filthy cushions, and dropped the chain next to Cisca.

'You can carry your own chain,' he said, then he turned and strode towards the balcony chamber.

Cisca cursed herself again as she picked up the chains and got to her feet. Bauchlie was nothing but a vile criminal, who had imprisoned her and bound a young dragon in chains; a man who murdered people for a living. And yet she thought that he had been looking at her differently since she had saved his life from Travers. Was it respect that she had seen in his eyes? She glanced down at the sleeping form of Lord Kheran. The dragon child was her priority. If Bauchlie did, in fact, respect her a little, then perhaps she could use that to her advantage; perhaps she could persuade him to let Kheran go before the Gunstians attacked. The Bullan were still guarding the base of the balcony, and they might be able to smuggle Kheran out on a ship before the Gunstians overran the palace. She hurried after Bauchlie, and joined him in the balcony chamber. He was standing facing the large windows with his arms folded across his chest, and the moonlight was striking his face and shoulders.

She stood next to him, her arms holding on to the coils of chain, and peered through the glass. The moon was two days off full, and its light was spilling over the waters of the Cyasarta inlet. To their left, the hills above Chesson were bathed in the pale glow, and the stars were out, shining down as though the world was at peace. Cisca took a breath, savouring the warm, fresh air after hours of lying on the fetid cushions. Was this the last time she would ever see the moon? She remembered her idea, and glanced at Bauchlie.

'There are ropes in the storage room,' she said.

Bauchlie said nothing.

'You could use those ropes,' she went on, 'to lower Kheran to safety. Drop the Bullan a message, and tell them that you are going to free the dragon child. In return, ask for an hour's truce in which to make your escape. The Bullan will agree. The Bullan would do anything to save Kheran.'

Bauchlie remained silent. Was he even listening?

'The Gunstians' arrival has changed everything,' she said. 'They will kill Kheran – you said it yourself. Save him, and you might be able to save yourself.'

'Have you ever been to either of the island's two mountains?'

'What? No. I have never left Igatz.'

'If you climb to the top of either mountain,' he said, 'you can see the entire island spread out in front of you. It is only then that you realise how the island got its name. Zamata, the Serpent Isle – different languages, but the words have the same meaning. The snake. This palace stands at the head of the snake, and the Gunstians are at its neck. Without a ship, there is no escape, Cisca; not for Kheran, not for me, and not for you.'

'Are you giving up?' she said, trying to ignore the fact that he had addressed her by name rather than rank for the first time.

'No. When the Gunstians arrive, we will fight them and we will probably die.'

Cisca gazed back out at the view of the moonlight.

'Only the Dominion Fleet can save us,' she whispered.

'Not if the Gunstian Fleet gets here first.'

'Your rebellion has done this,' she said. 'If you hadn't rebelled, then none of this would be happening.'

'It was worth it,' he said. 'Even if we all die tomorrow, I will have no regrets about what we did. For one brief shining moment, we were free.'

Cisca fell into silence. Did Bauchlie really believe that? He sounded like a fanatic, someone who valued an illusory sensation over the lives and well-being of the thousands of people who lived on the island. The Dragon Dominion wasn't perfect – she realised that now – but surely the island was better off in their hands rather than under the rule of the Gunstians? The Dominion had built roads and schools, and had spent vast amounts of gold trying to improve the Serpent Isle; more importantly, they hadn't tried to exterminate the local population, and even the descendents of the old Gunstian colonists had been allowed to live in peace. What else did Bauchlie want from them?

'I miss home,' she said. 'I miss the sunsets. The mountains here block off the sunsets, and I miss them. I sent my parents a letter before the ships left Inopei, telling them I would be coming here, but I only expected to be on the island for a few days. Did you know that ten times as many people live in my city than upon the entire island? And Naeth isn't the largest city in Aucteran; over a million live in Teros. A million people, in a single city.'

'We all love our homes, Cisca,' he said.

'Yes. I suppose we do.'

A rebel fighter approached through the shadows. 'Sir?'

Bauchlie turned to him.

'The Bullan are back, sir,' the fighter said. 'It's the same routine as before. They want to speak to you under a truce. Shall we let them in?'

'Yes. Bring them to me here.'

The young fighter saluted. 'Yes, sir.'

'This is your chance, Bauchlie,' Cisca hissed, as soon as the fighter had hurried away. 'The Bullan are here to try to make a deal with you.'

Bauchlie said nothing.

'Please, Bauchlie.'

'I want you to stay here for the discussion,' he said. 'They will have questions about Kheran, and you can answer them.'

'No. I cannot. For the sake of my honour I cannot be seen standing out here in the moonlight with you. The Bullan will assume that I have compromised myself.'

'But you haven't compromised yourself.'

'Appearances count. I am a prisoner, and am being held here against my will, but that is not what it will look like to the Bullan. You must let me return to Lord Kheran.'

Bauchlie extended a hand. 'Give me the end of your chain. I will ensure that you look like a prisoner.'

Cisca stared at him, then she passed him the end of the long chain. He took it, and wrapped a few coils around his arm until the chain went almost taut, and she felt a tug on her ankle from the shackle.

'No one will mistake you for my friend now, Lieutenant,' he said. 'You can tell me about the sunsets over Aucteran another time.'

She bit her lip to stop herself from saying something stupid, and folded her arms across her chest. The sound of boots approached, and the young rebel fighter led three Bullan officers into the balcony chamber. Behind them was arrayed a line of other rebels, all with their crossbows aimed at the Bullan.

The senior officer tilted his head a fraction. 'It seems that you have miscalculated, rebel commander,' he said.

'How so?' said Bauchlie.

'I assume that you did not intend for the Gunstians to arrive so soon?' the Bullan officer said. 'Or am I wrong? Perhaps you welcome the arrival of the Gunstians. Is that so?'

'I am no friend of the Gunstians, Captain.'

'Then how do you intend to greet their arrival? Do you still pledge to keep Lord Kheran from harm?'

'Tell me what you want, Bullan,' said Bauchlie. 'Stop dancing around the conversation.'

'I want you to release Lord Kheran into our custody.'

'No.'

'You cannot win, commander. We are besieging you, and now the Gunstians are besieging us. You are trapped.'

'Nothing has changed,' said Bauchlie. 'If you attempt to take Lord Kheran by force, I will execute him. If you stay away, I will protect him.'

'Protect him? I saw Lord Kheran on the way in – his lordship is in a most pitiable state; he is weak, he is thirsty; he may even be dying. Do you call this protection?'

Bauchlie hesitated for a split second, and Cisca wondered if he had misspoken.

'I meant protect him from the Gunstians,' he said.

'I see,' said the Bullan. 'And why would you do such a thing?'

'Because Lord Kheran is a political target; he is not a demon. I know what the Gunstians would do to him if they capture him alive.'

'You damned hypocrite,' snapped the Bullan. 'Lord Kheran is a child! You chain him up and degrade his noble heritage, and now you claim to be better than the Gunstians? Did you know that I have been authorised to grant you a truce, commander? A truce that would allow you and your rabble to flee if you leave Lord Kheran in our custody? But after hearing such foul hypocrisy come from your lips, I am of a mind to refuse to grant you anything.'

'Who granted you that authority?' said Bauchlie.

'How is that relevant?'

'Does Lord Rufus live?'

The Bullan paused. 'Yes. His noble Grace Lord Rufus lives, but he has been unconscious since he was wounded by the Gifted on board the Gunstian ships. The commander of the Bullan regiments has assumed control until he recovers.'

'Do you intend to fight to the death when the Gunstians attack your lines?'

'Do not insult me, rebel. You know the answer to that. The Bullan will never surrender while either dragon lives.'

'Then here is my deal, Bullan,' said Bauchlie; 'fight the Gunstians when they attack, and we shall protect Lord Kheran from them. But I am not giving him up.'

An uneasy silence fell as the three Bullan glared at Bauchlie.

'You could relieve his conditions,' said Cisca.

They turned to her.

'You could remove his chains and allow him some food and water. Perhaps the Bullan could provide water for his lordship? Lord Kheran is too exhausted and unwell to try to escape; it will be days before he regains the strength to walk, let alone fly. If you mean what you say about protecting him from the Gunstians, Bauchlie, then do this to prove your intentions.'

'We would turn on your water supply if you were to agree to this,' said the Bullan officer, 'and we can provide clean bedding and food.'

'What do you have to lose, Bauchlie?' said Cisca.

Bauchlie's eyes narrowed, but he remained silent.

'You should know the anger in our hearts, Commander,' said the Bullan officer. 'Every Bullan in Igatz loathes you, not only because you invaded the palace and took Lord Kheran hostage, but for the dishonourable and cruel way you have treated him while he has been in your custody. If we catch you, we will kill you; but you needn't die with such shame attached to your name. Do as the woman suggests, and some of that shame will be lifted from your shoulders. It won't save your life, but it might salvage your reputation.'

'I care nothing for my reputation,' said Bauchlie.

'I think you are lying,' said the Bullan. 'You see yourself as a symbol of Zamatan freedom and independence, do you not? That is how you wish to be remembered, I suspect. At the moment, all you will be remembered for is the way you chained up a child and forced him to lie in his own excrement. Some reputation. I do not envy you.'

'Wait here,' said Bauchlie.

He handed Cisca's chain to another fighter, then turned and strode into the sleeping chamber.

The Bullan officer leaned in towards Cisca. 'Well done, Lieutenant,' he whispered. 'When I first saw you this night, I suspected you of collusion with the enemy; but now I think I see what you are doing. Does Bauchlie have any other weaknesses we should know about?'

'He hates the Gunstians more than he hates the Dominion,' she whispered back. 'Also, his fighters stopped stretching the ballista cords some days ago. They used to do it regularly, but some of the machines have been at tension for three days now.'

The Bullan officer smiled. 'Amateurs. Stay close to him, and if you get a chance to end this – take it. If Bauchlie dies, his men will surrender or flee.'

Bauchlie strode back into the balcony chamber. 'Follow me.'

They walked behind him as they returned into the dragon child's sleeping quarters. A group of fighters were clustered around Lord Kheran, untangling the nets from his wings, and loosening some of the chains.

'You mentioned fresh, clean bedding,' said Bauchlie.

'Yes,' said the Bullan officer. 'I shall ensure it arrives here this night. I shall also authorise that the water supply be turned back on. May we approach Lord Kheran?'

'You may.'

The three Bullan walked towards the dragon child. Cisca glanced at Bauchlie, and he nodded. Her chains were handed back to her, and she followed the Bullan to the great heap of cushions. Kheran had his eyes open, and he looked fearful as the rebel fighters swarmed around him.

'My lord!' cried the Bullan officer. 'How my heart suffers to see you suffer! Know that your faithful Bullan have never once forgotten your plight.'

A chain around the dragon's jaws was loosened, and Kheran gasped for breath. Red weals marked his scales from where the chains had been wrapped, and he opened his jaws a little.

'Cisca,' he whispered.

'I am here, my lord,' she said.

'Come closer.'

Cisca stepped up onto the cushions and blankets, and placed her left hand on Kheran's face. He closed his eyes again, and leaned into her.

'Has this woman been a faithful and true servant, my lord?' said the Bullan officer.

'Yes,' said Kheran. 'I love her. Take her with you when you leave, so that she does not die here.'

'No, my lord,' Cisca said. 'I will not leave you.'

'The Gunstians have blockaded the peninsula, my lord,' said the

Bullan. 'Even if we were to take the lieutenant with us, we would not be able to guarantee her safety.'

'I'm not going anywhere,' Cisca said.

'Gunstians?' mumbled Kheran.

'Yes, my lord,' said the Bullan. He glanced at his colleagues. 'His lordship needs to rest.'

They bowed before Lord Kheran, whose eyes remained closed, then the three Bullan walked back to where Bauchlie was standing. Cisca stayed where she was. She raised her glance to the rebel fighters, and saw that most of the chains and nets had been removed. Two large shackles were still fixed to the dragon's rear limbs, and were connected by chains to the wall of the chamber, but most of the other restrictions on his movement had gone. Kheran tried to stretch his wings, but grunted in pain and gave up.

'We can try that tomorrow,' Cisca whispered. 'Clean bedding is coming later tonight, and fresh water, too; and then you can get some sleep before you try to move your wings.'

'Is my father dead, Cisca?'

'No, Kheran; your father is alive. The Gunstians hurt him, but he is still alive. He misses you.'

'Lieutenant?'

She turned, and saw Bauchlie standing a yard from the heap of blankets.

'Where are the Bullan?' she said.

'They've gone,' he said. He held out his hand. 'Your chain.'

She stepped down from the heap, and handed the end to the chain to the rebel commander.

'Thank you,' she said.

Bauchlie took the chain and carried it over to the wall. He affixed it to its hook, then walked away without a word.

She remembered what the Bullan officer had said to her. If an opportunity arose, she should kill Bauchlie and end the siege. His men were hungry, tired and fed up – they would surely flee if their leader was killed. She wondered if that would help Kheran. Would the rebels leave him alive if they ran away? And if they did, then what would happened after that? The Bullan would try to protect the young dragon, but they were heavily outnumbered by the Gunstians. Was there any point in killing Bauchlie if all it led to were two hundred fewer men willing to fight to protect Kheran? Would it not be better to keep the rebels where they were, as a last line of defence?

Yes, she told herself – that was why she shouldn't kill Bauchlie.

There was no other reason.

CHAPTER 24
BAREFOOT

Igatz, Serpent Isle – 12th Nethinch 1588

Two soldiers shoved Leona into the dark office, and her bare feet almost stumbled on the floorboards. Her wrists had been bound before her, and the soldiers had kept her awake all night, constantly moving her from room to room around the vast naval base of Handshore.

'What is your name, girl?' said a voice with a Gunstian accent.

'Leona of Kaugatz,' she said, keeping her head down.

She heard a few whispered comments in Gunstian regarding her identity, and she wondered if she should keep her knowledge of the language a secret.

'Are you Colonel Laimos's secretary and assistant?' said the voice.

'I am.'

'Look at us while we address you, Leona of Kaugatz.'

She raised her head and saw two men and two women in long grey robes sitting behind a desk. The pre-dawn light was penetrating the half-closed shutters, adding a silvery hue to the small office.

'Have you ever believed the demon dragons to be gods?' said one of the men.

'When... when I was younger,' she said.

'And now?'

She remembered what she was supposed to say. It was the truth, but that seemed almost irrelevant.

'I do not consider the dragons to be gods,' she said.

The four Gunstians nodded, and one wrote something in a ledger. Did they know about her Gift? If the colonel was being questioned with the Gift of Pain, then was there any reason to believe that he hadn't supplied them with that information? She tried to calm herself.

'Do you believe in the one, true god of this universe, Leona?' said one of the women.

'Do you mean the Gunstian religion?' she said.

'I do,' said the woman. 'Do you believe in Chadura, the almighty, the creator and saviour of humanity?'

Leona swallowed. 'I don't know enough about Chadura to be able to say.'

The panel nodded.

'This poor girl is nothing but another lost Zamatan peasant,' said one of the Gunstian men. 'We should not punish her for her ignorance.' He glanced at Leona. 'Are you prepared to learn about our faith?'

'Yes,' she said.

'We shall be holding lessons in religious instruction for the benighted inhabitants of this island,' said one of the women. 'Do you agree to attend?'

'I do.'

The Gunstians nodded again, and another note was added to the ledger.

'Now,' said one of the men, 'let us discuss your relationship with Colonel Laimos. We have it on good authority that you were present with the Colonel while he met with various agents of the Gunstian Empire. Is this true?'

'Yes,' she said.

'What was your role at these meetings?'

'I acted as the colonel's assistant,' she said. 'I made the travel arrangements, and organised his laundry. I also kept his diary, so that he would know his daily schedule.'

Here it comes, she thought; they knew about her Gift, and had been stringing her along.

'You are a pretty young woman,' said one of the Gunstians. 'Did the colonel take advantage of this?'

Leona blinked. Was this a trap?

'The colonel has confessed to carrying out a large number of affairs with wealthy Aucterian women,' the Gunstian went on, 'so we are aware of his corrupt and decadent ways. He has also confessed to treating you as little more than a common prostitute. Is that true?'

Leona's mouth went dry. None of what they had said had triggered the tingle in the back of her head.

'Did you abase yourself, Leona?' said one of the Gunstian woman. 'If the colonel abused his position of authority over you, then that was not entirely your fault.'

'Yes,' Leona whispered. 'It's true.'

The four Gunstians sighed and shook their heads as they exchanged glances, and yet another note was added to the ledger.

One of them looked up at her. 'Do you repent of these wicked deeds?'

'I do.'

He nodded. 'You are free to go.'

Leona remained where she was, her eyes narrowing.

'Didn't you hear me, girl?' said the Gunstian. 'The details regarding the classes in religious instruction will be posted up over Igatz in the following days – be sure to attend. Other than that, we have no further interest in you. You are free to go.'

A soldier stepped forward and cut the cords binding Leona's wrists, then he turned her by the shoulder and shoved her towards the door. Leona almost stumbled again, then the soldier led her out of the office.

'Get out of here, girl,' he mumbled at her.

Leona set off, and hurried down the long hallway. She passed more Gunstian soldiers by a large entrance, but they ignored her as she passed out into the open air. What had just happened? Could it be true? Had the colonel told them that he had been taking advantage of her in order to conceal the truth about her Gift? She had seen pity in the eyes of her interrogators, as if she were just a helpless and ignorant peasant girl ensnared by the vile Colonel Laimos. She ran across the large, empty forecourt of the Handshore Naval Base, and passed through one of its many gates. The Gunstian soldiers there glanced in her direction, but did nothing to stop her. She kept running until she was out of sight of anyone, then she stopped and put her hands on her knees as if she was going to throw up into the street.

Her head spun, and not just from the lack of sleep and the fear that had riven her heart. Her first thought was to get far away from Handshore as quickly as possible. If the colonel was still being tortured, then he might eventually reveal the truth to the Gunstians about her Gift, and then she would be hunted down and taken back into custody.

Her eyes welled. How could she be so selfish? The colonel was being tortured, and all she could think about was her own safety. But he had saved her; shouldn't she run and hide? That was what the colonel would want her to do, wasn't it? She straightened her back and gazed around at the empty street as the dawn light started to spread across the eastern horizon. She was in the Naval District, surrounded by tenements that had housed the Dominion personnel that had worked on the base. A few had been ransacked, their windows smashed, and the breeze was blowing discarded items of clothing along the cobbles.

Paralysed by indecision, Leona stood in frozen silence for several moments, torn between her duty and her survival instinct. She had never walked about Igatz on her own, never once in all the years since the colonel had approached her while she had been begging for food in the slums of Kaugatz. He had always been with her. She knew the street layout as well as anyone, though. Less than a mile away to her left were the Bullan barricades and defences that blocked access to the Temple, Harbour and Palace Districts; while to her right was the western ferry terminal that led to Kaugatz.

Kaugatz, she thought. Yes. She would report to the rebel leadership in Tsallon Anura, if any rebel leadership still existed. She wondered if the ferries were still running across the Cyasarta, as she walked south-west towards the terminal. What would the Gunstians do to restrict movement? Their priority would be to assault the Bullan and kill the island's remaining dragons; surely large areas of Kaugatz would remain beyond their control?

The sun breached the horizon to her left, and she heard whistles and horns blow behind her, followed by a low roar of voices and a rumble of boots. The attack had begun. The Gunstians would be charging the Bullan lines, and showering their defences with crossbow bolts. The Gifted would also be in action, using their talents to push back the Bullan. She urged the Bullan on in her mind. The more Gunstians they killed, the fewer would remain to occupy the island, and Zamata might still have a chance. She laughed at her own thoughts. A chance for what? The colonel's rebellion had done nothing but allow the Gunstians to land, and there was nothing more certain than the fact that more ships were on their way to the island – from Gunst, and from the Dominion. More ships, and more soldiers. The Gunstians and the Dominion would rather destroy Zamata than let their enemy occupy it, and the colonel's vision of freedom had been nothing but a naïve dream.

She frowned. Was that what she truly believed? Had it not also been her dream? She, too, longed for a day when the island was free to pursue its own destiny; but was such a thing even possible?

Leona stuck to the back streets, then heard the sound of a woman screaming to her left. She paused. She should keep going, she told herself. The scream rose up again, and Leona cursed, and changed direction, heading towards the sound. She followed a narrow lane between high townhouses, and peered out at the main road. Dozens of Gunstian soldiers were herding Aucterian civilians towards a large open junction where three roads met. A few Zamatans were also outside, but they were keeping their distance in the shadows by the side of the street. Leona stepped out of the alleyway and joined them.

'What's happening?' she whispered to an old Zamatan woman.

'The Gunstians are rounding up every Aucterian between Atzoun and the Bullan, lass,' the old woman said. She pointed to the junction. 'They're butchering them over there.'

Leona turned and gazed at the road junction. A mound of bodies three feet high had already formed, and Gunstians were standing around it with crossbows, waiting for the latest batch of Aucterian civilians to reach them.

'Why?' Leona gasped.

'Did you expect anything different?' the old woman said. 'The dragons, the Bullan, the Aucterians – the Gunstians will kill them all by the time they're through. And then the Zamatans will have to kneel before them and pretend that we worship their god. Don't you know your history, girl?'

The Aucterian civilians were shoved closer to the junction, and a few tried to break free. A woman and a man made a run for it, but the soldiers brought them down, using their crossbows as clubs, and killed them both on the cobbles where they had fallen. Another man made it as far as the edge of the road, and two crossbow bolts struck him in the back. He turned, then fell to the ground. A few children screamed and wept, and the civilians were pushed together and shoved towards the junction.

'Is no one helping them?' said Leona.

'If you help them, then you'll die, too. Go home, girl. You're too young to be watching this.'

Leona looked away as the civilians reached the junction, then she ran back down the alleyway, the sounds of their screams ringing in her ears. She took a left, and kept running, racing down the narrow lanes away from the Naval District. She came to a small park – a square area of plants and trees nestled among the tall townhouses, and stumbled to a halt. The park was full of bodies. Aucterian men, women and children lay in bloody heaps, their bodies riddled with crossbow bolts. Flies were already buzzing among the corpses, and a stray dog bolted into the shadows as soon as it saw Leona. She stared at the bodies. Was she partly responsible for their fate? The whirlwind days of the early rebellion seemed to mock her – had they really believed that they could disrupt everything without the island paying the price? She stepped among the bodies, her bare feet avoiding the touch of the dead, and left the square. She took another back road to the ferry terminal, and slowed as she saw the Gunstian soldiers on duty by the palm trees along the quayside. Two ferry boats were tied up at the docks, but there were no vessels crossing the inlet.

She approached a small group of Gunstian soldiers, and kept her glance lowered. They ceased their conversation and watched her as she walked towards them.

'Are there any ferries to Kaugatz?' she said.

'No,' said one of the soldiers, his accent thick. 'It's too dangerous over there at the moment. All Zamatan civilians in Igatz are to stay here until more soldiers arrive.'

Leona nodded.

'If you need somewhere to sleep,' said another soldier, 'report to Handshore Naval Base. They are assigning Aucterian houses to the native Zamatans.'

'Thank you,' she said.

She turned, and walked along the shoreline until she had moved out of sight of the ferry terminal; then she sat on a low stone wall and gazed out over the Cyasarta, as the dawn sunlight spread over the waters. A young man appeared a few yards to her right. He pulled off his tunic, and then crouched down and unlaced his boots.

'What are you doing?' she said.

He turned his head to glance at her. 'What does it look like? I'm going to swim over to Kaugatz.'

'The far shore is a mile away,' she said, 'and the currents are strong.'

'So? I'd rather drown than stay here.'

He glanced to either side, then he jumped up onto the wall and dived into the Cyasarta. She saw the splash of his arms and legs as he moved through the water, and then her eyes followed him as he swam out from the shore of Igatz.

She stood. If he could do it, then why couldn't she? She hadn't swum for any notable distance for a few years but, like most Zamatans, she had learned the basics as a child. Her dress would be cumbersome, but she wasn't going to strip down to her underwear, not when half of Kaugatz would be able to see her stagger out of the water at the other end. She looked to her left and to her right, then she got to her feet on top of the wall and jumped in. The water was freezing cold, and she immediately regretted her decision. She shivered, and told herself to start swimming. She struck out, kicking with her feet, and moving her arms just as she had been taught. Her saturated dress was weighing her down, but it was only slowing her a little, and she pulled away from the coastline of Igatz.

An hour later, two fishermen hauled her into their small boat. She coughed and spluttered, her limbs shaking with cold, and her lungs aching. She had never felt so tired or so cold.

One of the fishermen laughed. 'Look at her; she's floundering like a fish.' He handed her a blanket. 'Wrap that round yourself, girl.' She looked up, and saw three other wet and bedraggled swimmers sitting on the deck of the small boat, each with a blanket wrapped round their shoulders.

'That's right, girl,' said the fisherman; 'you're not the first we've pulled out of the Cyasarta this morning. But, you're our first Zamatan – you are Zamatan, yes?'

'Yes,' she gasped. She sat up and leaned her back against the side of the vessel. She rubbed her face with the blanket, then covered herself with it. 'How far did I get?'

'You swam for over a mile,' said the fisherman; 'the only problem was that the current was taking you north.' He nodded at the three others. 'Same thing happened to them.'

'Are they Aucterian?'

'They are.'

'And you rescued them?'

The fisherman scowled at her. 'Of course we did. Do you think we would let them drown?'

'I'm glad you rescued them,' said Leona; 'it's just... I'm glad to know that there are still good people on Zamata. The Gunstians are slaughtering Aucterians on the streets of Igatz.'

'We know,' said the fisherman. 'These three were lined up for execution, but they managed to get away.'

The other fisherman tossed her an orange. 'Eat.' He glanced at his colleague. 'I can't see any more swimmers out here – should we turn back, boss?'

The other man nodded, then he gestured to the crew positioned by the sails. 'Take us back to harbour, lads.'

The crew got to work, and the vessel turned into the wind. The sails were adjusted, and the craft sped off, its bow bucking up and down in the waves. Leona got up, and walked to where the three Aucterians were sitting.

'I'm sorry about what's happening,' she said, as she peeled the orange.

The Aucterians stared at her, but said nothing.

'Do you have anywhere to stay in Kaugatz?'

'No,' said the only woman among the three, her eyes narrow as she stared at Leona.

'I know people who can help,' Leona said. 'I can find you a safe place to stay. Are your families in Igatz?'

'We just watched our families be murdered,' said one of the Aucterian men. The woman sobbed, and he put his arm round her shoulder. 'Why should we trust you, Zamatan?'

Leona glanced at the vessel's captain. 'The Gunstians told me that Kaugatz isn't safe,' she said. 'What did they mean?'

The fisherman turned. 'They mean it's not safe for them, girl. They landed two thousand soldiers by the eastern ferry terminal yesterday afternoon, and they've been holed up there ever since. There aren't enough of them to occupy Kaugatz. They haven't even tried to attack the walls of Tsallon Anura.'

'Then the monastery is still in our hands?'

'That it is. Is that where you're going?'

'Yes.'

'We can't drop you off there,' the fisherman said; 'to do that would mean sailing out right in front of Handshore, and I'm not taking the risk. You'll have to walk from the central ferry terminal.'

Leona nodded. 'Thank you for pulling me out of the water.'

The fisherman smiled, then went back to work. The vessel berthed a few minutes later, and Leona followed the three Aucterians over the gangway and back on to firm ground. The sun had risen a little, and her dress was starting to dry in its warm rays. The only thing she was missing was a pair of shoes, she thought, as she glanced at the rough gravel lining the long quayside. She gave a last wave to the fishermen, and started to walk.

'My offer is still open,' she said to the Aucterians. 'I can take you somewhere you can get warm food and a room where you can sleep.'

'Tsallon Anura?' said the woman, her eyes dark. 'The headquarters of the rebellion?'

'Don't speak to us, rebel,' said one of the men. 'This is all your fault. Damn ungrateful Zamatans. You were living in mud huts and eating dirt before the Dominion got here. We gave you everything – schools, irrigation, proper houses – and this is how you treat us? You butcher Lord Meer and let the Gunstians land?'

'You oppressed us,' said Leona, her temper snapping. 'You had two sets of laws – one for the colonists, and one for us. You treated the Zamatans as ignorant peasants, while you all bathed in luxury; and you call us ungrateful? Perhaps if you hadn't been so arrogant, then we wouldn't have rebelled.'

One of the men raised his fist, but the other pulled his arm down. 'Leave it,' he hissed. 'We are surrounded by Zamatans. They'll lynch us if you hit her.'

Leona halted as the three Aucterians hurried away. She waited until they were out of sight, then she glanced in the direction of Tsallon Anura, and started to walk.

. . .

Her feet were in agony by the time she reached the gates of the fortified monastery, but the sun had dried out her dress. The rebel fighters at the entrance recognised her, and opened the doors to let her in.

'Where's the colonel?' one asked, but she was too tired to respond. It was hard to believe that she had been in Tsallon Anura the previous morning, when she and the colonel had visited Reyn to see how she had been recovering from her injuries. Her thoughts went to Lahnos. He had a right to know what had happened to his uncle, and she decided to tell him in person, rather than let him hear the news from another source.

She made her way through the monastery complex, limping as she walked, then ascended the stairs to Lahnos's apartment. She rapped her knuckles on the door, and waited.

'Who is it?' came a voice from the interior.

'Leona,' she said.

Reyn opened the door, the bandage still wrapped round her head. She glanced at Leona and her eyes widened.

'What happened to you?' she said.

Leona tried to smile. 'Do you have any spare shoes, Reyn?'

Reyn pulled her into the apartment by the arm, and sat her down on the bed. She crouched down, and looked at Leona's feet.

'Shit,' she muttered. 'Have you walked all the way from Igatz?'

'I swam, and then I walked.'

Reyn stared at her. 'You swam across the Cyasarta?'

'The colonel has been arrested,' she said. 'Where's Lahnos?'

'He's with his new... friends. I'll take you to him after I've cleaned your feet up. There are bits of gravel mixed in with all the blood.'

Reyn rushed away, then she returned with towels, soap and a basin full of water.

'This will hurt,' she said to Leona. 'Sorry. Stare at my horns to distract yourself.'

Leona clenched her fists as Reyn began wiping her feet clean.

'Why did they let you go?' she said, as she washed Leona's feet in the basin. 'I assume they arrested you, too? I can't imagine that you abandoned the colonel.'

'They... ouch! They released me at dawn.'

'Why?'

'The colonel told them that I was just a simple peasant, and that he had been... uh, that I had been... He told them I was a prostitute. They took pity on me and let me go, after I had promised to attend lessons on religious instruction.'

Reyn glanced up at her. 'The colonel told the Gunstians that you were a prostitute? And it worked? Shit.'

'They think the colonel is a corrupt womaniser.'

'He is a corrupt womaniser.'

'Yes, but he saved me; don't you see? They wanted to know why I had been with him all the time, but he didn't tell them about my Gift. He saved me.'

'He didn't save your reputation.'

'It's better they think me his mistress rather than the truth. Besides, I don't care what the Gunstians think of me. They're slaughtering Aucterians in the street. Children, Reyn. I had to get out of there.'

Reyn dried Leona's feet, then she applied some sticky ointment from a tub and wrapped her feet in bandages.

'How's your head?' Leona said.

Reyn shrugged. 'Getting better. My hair will take months to grow back, though. There. Do you think you can stand?'

Leona got to her feet and winced. 'Thank you,' she said.

Reyn pulled a pair of boots on, then found a spare pair of shoes for Leona.

'My feet are bigger than yours,' Reyn said, 'but with all those bandages, these shouldn't be too loose. Try them on.'

Leona knelt, and strapped the shoes to her feet. 'I'm ready.'

'I don't know how,' said Reyn. 'Your feet were in a terrible state. If that were me, I'd be unable to walk for days.'

Leona smiled. 'I've spent most of my life without shoes. I guess I'm used to it.'

Reyn narrowed her eyes. 'What is that supposed to mean? You spent most of your life with no shoes? Where did you grow up, Leona?'

'On Zamata.'

'Clearly, but where? Did your parents not buy you any shoes as a child?'

'I'd rather not talk about that. Could you take me to Lahnos, please?'

Reyn frowned, then she walked to the door and opened it. 'Come on.'

Leona noticed a crossbow sitting in the corner of the room by the bed, but didn't say anything about it. They left the apartment, and Reyn locked the door.

'Have the Gunstians attacked the monastery?' Leona said, as they walked down the stairs.

'No,' said Reyn. 'They have soldiers up on a roof a few streets away, watching us, but they haven't left the old Aucterian enclave.'

'So, there's been no trouble?'

Reyn smirked. 'I wouldn't say that. You know Lahnos – he attracts trouble.'

'What did he do?'

'Something that was brave, but also incredibly stupid that nearly got him killed. He said the voice in his head told him to do it. I expect he'll be using that as his excuse from now on – his excuse to do stupid things.' She glanced down. 'How are the shoes?'

'They're fine; thank you.'

Reyn led her to a long, low building close to the northern curtain wall of the monastery. Two rebel fighters nodded to them as they entered, and Leona heard the sound of deep voices locked in a debate. Reyn took her to a large hall, and opened the door. Inside, more than two dozen Bullan soldiers were sitting down with a dozen rebel officers, including the captain that the colonel had left in charge of Tsallon Anura.

'I've brought a visitor,' said Reyn.

The voices in the hall quietened, and everyone turned to look.

Lahnos got to his feet. 'Leona?'

He hurried towards her between the two rows of tables, as the Bullan and rebel Zamatans watched.

'She swam across the Cyasarta,' said Reyn.

'I'm glad you're alive,' said Lahnos, as he reached them, 'but where is my uncle?'

'Yes,' said a Bullan. 'Where is Colonel Laimos?'

Leona eyed the crowd. 'The colonel is being held in Handshore Naval Base by the Gunstians.'

'They're torturing him, aren't they?' said Lahnos. 'Torturing him with the Gift of Pain?'

'Yes. How did you know?'

Lahnos leaned in close. 'You know how I know,' he whispered. He pulled back. 'Tell us everything,' he said; 'and then we will work out how to rescue him.'

CHAPTER 25
AWAKENING

Kaugatz, Serpent Isle – 13th Nethinch 1588

'I disagree,' said the Bullan sergeant, his wide nostrils flaring; 'our priority is, and must be, the safety of the dragons in the palace. I know that you sympathise with the plight of Colonel Laimos, but the oaths we swore were to the Dominion, and the man you wish to rescue was responsible for the uprising. If Colonel Laimos had remained loyal, then the Gunstians would not be here.'

Several of the other Bullan muttered agreement, while, on the other side of the hall, the Zamatan rebels remained silent.

Leona got to her feet. 'No one is asking the Bullan to go to the aid of the colonel,' she said. 'We understand how you feel about the uprising, but the Gunstians threaten us all. If we remain here and do nothing, they will crush Igatz.'

'We are not suggesting inaction, ma'am,' said the Bullan sergeant. 'If the rebels wish to lend us boats, then my kinsfolk and I will cross the Cyasarta and go to the aid of our regiment.' He stood, and gazed at the other Bullan in the refectory. 'We should sail as soon as it gets dark, and attack the Gunstian positions from the rear. The Zamatans can do as they wish.'

'If you sail to the palace, you will all die,' said the rebel captain.

'Leona has told us enough about the strength of the Gunstians in Igatz. You would be throwing your lives away.'

'Then so be it!' cried the Bullan. 'We serve, we fight, and we die. I mean no disrespect to young Laimos – he saved our lives and we are grateful; but he did not save us so that we could sit here idly while the Gunstians attack our kinsfolk. For a day and a night, they have been pushing the Bullan regiments back to the Dragon Palace, while we have done nothing.' He shook his head, as if struggling to retain his composure. 'We thirty, the ones young Laimos rescued, are already living in shame – do none of you understand that? We were ordered to return to Igatz with the other Bullan units, but we were delayed, and we missed the last ferry transports. We should be with our kinsfolk; we have let them down.'

The hall fell into silence, and Lahnos glanced at the faces of the Zamatan rebels. From their expressions, it seemed clear that none were willing to accompany the Bullan on any voyage to the besieged palace; while the same was true of the Bullan – none wished to risk their lives to save his uncle.

He got to his feet. 'I need some fresh air,' he said. 'Perhaps a break will give us time to think about our next course of action.'

'Shall we say ten minutes?' said the rebel captain.

A few of the Bullan looked displeased at the suggestion, but none spoke up, and the crowd began to rise and disperse. Lahnos found Reyn and Leona, and walked with them out of the hall and into the warm sunshine.

'That didn't achieve much,' said Reyn. 'The Bullan you rescued seem determined to kill themselves as soon as possible.'

'I can see their point,' Lahnos said. 'Each one of them feels as though they have abandoned the other Bullan, because they couldn't cross the Cyasarta in time. The guilt is weighing upon them.'

'How do we turn that guilt into something positive?' said Leona.

'I have an idea,' said Lahnos, 'but I don't think anyone will agree to it.'

'Did the voice give you this idea?' said Reyn.

Lahnos frowned. 'No. I can occasionally come up with ideas on my own, you know. And I haven't heard from the voice since we got back from the ferry terminal a couple of nights ago. Who knows where she is or what she's doing? We can't rely on the Demon Witch to save us every time we get into trouble.'

'Let's hear your idea,' said Leona.

'All right,' he said. 'We are holding five hundred prisoners from the Dominion Navy in Tsallon Anura, and I think we have another five hundred being kept elsewhere in Kaugatz. That's a thousand extra men at our disposal. We should release them, arm them and send them over to Igatz, along with every single Zamatan fighter who is willing to go. Let the Bullan go to the palace, and the rest of us will take on the Gunstians from the other direction.'

'We would need to keep fighters here to watch the Gunstians who are already in Kaugatz,' said Leona, 'and I'm not sure the rebels would agree to the release of the sailors.'

'And how many Zamatans would volunteer to go?' said Reyn. 'Igatz will be a bloodbath, and you will be asking them to fight alongside Aucterians and Bullan.'

'It's the only way we're going to beat the Gunstians,' Lahnos said; 'and that's the truth.'

Leona and Reyn glanced at each other.

'You both know what I thought about this rebellion,' Lahnos went on. 'I have never liked the Dominion, but at least they aren't hunting down the part-Bullan and calling us demons. But if we beat the Gunstians, then maybe there's a chance that the Zamatans will sit down with the Bullan and the Aucterians when it's all over, and we can hold a civilised discussion about the future of this island.'

'I admire your optimism,' said Leona, 'but for years I watched the colonel try to persuade the Aucterians to treat the Zamatans with more respect, without any success. He argued over the laws, and property rights, and everything else imaginable. We have tried to reason with the Dominion, and they ignored our pleas at every turn. The Aucterians see us as inferior. Your uncle was one of the highest-ranking

Zamatans on the island, Lahnos, and they barely treated him with any respect.'

'We have to do something that proves we are not inferior,' said Lahnos. 'If the Zamatans help defeat the Gunstians, the Aucterians will have to listen to us. That's what I did with the Bullan I rescued – I showed them that we were capable of being their allies and equals against the Gunstians; we now have to make the Aucterians see it, too.' He lowered his gaze and rubbed his tired eyes. 'I think I need to be alone for a minute. I need to clear my head.'

'All right,' said Reyn. 'Don't be long.'

Lahnos strode off towards the western curtain wall, and ascended the worn steps to the parapet. On the roof of a building in the distance, he could see a squad of Gunstian soldiers spying on the monastery from the safety of their sealed-off enclave. He turned away from them, and gazed out over the Cyasarta.

Where was the damn voice when he needed it? He had never felt so confident and certain about himself as he had when he had been leading the raid, and his resolve had dwindled in the following days. There was only one possible explanation, but he was loath to embrace it. If the Demon Witch was able to persuade people to change their minds, then she must have done something to Lahnos's head – something which had made him braver than he really was. She had told him to be fearless, and it had been so. He had been scared of nothing that night, and had earned the Bullan's respect and admiration; but it was false; a trick. What if they realised that he wasn't as brave and clever as he had been when he had rescued them?

Do you hate me?

Lahnos gasped in relief. 'Demon Witch.'

You have realised what I did to you – do you hate me for it?

'I don't hate you. I'm just... disappointed in myself. I know that it wasn't me doing those things.'

It was you, Lahnos. I didn't create your courage out of nothing; I used what was already inside you.

'How do I find that courage on my own?'

It will come, Lahnos. You will do great things. I listened to your plan – it is a fine idea. Unity, Lahnos – that is the only way to defeat the Gunstians.

'Will you give me the courage to carry it out?'

No. I have interfered in your mind too much already. You will have to do this on your own, Lahnos; I will help, but I will not influence your emotions again.

'Will you watch over me?'

Of course I will, Lahnos. I will guide your steps, but I will not instil you with courage or false confidence. Fear is natural, and what I did to you was unnatural. True courage comes from facing your fears, not from a rash sense of fearlessness. You know this.

Lahnos lowered his gaze. 'Why me? Out of all the people you could have chosen, why did you pick me?'

Perhaps I will tell you one day, but not today. Inform the Bullan and the rebel officers of your plan. The Bullan will agree to it; that will be the easy part. It will be more difficult to persuade the rebels to release the imprisoned sailors, but I shall help with this aspect. Return to the hall with Reyn and Leona, and trust yourself.

The voice disappeared. Lahnos took a breath, then he descended the old steps of the curtain wall.

Two hours later, Leona and Reyn were staring in disbelief as the officers in charge of Tsallon Anura opened the prison and allowed the five hundred Dominion sailors to walk out into the sunshine. The thirty Bullan soldiers were waiting there to greet them, and to reassure them that their release was genuine and not a vile rebel trick. The sailors squinted in the light of the sun, as bemused rebel fighters removed their bonds and handed out supplies of fresh water and food.

Leona's mouth opened. 'How, Lahnos? How did you do that?'

Lahnos shrugged.

'How do you think?' muttered Reyn. 'He had help.'

'Help from whom? Oh. Our mysterious friend?'

'Exactly,' said Reyn. She shook her head. 'She's sending Lahnos off on another mad expedition. I'd like to have a little word with this Demon Witch, woman to woman, to ask her why she's decided to stick her claws into my Lahnos.'

'I asked her why,' he said. 'She gave me the usual answer.'

'Is she in love with you?' said Reyn.

Lahnos frowned. 'No.'

'If she was in love with him,' said Leona, 'then it would be unlikely that she would keep sending him into danger. Besides, she could be a hundred years old for all we know.'

'She sounds younger,' said Lahnos.

'How young?' said Reyn.

'I don't know – older than us, but younger than an old person.'

Reyn rolled her eyes.

The rebel captain approached.

'That's the five hundred sailors released,' he said, 'and we've managed to rustle up fifteen hundred Zamatan volunteers to make the crossing to Igatz.'

'What about the other five hundred sailors locked up elsewhere in Kaugatz?' said Lahnos.

'We only have enough boats to transport two thousand men,' the captain said. 'Will you be joining the assault on Handshore Naval Base in person?'

Tell them you are going to the palace with the Bullan.

'No,' he said. 'I'll be on the boat with the thirty Bullan going straight to the Dragon Palace.'

Leona and Reyn stared at him.

'What?' said Leona. 'I thought you were coming with me to free your uncle?'

'I want to go with the Bullan.'

'Why?' said Reyn.

Lahnos hesitated. 'Because... I think it's where I need to be.'

Reyn narrowed her eyes at him.

Lahnos nodded at the rebel officer. 'I'm going to the palace.'

'Very well,' said the captain. 'Your boat will be leaving first, young

Laimos, and the other vessels shall depart for Handshore as soon as it gets dark. Good luck.'

'Thank you, sir.'

The rebel officer turned and strode away.

As soon as he was out of earshot, Reyn leaned in closer to Lahnos. 'Was this the Demon Witch's idea? Did she tell you to go to the palace?'

Lahnos nodded.

'If that damned witch gets you killed, I will find her, Lahnos; you tell her that.'

'I will.'

'I think I can see the logic,' said Leona. 'We talked about proving ourselves to the Aucterians, but maybe we were wrong. Perhaps we need to prove ourselves to the dragons first. If you can save Lord Kheran, Lahnos, then Lord Rufus will have to listen to us; and then the Aucterians will change their minds about the Zamatans on their own.'

'We don't even know if Lord Rufus is alive,' said Reyn.

He is alive.

'He's alive,' said Lahnos. 'I will do what I can to get his son out of danger.'

Leona frowned. 'Bauchlie might not cooperate,' she said. 'Be wary of him, Lahnos. He has done some terrible things.'

'I can handle Bauchlie,' said Lahnos, then he turned to Reyn. 'I'll be back in a day or so.'

'You'd better be,' she said.

He glanced over and saw the Bullan gathering by the freed sailors in the courtyard. 'I'd better tell them that I'm coming with them to the palace.'

They kissed, and Reyn pulled him close.

'I'll be waiting here for you,' she said, 'but one of these days, I'll be coming with you, and fighting by your side.'

Lahnos smiled, then he let go of her hand and strode over to the Bullan soldiers. He found the sergeant, and walked up to him.

'I've decided to come with you to the Dragon Palace,' he said.

'Good,' said the Bullan sergeant. He turned his head. 'Did you hear that? Young Laimos is coming with us to rescue the dragons.'

The Bullan gathered round, and several of them slapped Lahnos on the back.

'Our lucky Laimos,' said one.

'Make your way to the jetty,' the sergeant said. 'We are leaving in twenty minutes.' He glanced at Lahnos. 'You had better fetch that war axe of yours, lucky Laimos; you're going to need it.'

The waters of the Cyasarta were calm and clear as the fishing boat sailed away from the monastery jetty. A handful of Zamatan rebels were watching from the ancient battlements of Tsallon Anura and among them Lahnos could see Reyn. She hated being left behind, but her head injury had yet to fully heal, and Lahnos felt uncomfortable about placing her in danger.

A Bullan soldier sat down next to Lahnos by the bow of the boat, and then nudged him with an elbow.

Lahnos turned to him.

'Your woman wants to fight, Laimos,' said the soldier.

Lahnos said nothing.

'I could see it in her eyes,' the Bullan went on. 'She wants to kill Gunstians as much as you do.'

'She'll be safe in the monastery,' Lahnos said.

'No doubt, but she does not desire to be safe; she desires to fight by your side.'

'The stitches in her head are still healing.'

The Bullan gave him a wry smile. 'If she had fully healed, then would you have allowed her to accompany us?'

Lahnos turned back to gaze at the waters of the Cyasarta.

'Why do the Zamatans not permit their womenfolk to fight, Laimos?'

'Fighting is... men's work.'

The Bullan laughed.

'You think it's funny?' said Lahnos. 'I have never seen a single female Bullan soldier; I assumed you thought the same as we did.'

'No, my young friend,' said the soldier; 'you would not assume such things if you had ever met the women of my homeland. The Dominion only recruits male Bullan for their armies – that was the deal we made with the dragons centuries ago – but our women are as disciplined and as warlike as any man.'

Lahnos narrowed his eyes. 'What is your name?'

The soldier said nothing.

'Why won't you tell me?' said Lahnos. 'My uncle knew the names of several Bullan.'

'Colonel Laimos is a traitor,' said the soldier, 'but he earned the respect of my kinsfolk a long time ago.'

'Have I not earned your respect?'

'Do not be insulted, young Laimos – we respect what you did for us. My concern is that you see us all as the same. Tell me truthfully – would you recognise me again if you saw me tomorrow? To your human eyes, do I not appear identical to my comrades?'

'I am not fully human,' said Lahnos. 'I would recognise you.'

The soldier glanced at the coast of Kaugatz on their left. 'We shall see.' He pointed at the ferry terminal. 'Look; the Gunstians are watching us from the harbour. They will be wondering what we are doing.'

Lahnos watched as several Bullan shouted out something in their own language at the Gunstian soldiers standing on the ferry terminal's damaged quayside.

'What are they saying?' he asked the soldier.

'Our language is our own, friend,' said the Bullan; 'we do not teach it to others.'

'The dragons must know it.'

'Why do you make so many false assumptions? Not even King Gahad the Mighty learned our tongue; and if he knew nothing, what makes you think any of his kin would have learned?'

Lahnos frowned. 'You hate us, don't you? Not just the Zamatans; I mean that you hate all humans.'

'Hate is not the appropriate word for what we feel towards the humans of this world. We swear oaths and we serve. That was the deal we made.'

The Bullan on board the fishing vessel turned as they passed the ferry terminal, and their gazes went to the opposite shore. Movement could be seen along the densely-packed coast of Igatz, and flames were licking the sides of a large barrack block close to the boundary of the Dragon Palace. A scream rose up amid the grey smoke, and the eyes of the Bullan soldiers tightened. On the inner side of the walls surrounding the ornate gardens, Bullan were pulling back towards the white marble buildings of the palace.

'Were it not for their Gifted,' said the soldier sitting next to Lahnos, 'we would have already defeated the Gunstians.'

Two of the retreating Bullan burst into flames as they were running from the walls, and they fell to the ground screaming.

'Do you see, young Laimos?' said the soldier. 'Bravery counts for nothing when set against the Gifts of Theodora.'

The Bullan adjusted the sails, and the fishing vessel turned to the south-east. The craft began to slow as it neared the gardens, its bow riding up and down on the gentle waves. No Gunstians had yet broken through the walls, but the Bullan were pulling back in large numbers towards the palace.

The Bullan sergeant walked up to the bow of the vessel and crouched next to Lahnos. 'We will be landing soon, lucky Laimos,' he said. 'Say nothing until I speak to an officer, and remain at the rear. You should be safe from my kinsfolk once I have explained what you did for us.'

Lahnos nodded.

'Furthermore,' the sergeant went on, 'you should know that we intend to volunteer to hold the walls of the garden, as a penance for the shame we bear for not fulfilling our orders to return to Igatz several days ago. We will likely be dead soon.' He bowed his head. 'Thank you for allowing us a chance to redeem our honour, friend of the Klediomira Haga.'

The sergeant stood before Lahnos could respond, and returned to the main mast, where he began to issue orders to the others.

'Friend of the what?' Lahnos whispered.

The soldier next to him smiled. 'You did not think that *Bullan* was our real name, did you?'

The craft bumped against the low stone wall guarding the shore of the gardens, and the soldier next to Lahnos slapped him on the back then joined his comrades as they climbed up onto dry land. The wall was being guarded by dozens of Bullan, and a few squads ran to meet them. Lahnos heard the sergeant speak to them as he got to his feet on the deck of the fishing vessel. The sergeant pointed in Lahnos's direction, and several Bullan stared at him. An officer nodded, then the thirty soldiers Lahnos had rescued from the Gunstians started hurrying towards the defensive walls – a small stream flowing against the main current of retreating Bullan. Lahnos pulled himself up onto the low wall, and dropped down into the gardens. The sound of the conflict rang in his ears, though he could see no fighting, and he felt his nerves jangle. The officer strode towards him, flanked by two soldiers.

'Young Laimos?' the officer said; 'nephew of the traitor colonel?'

'I am Lahnos Laimos,' he said.

'Your rebellion has doomed us all.'

'It wasn't my rebellion,' said Lahnos. 'I want to fight alongside the thirty soldiers I arrived with.'

The officer glanced at his horns, then shook his head. 'No.'

'Do you doubt my fighting abilities?'

'I have been told that you can fight, young Laimos,' said the officer. 'The thirty you saved were tried for desertion in their absence; their sacrifice this hour will clear their names of the shame they have brought to their families. You are now under our protection.' He nodded to the two soldiers next to him. 'Take him to the palace.'

Lahnos tried to move towards the walls, but the two Bullan gripped his arms and led him away in the opposite direction.

'Don't struggle, boy,' said one, as the soldiers dragged him along a gravel path.

A low whistle rose up, and a huge boulder smashed into the gardens, killing three Bullan as it ploughed into the ground. The retreating soldiers picked up their pace, flooding through the wide open doors of the marble palace. More boulders fell, smashing into trees, while one struck the façade of the palace in an explosion of noise, destroying a balcony and shattering a dozen tall panes of glass. Lahnos was bundled into the interior of the palace, where Bullan were assembling barricades by the entrances.

'I want to fight,' Lahnos cried, as he was forced along a marble-lined passageway, past rows of injured Bullan.

'You will get your chance soon enough, boy,' said one of his escorts. 'The Gunstians are on their way.'

Lahnos was shoved through an arched entrance and into a huge, domed hall, where dozens of unarmed humans in Dominion uniforms were huddling. Upon a circular platform in the centre of the hall lay a great dragon, its head resting on the cold, marble floor, and its eyes closed.

'Stay in here with the others,' yelled one of Lahnos's Bullan escorts, as his shoulders were released.

Lahnos fell to his knees, then turned to see his escorts hurry back out of the hall. Several Aucterians were staring at his horns, he realised, and he got back to his feet and raised his chin, challenging them to say something.

'That's right,' he said, as he eyed the high-ranking Dominion officers; 'I have horns.' He shook his head. 'Look at you all – cowering in here while the Bullan fight and die for you. Have you no pride?'

'How dare you?' said a naval officer.

'He is a rebel,' said another. 'An ungrateful piece of Zamatan trash.'

Ignore them, said the voice in his head. *Go to the dragon, Lahnos. Open one of his eyes, so that I can reach his mind.*

Lahnos turned to face the still form of the dragon. For a moment, he thought that Lord Rufus was dead, but then he saw the dragon's chest rising and falling. He started striding towards the central platform, and a few Dominion officers raced forward to block his path.

'Stay away from him,' cried one, raising his fists. 'The blessed Governor is dying – leave him in peace.'

Tell him to go to sleep.

Lahnos stared at the officer. 'Go to sleep.'

The officer's eyes rolled up into his head, and he collapsed to the marble floor as the other Aucterians gasped.

'He is Gifted!' one shouted. 'We are doomed.'

Lahnos reached the great head of Lord Rufus. He raised a hand, and lifted the dragon's eyelid.

The Gunstians have paralysed the dragon's mind, Lahnos. I shall awaken him, and then you shall order him to go to the defence of the palace.

'Will he listen to me?'

He will listen.

Lahnos smiled.

That's the good news, said the Demon Witch. *The bad is that my powers will be exhausted by what I am about to do to Lord Rufus's mind. I am not as strong as I once was, and I will need time to recover. I will be watching, but I will not be able to offer you any more assistance. Do you understand?*

'I do.'

Lord Rufus's body trembled, and Lahnos released his eyelid. The Aucterian officers cried out in alarm at the sight of the dragon convulsing on the floor, and four bundled into Lahnos, knocking him off his feet. Two pinned down his arms, while another tried to rip the war axe from his belt.

A great roar shook the hall. 'Release him!'

The Aucterians turned and stared as Lord Rufus raised his enormous head from the marble floor. The dragon's eyes were glowing like burning coals, and several officers fell to their knees, their heads bowed.

'The Governor has arisen!' cried one. 'It is a miracle.'

'Release the boy!' Rufus cried. 'He healed me from the Gifts of the Gunstians.'

Lahnos pulled his right arm free, and pushed an Aucterian off him. Rufus lowered his head, then shoved the others out of the way with a giant forelimb. Lahnos got back to his feet, and stared at the dragon standing a yard in front of him. Sparks and licks of flame were rolling over Rufus's jaws, and his eyes seemed to pierce Lahnos's soul.

'Thank you,' said Rufus. 'My mind was imprisoned in torment, but now it is free. I am in your debt, Bullan-boy.' He lifted his head a little. 'I hear the sounds of battle.'

'The Gunstians are besieging the palace, my lord,' cried one of the Dominion officers; 'they have pushed the Bullan regiments back.'

'And my son?'

'If you fight the Gunstians, Lord Rufus,' said Lahnos, 'I will free your son.'

A flicker of fear passed over the dragon's eyes.

'The Gifted brought you down last time,' Lahnos went on, 'but they believe you to be paralysed or dead. Fly low over the Cyasarta and attack them from behind. Burn them, and I will save your son.'

'My son is all that matters now,' said the dragon. 'He has King Gahad's blood flowing through his veins. If you save him, then I will gladly fight.'

A squad of Bullan soldiers burst into the hall, alerted by the noise. They stared at Lord Rufus, then bowed their heads.

'Open the northern gates of the palace,' the dragon said. 'It is time to make the Gunstians pay.'

More Bullan arrived, and they shoved the Aucterians out of their path.

Lord Rufus gazed down at Lahnos. 'Farewell. Fulfil your task, and I shall fulfil mine.' He glanced at the Dominion officers. 'Do whatever this boy asks of you. The life of Lord Kheran is in his hands.'

The dragon turned, and the Bullan formed up to flank him as he strode from the hall.

An Aucterian major stared at Lahnos. 'You bewitched the Governor,' he cried. 'Lord Rufus was dying, and you made him get up and fight.'

'I did what I had to do,' said Lahnos.

'Who are you?' said the officer, his eyes wide.

'I am Lahnos Laimos.'

'A part-Bullan?' said a captain.

'A Zamatan.'

The Aucterian officers glanced at each other.

'What do you want?' said one.

'I want to see Lord Kheran,' said Lahnos. 'Take me to the rebels.'

CHAPTER 26
BEWITCHED

Igatz, Serpent Isle – 13th Nethinch 1588

The dragon child whimpered as the sound of fighting grew closer. Shouts, screams and the roar of fires were reaching his sleeping quarters, and the rebels under Bauchlie's command were on alert, each grasping their weapons as if they expected Gunstian or Bullan soldiers to burst through the doors at any moment.

'The Gunstians are bombarding the gardens!' cried a fighter, running through from the balcony chamber. 'They're surrounding the palace!'

'Remain calm,' said Bauchlie, a hand resting on the hilt of his sword. He walked over to where Cisca was sitting next to Kheran, and gestured for two rebel fighters to approach. 'Remove her shackles. All of them.'

The fighters came closer. One held a hammer, while the other had a pair of long-handled pliers.

'No,' said Cisca. 'The shackles prove that I am a prisoner. I will not have anyone think otherwise.'

Bauchlie narrowed his eyes. 'How do you expect to run weighed down by a chain?'

'I do not expect to run,' she said. 'Lord Kheran cannot run. I expect to die by his side.'

Bauchlie glared at her, then he nodded to the two fighters. 'Remove most of the chain, but leave a yard attached to her shackle.'

The fighters ran to Cisca's side. One laid out the chain running from her ankle, then he gripped one of the iron links a yard from the shackle. The other brought the hammer down, and the link buckled under the force of the jarring impact. The two men forced it open with the pliers, and the rest of the chain fell loose.

'Happy now, Lieutenant?' said Bauchlie.

Cisca glanced at the yard-long length of chain attached to her ankle. 'Yes.'

Bauchlie shook his head at her, then he dropped a sword by her side, and strode away. Cisca picked up the sheathed weapon, then glanced at Kheran.

'He gave me a weapon,' she whispered to the child dragon. 'I will use it at the end.'

'Will you slay me with it, Cisca?' the dragon whispered back.

Cisca's eyes widened. 'Of course not! I will use it to defend us.'

Kheran glanced down at the floor. 'I would rather die at your hands,' he said. 'The Gunstians will torture me and make me suffer. You would make it quick. You would, wouldn't you, Cisca, my dear?'

'Don't say such things.'

'What else is there to say? I don't want to be tortured. Promise me that you won't let the Gunstians take me alive.'

Cisca stared at the sword in her hands.

'Promise me, Cisca.'

'I promise.'

She jumped as a pounding came from the door in the storage room. Several rebel fighters hoisted their crossbows and ran through the entrance, and Bauchlie re-appeared, his eyes grim as he waited to see who had arrived.

'It's the Bullan, sir,' cried a fighter; 'and... and a part-Bullan. They are requesting to speak to you under truce.'

'Let them in,' said Bauchlie.

A young man strode into the chamber, flanked by four Bullan soldiers. Cisca stared at the man. He was tall, with broad shoulders, but it was the horns on his head that drew her attention.

'You?' said Bauchlie, his dark eyes burning. 'Did your uncle send you?'

'My uncle was captured by the Gunstians two days ago,' said the young part-Bullan. His glance went over to the dragon child. 'I'm here to free Lord Kheran.'

Bauchlie laughed, but it sounded hollow. 'You have some guts, Lahnos, turning up here like this,' he said; 'but Lord Kheran goes free when I say he does.'

'I made a deal with his father,' said Lahnos. 'Lord Rufus will fight the Gunstians, but only if his son is spared.'

Bauchlie frowned. 'Rufus was brought down by the Gifted. How can he fight?'

'He has recovered,' said Lahnos.

The dragon child raised his head from the mound of blankets. 'My father is going to fight?'

Lahnos walked over to Kheran, and Cisca narrowed her eyes at the young man.

'Lord Rufus is prepared to do whatever it takes to protect you, Lord Kheran,' Lahnos said. 'Are you ready to leave the palace?'

'Wait,' said Bauchlie. 'You might have made a deal with Rufus; but I didn't.'

Lahnos eyed him. 'What was the purpose of taking this dragon as a hostage? You wanted to gather the Bullan here, and you achieved that aim. But things have changed. The Gunstians will kill us all if we stay. It is time to let the child go.'

Bauchlie stared at him, but said nothing.

'Should we take this part-Bullan into custody, sir?' said one of the rebel fighters.

'We entered these quarters under a flag of truce,' said one of the four Bullan who had escorted Lahnos. 'Do not shame yourselves by breaking your word.'

'No one is being taken into custody,' said Bauchlie, 'but I cannot honour a deal I did not make. Lord Kheran stays here.'

'If the dragon child remains in the palace,' said Lahnos, 'then Lord Rufus will not fight, and you will have doomed us all.'

Cisca got to her feet. 'Listen to the boy, Bauchlie. You have always said that you didn't intend to kill Lord Kheran, and I believe you. Now, prove it. You shall not harm your cause by showing mercy; and think of your men. If there is a chance to escape, we should take it.'

Bauchlie's eyes darkened, then he turned back to Lahnos. 'Do you have a plan?'

'We will lower the dragon off the balcony,' said Lahnos, 'and escape through the gardens. The Gunstians are attacking from the west, but if Lord Rufus is successful, then we should be able to slip past their lines to the south.'

'And then what?' said Bauchlie.

'Two thousand Zamatans and Aucterian sailors are crossing over from Kaugatz to Igatz. They will attack the Gunstians from the rear. We can defeat them, Bauchlie, but not if we stay here.'

Bauchlie shook his head. 'This is insane.'

'So was infiltrating the palace in the first place,' said Lahnos.

The walls shook as a low rumble sounded.

'The Gunstians are getting closer,' said one of the fighters.

'You have to make a decision, Bauchlie,' said Cisca. 'Stay and die, or run and fight.'

Bauchlie turned to one of his officers. 'Have the Gunstians made it as far as the gardens under the balcony?'

'Not yet, sir,' said the officer. 'We still have time.'

Bauchlie exhaled, then he raised his eyes to the crowd of rebel fighters in the hall.

'New orders,' he said. 'We are going to follow Lahnos's plan. Gather ropes, and we'll rig up a pulley to lower Lord Kheran to the ground. All fighters will shield and protect the dragon child. Get to work.'

The rebel fighters began to scatter. Some headed for the storage room, and began to carry long coils of rope through to the chamber that held the balcony, while others checked their armour and weapons. Cisca smiled. She strapped the sword to her waist, and threaded the yard-long length of chain over her belt.

Bauchlie nodded to the four Bullan who had escorted Lahnos. 'Return to your posts and report to the Aucterians that we will be taking Lord Kheran out this way. Hold the Gunstians back until we are free.'

The four Bullan soldiers glanced at each other.

'Young Laimos,' said a Bullan sergeant. 'We cannot leave the dragon in the custody of rebels.'

Lahnos nodded. 'Then come with us.'

The Bullan frowned, but remained where they were.

Lahnos gazed into the dragon's eyes.

'Trust me,' he said to Lord Kheran. 'Your father will do everything he can to keep the Gunstians back; and I will do everything I can to make sure you get out of this alive.'

'Thank you,' said the young dragon.

'I will go out on to the balcony,' Lahnos said, 'and help the rebels rig up the pulley.'

Cisca watched the young part-Bullan stride away, then she walked over to Bauchlie, who was keeping an eye on his men as they worked.

'You are doing the right thing,' she said.

Bauchlie eyed her. 'We shall see about that. I have no desire to sacrifice the lives of my men for a dragon. Do you think Lord Rufus will thank me for what I have done, even if we manage to get Lord Kheran to safety?'

The four Bullan approached, and stood between Bauchlie and the child dragon.

'You are a condemned traitor and a terrorist,' said one. 'Your present actions, even if successful, shall not spare you from the noose.'

Cisca stepped in front of Bauchlie. 'You shall not harm him, not while he is trying to protect Lord Kheran.'

'Get out of the way, Lieutenant.'

She folded her arms across her chest. 'No.'

One of the Bullan reached out to grab Cisca's arm, and the dragon child growled and raised a clawed forelimb.

'Do not touch her,' Kheran said.

'But, my lord,' said the Bullan; 'this officer is siding with an enemy of the Dominion.'

'I trust her more than I trust you,' said Kheran. 'Go – I command it.'

The four Bullan turned and hurried from the chamber. Several rebel fighters approached as soon as they had left, and approached Lord Kheran.

'Lahnos asks that you come to the balcony,' said one. 'The pulley is ready.'

Cisca glanced at the dragon child. 'Can you walk?'

'I can try,' Kheran said.

He lifted his forelimbs, and stepped down from the mound of blankets and cushions. Lines of pain creased his scaled features, but his eyes were undimmed, and Cisca stood back as he swayed. The rebels formed up around Kheran, Bauchlie and Cisca, and flanked them as they made their slow way from the large sleeping chamber. Lahnos was standing out on the balcony, where dozens of fighters had rigged up a large pulley. A harness fashioned from straps and ropes had been laid out on the floor next to the wide balcony, and the rebels directed Kheran to place his limbs into it. He did so, his movements unsteady and halting, then the fighters fastened the straps around his body. Cisca walked out on to the balcony for the first time since Bauchlie had infiltrated the palace, and stared down at the view. The strip of gardens between the palace and the Cyasarta was empty of the Bullan soldiers who had been besieging the rebels, and the daylight was fading as the sun set in the west.

Lahnos eyed her. 'Thank you for helping to persuade Bauchlie.'

She nodded.

'Who are you?' he said.

'My name is Lieutenant Cisca of the Dragon Corps,' she said. 'I am assigned to Lord Kheran as his assistant, and I have been imprisoned here with him for... for... I can't remember how many days.'

'If you are a prisoner,' said Lahnos, 'then why do you have a sword strapped to your waist?'

'Bauchlie gave it to me.'

Lahnos glanced over at the rebel leader, who was directing the fighters on the balcony. 'Why?'

'I don't know,' she said.

'Did he hurt you?'

'I… No. Are you… his friend?'

'No,' said Lahnos. 'I wanted no part of the rebellion, but whatever I do, I can't seem to escape it.'

A rebel fighter approached Bauchlie. 'Sir, the harness and pulleys are ready. Shall we begin lowering the dragon into the gardens?'

'Yes,' said the rebel commander. 'Let down more ropes, so that the fighters can also descend. I want twenty men at the bottom ready to help Lord Kheran down.'

The fighter saluted. 'Yes, sir.'

Lahnos turned back to Cisca. 'Go down with the first batch of fighters and wait for your dragon.'

Cisca wanted to ask the young part-Bullan more questions, but she ran to Kheran, kissed him, then went to the side of the balcony. Fighters were securing more ropes to the railings, and she climbed up and over the edge, then took hold of a rope and lowered herself down. She passed a set of tall windows on the ground floor, but the large rooms beyond were still and empty, and then her feet touched the gravel of a wide path. She let go of the rope and took a few steps back. The gardens showed evidence of the Bullan's siege, but none of their soldiers were in sight. She could hear the sounds of battle coming from the far side of the palace grounds, and saw the red glow of flames amid the smoke staining the darkening sky, but the waters behind her were calm and peaceful. The ocean lay in that direction, and then, after thousands of miles, her home in Naeth. She longed for a ship at that moment, a tall dragon carrier that could take her back to where she belonged.

Shouts from above drew her attention, and she looked up to see several dozen fighters begin to lower Lord Kheran out from the balcony.

They lifted him until he had cleared the railing, then guided him out away from the wall of the palace, the ropes straining. The dragon child swayed back and forth, and collided with the smooth marble of the palace, then the ropes were eased down, and Kheran jerked and juddered as he was lowered through the air.

'Stand clear!' cried a voice, and the dragon child landed onto the ground next to Cisca. Fighters gathered round Lord Kheran, unfastening the buckles and straps, and freeing him from the harness, while the last of the rebels clambered down the ropes from the balcony. Lahnos and Bauchlie were the last to descend and, as soon as their boots were on the ground, the two men stared at each other. They said nothing for a long still moment, then Bauchlie nodded at the younger man. Lahnos pulled a war axe from his belt and strode through the crowd of rebels.

'Follow me,' he said.

The rebel fighters glanced back at Bauchlie.

'Do as he says,' said the rebel commander. 'Lahnos Laimos shall lead us out of the gardens. Protect Lord Kheran with your lives.'

Lahnos set off towards the south, his boots crunching on the gravel of the path that ringed the palace. Kheran got to his feet and staggered onwards, while the rebel fighters crowded round him. Bauchlie fell in beside Cisca as they walked to the rear of the dragon child, his eyes troubled. They reached a corner and slowed as Lahnos gazed across the gardens. To their left was the small jetty where Cisca had first set foot upon the island, while to their right the main part of the gardens was in ruins, the ground churned up by huge boulders and littered with the bodies of fallen Bullan. Dozens of trees that had lined the paths were smashed, their trunks split by the Gunstian bombardment, but no more rocks were falling.

Bauchlie pointed towards the walls that encircled the gardens. 'They are coming.'

A few rebel fighters gasped as the first Gunstians appeared on the walls. Ladders had been placed all along the length of the wall and the slow trickle of Gunstians became a flood as dozens, then hundreds of them dropped down into the gardens.

'We're trapped!' cried a rebel fighter. 'There's no way out!'

Gunstian soldiers in the gardens opened the main gates, and hundreds more began to pour into the complex, forming up into thick shield walls and advancing towards the palace buildings. A few Bullan had remained hidden in the gardens, and they sprang up and attacked the advancing Gunstians. Soldier for soldier, the Bullan were the better, and they cut down several Gunstians, their swords and axes hacking through the enemy shields; then several robed figures strode forwards, raised their hands, and the Bullan out in the gardens began bursting into flames.

'The Gift of Immolation,' cried one of the rebels by Kheran. 'We're going to be slaughtered!'

'Silence,' said Bauchlie, and the rebel closed his mouth.

Cisca and Bauchlie pushed their way forward to stand by the side of the young part-Bullan.

'It was worth a try,' said Bauchlie, 'but your plan has failed, Lahnos. There is nowhere to run.'

'My plan hasn't failed; not yet. Wait,' said Lahnos.

'For what?' Cisca said.

A great shadow rose up from the north as the sun set. Before Cisca could see what was causing it, the sky was lit up by flames as an inferno bore down upon the Gunstians advancing through the gardens. Dozens were incinerated in an instant, their bodies disappearing within the almighty conflagration that tore through the ranks of Gunstians soldiers. The robed figures turned, but too late, and the flames ripped through them before they could unleash their Gifts upon the dragon.

'Father!' cried Kheran, his voice piercing the air.

Lord Rufus passed over the gardens, the flames unceasing from his jaws. Trees burst alight, their branches burning briefly like lanterns, while the death toll among the Gunstians grew. Ballista bolts tore through the sky, and the Gunstian catapults went back into action, sending rocks hurtling towards the dragon as he wheeled and banked.

More robed figures appeared by the wall enclosing the gardens. They raised their arms and Lord Rufus screamed in agony; but his flames did not stop, as though he was being driven on by an indefatigable will to destroy the enemy. He reared up, and three ballista bolts rammed into his chest and flank, while a rock tore a great hole in his right wing. He cried out again, a terrible cry that shook the ground, then he crashed into the high palace wall where the robed figures were standing, obliterating an entire stretch of the defences. A great cloud of dust and smoke arose, then the remaining Bullan emerged from the palace, and charged at the surviving Gunstians.

With their Gifted dead, the Gunstians broke. Hundreds began fleeing from the palace grounds, while others scattered through the gardens, trying to escape the onslaught of the Bullan. A large detachment of Gunstians ran south, attempting to get behind the palace, and slammed into the rebel fighters surrounding Kheran.

Bauchlie raised his sword. 'Fight!' he cried, then he led the rebels into the panicking Gunstians.

Cisca drew her sword as chaos descended. The sun had set, and no lamps had been lit in the palace or gardens, and the only light was coming from the burning corpses that were piled in heaps by the manicured lawns and neat paths. Cisca peered into the gloom, but could see no sign of Bauchlie or his rebel fighters. She glanced at Lahnos, who had remained close by, his war axe in his right hand. Three Gunstians emerged from the darkness next to Lord Kheran's flank, and Lahnos swung the axe, driving its blade into the side of the first Gunstian's head. One of the other Gunstians turned and ran, and Lahnos sprinted after him. The last Gunstian lunged wildly at the dragon child with a mace, and Cisca brought her sword down, slashing the blade across his back, his blood spattering the front of her clothes. The soldier fell, then tried to raise his weapon again, and Cisca rammed the point down into his chest, wielding her sword two-handed as she stabbed through his leather armour. His eyes looked up into hers for a moment, and she saw the terror in his gaze as she ended his life. She let go of the sword hilt, transfixed by what she had done, then the chaos seemed to move on, and she fell to her knees by Lord Kheran.

'Father!' the dragon child cried.

Cisca pulled her gaze from the man she had killed. Dead and wounded Gunstians and rebel fighters lay scattered around the dragon child, their blood spilling into the gravel by their torn and broken bodies.

'My father, Cisca,' sobbed Kheran.

'It's all right,' Cisca said, though she scarcely believed her own words. 'Everything's going to be all right.'

Lahnos appeared through the smoke and dust, his war axe bloodied, and his eyes gleaming. His gaze went to Cisca and the dead Gunstian lying next to her, then he turned to Kheran.

'The Bullan are pushing the Gunstians back,' he said. 'You are safe. Lord Rufus gave his life to protect us. He killed the Gifted. The Gunstians are fleeing back towards Handshore.'

Kheran wept. Cisca placed her hand onto his scaled neck, but her eyes remained on the young part-Bullan.

'You killed a Gunstian,' said Lahnos.

'I did,' she said.

Lahnos nodded, but said nothing. He turned, and they watched as several squads of Bullan soldiers approached. They fanned out until they were surrounding the dragon child, then an officer stepped forward. His eyes went over Lord Kheran, then he bowed his head.

'My lord,' he said; 'my soul sings with relief and joy to see you alive and free.' He turned to Lahnos. 'You kept your word, Laimos,' he said.

'I did.'

'Lord Rufus is dead.'

'Yes,' said Lahnos. 'Lord Kheran is now the highest-ranking Dominion representative on the island.'

'Was this your plan, young Laimos?' said the Bullan officer.

'My plan was to defeat the Gunstians,' Lahnos said. 'We succeeded.'

'Not yet,' said the officer. 'Thousands of Gunstians remain in Igatz.'

The officer glanced around. 'Where is Bauchlie? I have orders to arrest and execute him.'

'Bauchlie has gone,' said Lahnos. 'He and the surviving rebels from the palace are now out of your reach.'

'Bauchlie's gone?' said Cisca.

Lahnos and the Bullan officer turned to face her.

'I want to see my father,' said Kheran.

'Yes, my lord,' said the Bullan officer. He gestured to his men. 'Escort Lord Kheran and Lieutenant Cisca to the site of Lord Rufus's death, then bring them back to the palace. Igatz remains unsafe for the present time.' He hesitated for a moment. 'I also have orders, my lord, to arrest Lahnos Laimos as a rebel and a criminal, but I wished to ask for your advice before proceeding.'

The dragon child said nothing.

'He is too upset for such things, Major,' said Cisca. 'Can this wait?'

'Who gave the orders?' said Lahnos.

'The Aucterian officers in the palace,' said the Bullan major. 'Will you accompany us for now, young Laimos, until his lordship has time to reach a decision?'

'I will,' said Laimos.

'But he saved us,' said Cisca. 'How can we arrest him?'

'Several senior officers among the Aucterians have accused him of bewitching Lord Rufus and sending him to his death, Lieutenant,' said the Bullan major.

Kheran glanced up, his eyes burning.

'Nonsense,' said Cisca. 'How could a boy bewitch a dragon?'

'There were over a dozen witnesses,' the Bullan officer said; 'and they are all saying the same thing.' He gestured to his men. 'This way.'

The Bullan soldiers flanked Kheran, Lahnos and Cisca as they made their way through the smoking ruins of the gardens towards the high wall that separated the palace from the rest of Igatz. Some of the heaps of dead Gunstians were still smouldering, and many trees were ablaze.

'My father did this,' said Kheran. 'He killed all these Gunstians.'

'Yes, my lord,' said the major. 'If anyone saved us, it was him.'

Cisca said nothing as they traversed the gardens. Could it be possible? Had Lahnos somehow bewitched Lord Rufus? No, she decided – it was clearly a lie, fabricated by Aucterian officers who despised and mistrusted the part-Bullan. She glanced at the young man, but his face was giving nothing away. And where was Bauchlie? After all she had been through, it seemed wrong to be unable to see the rebel leader one more time, to tell him exactly what she thought of him. He had chained them, imprisoned them, and had been the cause of so much suffering, and for what? Her heart burned red with anger, and yet she felt relieved that Bauchlie hadn't been caught and executed. It was because she wanted to kill him, she told herself, even though she knew it was another lie.

They reached the destroyed section of wall, and Cisca saw the body of the fallen dragon, lying sprawled out amid the ruins and carnage. Multiple ballista bolts were embedded into his scales, and his neck had been broken. His wings were tattered and trails of blood were seeping from his open eyes. Monks from the nearby Temple of the Undying Serpent had gathered round the gigantic corpse, and were chanting prayers and lamentations amid the scattered Gunstian bodies; and Kheran pushed his way through them to stand by his father's side. The voices of the monks rose up at the sight of the rescued dragon child, and Cisca stood back, watching as Kheran was worshipped as a god.

Cisca walked over to Lahnos, who was gazing at the body of the dead dragon.

'Did you bewitch him?' she whispered.

Lahnos kept his eyes on Lord Rufus, but he said nothing.

'Where is Bauchlie?' she went on.

'I know how you feel about Bauchlie, Cisca. He's safe.'

Cisca's anger flared. 'What do you mean you know how I feel?'

'I saw the way you were looking at him.'

'Bauchlie is a vile criminal,' said Cisca. 'He deserves to hang.'

'What will you do now?' said Lahnos.

'Whatever happens next has nothing to do with me,' she said.

'You are wrong, Cisca,' Lahnos said. 'Lord Kheran is in charge now, and you are the only human he listens to, the only one he trusts. You have more power than you think; possibly more than you can imagine.'

The Bullan major stepped forward. 'Lord Kheran,' he said, 'we should return to the palace. Armed Gunstians are still in control of much of Igatz; it might not be safe to linger.'

The dragon child turned. 'My father saved us.'

'Yes, my lord.'

'He sacrificed himself to save us.'

'Yes, my lord.'

'If... if he was bewitched,' said the dragon child, 'then his sacrifice was a mockery. I cannot believe that. Cisca, tell me – do you think he was bewitched?'

Cisca swallowed. 'No, my lord.'

Kheran lowered his gaze. 'Then my mind is made up,' he said. 'My father was a hero. He was not bewitched. Let Lahnos go free. That is my order.'

The Bullan major saluted. 'Yes, my lord.' He turned to the young part-Bullan. 'You heard his lordship. Get out of here, young Laimos.'

Lahnos nodded, then he disappeared into the crowds of chanting monks. Kheran withdrew from the body of his father, as the Bullan set up a cordon to seal off the area.

'The palace, my lord?' said the major.

'Yes,' said Kheran.

The major signalled for his men to begin escorting Lord Kheran away from the collapsed section of wall.

The dragon child turned his face to Cisca, as they retraced their steps through the ruined gardens. 'And then we burn my father's body,' he whispered.

Cisca nodded.

'After that, my dear Cisca,' the dragon child went on, 'what should we do?'

Cisca said nothing for a moment. She hated the island, but her heart was torn between her desire to return to Naeth to see her family again, and her duty to the Dragon Corps and to the Dominion. She considered Lahnos's words to her – should she try to use her influence over Kheran to persuade him one way or another?

She placed her hand on to the side of the young dragon's head. 'I don't know, my lord. Only you can make that decision.'

'I know what I want, Cisca,' the dragon said.

She looked into his eyes. 'What, my lord?'

Lord Kheran gazed at a smouldering mound of dead Gunstians. 'I want to go home.'

CHAPTER 27
THE VESSEL

Cyasarta, Serpent Isle – 13th Nethinch 1588

The flotilla of vessels sailed down the Cyasarta in silence as the sun set in the west, the light framed by the twin mountains of Medamuna and Hodzulat, which were rising into the deep red sky like horns. Leona sat huddled on the deck next to a company of rebel fighters, the only woman on board any of the twenty vessels that were making the crossing from Kaugatz. She had no weapon or armour, but that suited her; unlike Reyn, she had no desire to fight Gunstians.

As the dark coastline of Igatz approached, she wondered if the colonel was already dead. She had been trying to harden her heart, in case her worst fears had materialised. Life would go on without him; she knew that, but she had no idea what she would do if she got to Igatz to discover his body hanging from a lamppost. He had been an integral part of her life for so long that it would feel like starting everything from scratch if the colonel was dead. Her life had been like that for as long as she could remember – broken routines and false restarts every few years. Of all the periods of her life, her time with the colonel had been by far the best, and not only when measured in material comforts. He loved her, though he had a strange way of showing it, and his love had been the rock upon which she had reconstructed her own identity.

'Five minutes,' whispered an officer, as he made his way down the deck; 'five minutes to landfall.'

The fighters around Leona began to get ready. Their vessel was due to reach the shore not far from where she had dived into the waters of the Cyasarta to escape Igatz only a day and a half before, while the other ships in the flotilla were to land all down the coast, from Handshore Naval Base to Atzoun Fortress. Leona peered into the gloom. Barely any streetlights had been lit, and Igatz sat in sullen darkness, its misery almost tangible. Her eyes flickered across the horizon, then she was nearly blinded by a massive burst of light coming from the Palace District. The fighters on the vessel gasped as the flames rose high into the evening sky.

'By all the serpents,' cried a fighter, unable to restrain his tongue. 'Dragon!'

Leona's eyes went back to the coastline, where the glow from the flames was illuminating several Gunstian soldiers on the low coastal wall.

'They've seen us!' she said. 'The soldiers have seen us!'

'Keep your heads down and prepare to loose!' cried the officer. 'This landing is about to get messy.'

A few crossbow bolts whistled past the bow of the vessel and splashed into the water as the Gunstians on the shore scurried into position. A rebel fighter took it upon himself to push Leona down against the deck, almost crushing her arm in the process, as the Zamatans loosed back at the soldiers. A fighter by the port railings was hit in the throat and fell into the inlet, and then the craft bumped against the low wall.

'Out! Out!' cried the officer, then he was struck in the face by another bolt.

Rebel fighters clambered up the wall and into the chaos as the Gunstians began to pull back. All along the coast, other vessels were disgorging their cargoes of rebels and Dominion sailors, and Leona remained where she was amid the screams and yells, her hands covering her head. The noise began to fade away, and she risked a quick glance up, to see that the vessel was empty, apart from its small crew, two dead rebels, and three with crossbow injuries who were rolling about the deck in agony.

'You all right, love?' said one of the crew.

Leona nodded.

'Then take a look at those wounds,' said the crewman. 'The boy by the bow has got a bolt in his chest – start with him.'

'No,' she said, as she got to her feet. 'Sorry, but I have a task to accomplish.'

The crewman narrowed his eyes at her. 'Task? What task? I thought you were a nurse or something.'

Leona shrugged, then walked to the front of the craft and climbed up the low wall, ignoring the cries of pain from the injured rebels and the dirty looks she was receiving from the crew. She got to the top of the wall and stepped down onto the road that ran by the shoreline. Several more dead and injured were littering the ground, and she walked past them, heading north towards the naval base. She pulled her cloak around her and took a narrow alleyway to her left, away from the sounds of fighting. The rest of the fighters, along with the freed Aucterian sailors, would be moving south to secure the gates of Atzoun Fortress, and then, once the besieged civilians inside had been released, they were due to push north towards Handshore and the Palace District. Beyond that, Leona had little idea of the rest of the plan, except that there was a vague idea to trap the Gunstians between the rebels and the Bullan.

She reached another junction, and gazed up at the sky. The flames from the palace were still burning brightly, but there was no sign of any dragon. It had to have been Lord Rufus, but how? As far as she knew, the acting Governor of the Serpent Isle had been incapacitated by the Gunstian Gifted. What could have made him fly again? More than that – what could have possibly persuaded him to risk his life again? She shook her head as she carried onwards. Lahnos and his Demon Witch – it had to be.

She crossed the road and stole down another alleyway, avoiding a panicked-looking Gunstian patrol who were scanning the skies.

Lahnos had too much power if he could persuade others to act against their will. The Demon Witch had proved useful when foiling the counter-attack staged by the Dominion Navy, but that was intelligence, not persuasion. Leona tried to make sense of it as she crept closer to the southern outskirts of Handshore. The Demon Witch had chosen Lahnos, that was clear, but it was also irrelevant. She could have chosen anyone. Regardless, she had chosen him, and now she was using him as the vessel to carry out her wishes. He had progressed from being a conduit for information to being a tool in her hands; but what did she want? She had killed King Gahad, so one might assume that she wanted the destruction of the Dragon Dominion, but now it appeared that she wished to see the Gunstians defeated. Why? Leona doubted that Lahnos knew; she doubted that anyone apart from the Demon Witch herself knew.

'Demon Witch,' she said in her mind, as she scaled the back wall of a townhouse garden; 'can you hear me?'

Silence.

Of course. What had she been expecting?

At some point, it might become essential to have Lahnos killed. It was a shame, as she liked him, but there was a possibility that the Demon Witch would drive him into becoming too dangerous. Would killing him anger the Demon Witch? Would she find someone else to use as her vessel? There were too many variables, and Leona disliked uncertainty. Her life begging on the streets had been much simpler. Back then, all she had worried about was day-to-day survival – obtaining enough food to live on, finding a place to shelter, avoiding the militia, and remaining out of the clutches of the crueller, unscrupulous elements among the inhabitants of Kaugatz. The colonel had changed all that. Now she had to contend with the future of the island.

She paused as she saw the high walls of the naval base on the far side of the street. The low rumble of conflict was closer than it should have been, and she waited in the shadows, listening. She heard raised

Gunstian voices, and slipped down another alleyway until she arrived by one of the many gates leading into Handshore. She crouched among the bushes by a line of orange trees, and watched. A crowd of Gunstian soldiers was attempting to get into the base, but they weren't fleeing from the combination of rebels and sailors in the south of Igatz – they were coming from the Palace District. Officers by the closed gates were urging them to return to their posts, but panic had taken hold of the lower ranks, who were babbling about dragons and the deaths of at least seven Gifted. There was no tingle in her mind, so Leona knew that they believed what they were saying. Gunstian civilians were also clamouring to be let into the base, fearful about revenge attacks by the Zamatans, Aucterians and Bullan.

Ignoring the officers, the massed crowd of Gunstians pushed at the gates, and they burst open. Leona got to her feet without hesitating, and joined the jostling crowd as it streamed through into Handshore.

'The boats!' cried a Gunstian. 'To the boats!'

'Get back!' shouted an officer. 'Back or we will loose!'

A double line of Gunstian soldiers had formed up fifty yards from the gates, with the front row down on one knee. They aimed their crossbows into the crowd and loosed. The air thrummed with bolts, and over a dozen were hit; then the crowd was upon the soldiers, pushing them aside and trampling over several in their panic. Leona slipped away in the confusion, darting between two buildings to her left.

She paused in the thick shadows of a doorway and took stock.

Discipline among the Gunstians had broken down – that was obvious. The dragon had killed seven Gifted, and incinerated hundreds of their soldiers, maybe thousands, and the rest were in a panic to flee – to get off the island before the rest were slaughtered. Sooner or later, the officers would accept the inevitable, and order the evacuation. What would that mean for the colonel, assuming he lived? Would they kill their prisoners before departing?

She felt the handle of the door by the entrance. Locked. She removed two tiny blades from a pocket, and picked the lock with practised ease, then slipped inside. She closed the door behind her and waited until her eyes had adjusted to the gloom, then she crept through the empty building until she found a set of stairs. She climbed, then walked out onto a balcony. The base was in chaos. From her elevated position, she could see at least three gates that were lying open, and hundreds of Gunstians were entering, heedless of any orders. On her right, she could hear the approach of the rebel force from the south, and Gunstians were starting to arrive from that direction, but most were still streaming in from the direction of the palace. Some gates were still closed and defended, but the officers there had lost control of their men in the general panic. Leona frowned, then she remembered that the soldiers had been rustled up from the coastal garrisons of the Gunstian Empire – they were the dregs of the army, a far cry from the well-disciplined and highly-trained forces that sailed with the main fleet. The Gunstians had gambled, and their second-rate soldiers had failed to rise to the challenge.

Over to her left, a small force that had remained loyal was guarding the quaysides that led to the Gunstian troop-carriers, as a mob surged towards them. Leona turned her gaze towards the building where she had been questioned by the robed Gunstians. A few lights were shining out from the windows on the upper storeys, and she imagined the leaders of the Gunstians gazing down in dismay at the collapse of their invasion. That was where she needed to go. That was where the colonel would be.

She froze as she felt the cold steel of a blade against her throat.

'You want to kill me, do you?'

Leona swallowed. 'No, Lahnos. I don't want to kill you.'

'Don't lie to me, Leona. The Demon Witch told me what you were thinking. She heard you call out to her, and she read your thoughts.'

Leona raised her hands and slowly turned. Lahnos was standing by the balcony door, the war axe held in his right hand.

'Please lower your weapon,' she said. 'I am unarmed.'

Lahnos narrowed his eyes, then pushed the axe into his belt. He gazed into her eyes, but said nothing.

'If the Demon Witch read my thoughts,' Leona said, 'then she would know that my fears and doubts about you have substance. Are we supposed to trust her without knowing what she wants?'

'She wants to defeat the Gunstians,' Lahnos said.

'But why?'

'Does it matter?'

'Yes, Lahnos – it matters a great deal. She killed King Gahad. If she could do that, then what isn't she capable of doing?'

'She wants the island to be free.'

Leona stared at him. There was no tingle, but all that meant was that Lahnos believed it to be true.

'Ask her why,' she said.

'She doesn't answer *why* questions.'

'And that doesn't bother you?'

'We're wasting time,' he said. 'I know where my uncle is.'

'Are you going to help me rescue him?'

'I have something else to do,' he said; 'but I can tell you where he is.'

Leona watched as he walked to the front of the balcony.

'Can the Demon Witch help me?' she said. 'Can she persuade the Gunstians to release the colonel?'

Lahnos kept his gaze on the chaos down in the base. 'The Demon Witch's powers don't affect Gunstians.'

'Why not?'

'Because she doesn't understand their language.' He pointed at a low structure by the quayside. 'My uncle is in that building.'

Leona frowned. 'Why is he being held in there?'

'The Gunstians are planning to ship him back to their Empire,' Lahnos said. 'Well, they were. After the events of this evening, I'm not sure any more.'

'How did the Demon Witch know what they were planning if she can't read their thoughts?'

Lahnos eyed her. 'Because she read my uncle's thoughts. I'm going to place the best route into your mind. Follow it, and you'll reach my uncle's cell.' He smiled. 'I'm sure you can pick the lock. Then go to the dockyard where the Dominion ships were refurbished – Quay Seventeen. A fishing boat will be waiting there to pick you up.'

'You came all this way to tell me this?'

He shrugged. 'You were going to look in the wrong place, Leona. You might not trust the Demon Witch, but I do. Now, hold steady.'

He gazed into her eyes, and a map of the base flashed into Leona's mind, along with a complicated route to get to the building where the colonel was being held, followed by another route to Quay Seventeen.

'Did you get all that?' Lahnos said.

Leona nodded. 'Thank the Demon Witch for me. But tell her this – if she wants me to trust her, she needs to start answering some questions.'

'I don't need to tell her,' he said; 'she is listening to you right now.'

'I might start brushing up on my Gunstian,' she said. 'I would quite like to keep my inner thoughts to myself if it's all the same to you.'

She eased past him and slipped into the darkness of the building.

'One last thing, Leona,' Lahnos said.

She turned. 'Yes?'

'The Dominion Fleet will be here at dawn.'

Leona raced away without another word, her mind spinning. She had been right about Lahnos and the power that the Demon Witch had concentrated within him. All the same, she decided to put her faith in him, and followed the route that had been impressed into her mind. It had been beautifully crafted, and she avoided every patrol and stayed clear of the chaotic mobs that were roaming the naval base. The building containing the colonel's cell had been ransacked, and was lying unguarded when she entered it. The door to his room was still locked, however, and it took all of her skill to get it open quietly. Inside, the colonel was lying on a filthy mattress of straw. She scanned his body, but he seemed uninjured.

She shook his shoulder, and he opened his eyes and smiled.

'I knew you would come for me,' he said. 'The bastards were going to take me to Gunst.'

'Is that right, sir?' she said. 'Can you walk?'

'Oh, I think I can manage that,' he said, swinging his legs off the mattress. 'That's the funny thing about the Gift of Pain – it hurts, oh does it hurt, but it doesn't do any lasting damage.' He groaned, and she helped him stand. 'Sorry about... you know.'

'Sir?'

'That whole prostitute business,' he said. 'I only told them that so they would leave you alone.'

'I know, sir. It's all right.'

They stumbled their way to the main entrance of the building and peered outside. The colonel frowned at the chaotic sounds of violence.

'I'll explain later, sir,' Leona said, keeping her arm around his waist to help support him. 'We should go – there's a boat waiting for us by Quay Seventeen.'

'It seems I trained you well, Leona,' he said, the old familiar smile back on his lips.

They set off to the left, and the colonel hesitated. 'Quay Seventeen is on our right.'

'Yes, sir, but we're going by a different route to avoid the trouble. Trust me.'

'You never have to ask me to trust you,' he said. 'I have always trusted you.'

There was no tingle, and she smiled.

The journey to Quay Seventeen took much longer than Leona liked. The area closest to the harbour was swarming with ill-disciplined mobs of Gunstian soldiers and civilians who were trying to gain access to the guarded troop-carriers; and while the colonel had no visible injuries, it was clear that he was in considerable pain. They were seen more than once as they made their tortuous way through the massive naval base, but no one paid them the slightest attention. Leona overheard snatches of soldiers' conversations as the night drew on – tales of Bullan forces advancing from the east, and rebel Zamatan forces mixed with Dominion sailors coming up from the south, all converging on Handshore. Fights were breaking out by the long quaysides and piers as the mutinous Gunstian forces began storming the troop-carriers, but Quay

Seventeen was located far from where the Gunstians had docked, and the area grew quieter as they neared their destination. They rounded the corner of a large warehouse and, in the moonlight, Leona saw a tiny fishing vessel tied up next to the vast repair yards. Sitting on a large iron cleat was a young man with horns.

The colonel smiled. 'My nephew? Leona, you didn't tell me that my nephew would be here.'

Leona helped the colonel limp the last few yards as Lahnos got to his feet and walked forwards.

'Your nephew organised this escape, sir,' she said, as Lahnos put an arm over the colonel's shoulder to support him, 'but I didn't know he would be here in person.'

'It's good to see you, Lahnos,' said the colonel.

'You, too, uncle,' he said. 'Let's get on board before the troop-carriers try to leave the harbour.'

Lahnos helped Friel step down into the small vessel, then he nodded to the crew, who began raising the sail. Leona jumped down onto the deck as the ropes were loosened, and the fishing boat moved away from the quay, the light breeze filling the sail. Lahnos sat the colonel down close to the bow, and Leona joined them.

'Keep as quiet as possible,' Lahnos said to the crew, 'and we'll slip out before the Gunstians even know we were here.'

The small craft ploughed through the calm waters of the harbour basin, keeping the tied-up troop-carriers on their right as they sailed. Several of the huge ships looked ready to depart, their decks crammed with soldiers and Gunstian civilians trying to flee the island. In a low voice, Lahnos told the colonel everything that had happened over the previous few days, while Leona sat and listened, her mind still conflicted about all that the Demon Witch had done for them. If the colonel also entertained such doubts, he kept them to himself, merely nodding and smiling as he learned of the rescue of the thirty Bullan, and the sacrifice that Lord Rufus had made to secure victory.

The first troop-carriers were casting off as the small fishing vessel passed between the massive breakwaters of the base. The crew of the little boat raised the sail fully as they reached the open waters of the Cyasarta, and they picked up speed, racing across the inlet under the light of the moon, as the dawn glow began to spread in the eastern sky.

'That's quite a story,' said the colonel. 'It seems Zamata owes a debt of gratitude to you and the Demon Witch, nephew.'

'He missed out a part,' said Leona.

'Yes? Which part?' said Friel.

'I was saving that for dawn,' said Lahnos, his horns glinting in the last light of the moon. 'Keep your eyes on the Cyasarta to the east.'

Leona and the colonel turned to their right, and gazed across the inlet where it narrowed between Igatz and Kaugatz. The predawn light was transforming night into day, illuminating the smoke still rising from the Palace District.

Friel gasped. 'Sails.'

Leona raised a hand to shield her eyes as the sun split the horizon. It was hard to see in the sudden glare, but the colonel was right – a thick forest of sails was visible in the distance. She turned back to look at the entrance to Handshore, and saw the Gunstians troop-carriers queuing up to leave the harbour, then she glanced back at the approaching Dominion fleet.

'By all the serpent gods,' muttered Friel.

'I thought you didn't believe in those, uncle,' said Lahnos.

The two troop-carriers berthed at the Kaugatz ferry terminal were attacked first. A long row of Dominion warships struck as they passed the tied-up vessels, sending flaming incendiary devices onto the decks of the Gunstian ships, and loosing a hailstorm of ballista bolts at the soldiers on the damaged quayside, then the main body of the fleet turned to the south-west, and began to encircle the vessels leaving Handshore.

The fishing craft neared the jetty at Tsallon Anura, but no one on board the small vessel reacted, their full attention on the two fleets. Without an armed escort, the over-loaded Gunstian troop-carriers were sitting targets, and the Dominion warships sank them one by one, their blazing hulls sending thick columns of smoke into the air before they disappeared beneath the gentle waves of the Cyasarta. Screams echoed across the inlet as the crowded troop-carriers succumbed, the passengers trapped in the holds. Many who had been on deck were attempting to swim to shore, and hundreds of Gunstians were dispatched by the armed sailors on board the Dominion fleet, their crossbows loosing in unceasing waves in the dawn light.

'The Cyasarta will be filled with bodies,' mumbled Friel, his eyes wide as he watched the slaughter unfold.

Leona heard a cheer as the last Gunstian troop-carrier was engulfed in flames, and she glanced over her shoulder to see the ancient monastery battlements crowded with rebel fighters.

'Listen to them, uncle,' said Lahnos; 'your rebels are cheering on the Dominion fleet.'

The colonel said nothing. He stood, winced in pain, then he stepped up onto the stone jetty as the crew secured the ropes. A tall, well-built man came hurrying down from the gate in the monastery walls.

'Bauchlie?' said Friel. 'I thought you were in the Dragon Palace.'

'I was,' said the colonel's son, as he strode along the jetty. 'That was before your horned nephew intervened.'

Lahnos smiled as he got to his feet. 'That was a strange way to say thank you for saving your life. Are you angry that I ruined your plan to become a glorious martyr for the cause?''

Bauchlie narrowed his eyes. 'Where is Kheran?'

'In the palace, where he belongs,' said Lahnos. 'Move aside, Bauchlie. I'm tired, and I want to see Reyn.'

Bauchlie stared at him, but did nothing as Lahnos stepped past him and walked along the jetty.

Leona got to her feet. 'He's right, you know,' she said. 'Were it not for Lahnos, you would be dead, Bauchlie.'

'How did he persuade Rufus to fight the Gifted?'

'I don't know,' said Leona; 'but whatever he did, it worked.'

Bauchlie's eyes darkened, then he turned to the colonel. 'What now?'

'There is much to be done, Bauchlie,' said Friel. 'Kaugatz still belongs to the Zamatans, as does every town and village in the outer island. The return of the Dominion fleet hasn't changed that. We shall also need to round up every Gunstian soldier in Kaugatz, but that can wait for now. Like Lahnos, I am tired.' He gazed out across the Cyasarta. Only three of the troop-carriers were still afloat, and each was ablaze, sending tall pillars of smoke rising into the dawn sky. 'Such carnage,' he said. 'We did this, son – you and I, and it is time to take responsibility for our actions.'

'Are you going to surrender?' said Bauchlie.

'Surrender, negotiate – we shall see,' said Friel. 'But first, I need to get some sleep. Leona, will you walk with me?'

She stepped up onto the jetty, and linked arms with the colonel.

'I will work while you rest, sir,' she said, as they walked towards the monastery gate.

Friel smiled. 'That's my girl.'

CHAPTER 28
THE AUDIENCE

K**augatz, Serpent Isle – 14th Nethinch 1588**

Lahnos opened his eyes and stretched. Next to him, Reyn was propped up on an elbow in bed, her hand on his bare chest.

'Did you sleep well?' she said.

He frowned. 'Yes. No nightmares. No dreams at all.'

'I'm glad,' she said.

He glanced at the shuttered balcony windows. 'What time is it?'

'Almost sunset.'

He lifted a hand and traced his finger along the scar on the side of her head. 'Does it still hurt?'

'A little,' she said. 'The ointment to keep it clean hurts more than the actual wound.'

'You are so beautiful,' he said. 'Let's just stay in bed for the rest of the night.'

'I'd like that, but your uncle might disagree. He wants you to meet him.'

'Why? I already told him everything that happened.'

'He's planning on travelling to the Dragon Palace, and he wants you to accompany him.'

'The Dragon Palace?'

'That's what he said. He was here an hour ago, with Leona. I refused to let them wake you, but I had to promise that I would pass on their message.'

Lahnos narrowed his eyes. He waited a moment to see if the Demon Witch would say anything, but he felt no sign of her presence in his mind.

'I'll go,' he said.

'I thought you would say that, Lahnos,' she said. 'Do you have to? You might be arrested and executed. Haven't you done enough?'

'Lord Kheran won't execute me,' he said.

'If you go, then I'm coming, too. You're not leaving me behind again.'

Lahnos opened his mouth to object, then he hesitated. 'All right.'

Reyn's eyes widened. 'You mean that?'

'Yes. Will you leave your horns uncovered?'

'Do I have to? To be honest, it's not the horns that I'm worried about; it's the side of my head with no hair. The scar is so ugly, and...'

'Nothing about you is ugly, Reyn. Hold your head high, and we'll stand side by side when we see Kheran and Cisca.'

'Cisca? Who's Cisca?'

'An Aucterian woman – Lord Kheran's personal aide. She was held hostage with the dragon child in the palace. I saw her kill a Gunstian soldier.'

Reyn frowned. 'A woman?'

'Yes.'

He swung his legs out of bed, stood, and walked to the balcony. He pulled the shutters open, inhaled a lungful of fresh air, then stared out at the Cyasarta. The Dominion fleet had anchored outside Handshore Naval Base, and bodies were bobbing up and down on the surface of the calm waters. Over by Igatz, the fires had been quelled, though patches of smoke still lingered over the Palace District. Reyn joined him, and he put his arm round her waist.

'So many dead Gunstians,' she said. 'What will become of us, Lahnos?'

'That all depends on Lord Kheran,' he said. 'And Cisca. She doesn't realise it, but she's probably the most important human on Zamata at the moment.'

'People are saying that you bewitched Lord Rufus. Is it true?'

'Yes. Well, no. I didn't do anything to him; it was the Demon Witch. She took away his fear and told him to fight – and so he did.'

'She scares me.'

'She scares Leona, too; but neither of you need to worry. Keep what happened to Lord Rufus a secret. It's better that everyone believes he willingly laid down his life to save the island from the Gunstians. No one needs to know the truth.'

They got dressed, left the apartment and went downstairs to the ground level of the monastery complex. Tsallon Anura was bathed in the light from the setting sun, its golden sandstone walls and buildings glimmering in the dusk. Rebel fighters nodded to Lahnos as he and Reyn walked towards the temple, and Lahnos nodded back to them, unsure how much they knew about his role in the previous day's events. An air of nervous expectation had fallen over Tsallon Anura following the celebrations at the destruction of the Gunstian invasion force, as everyone waited to see what the Dominion fleet would do now that a dragon child was in charge of the island. Lahnos and Reyn were about to enter the temple when Friel, Leona and Bauchlie emerged from the main entrance. Bauchlie's dark eyes narrowed at the sight of Lahnos, but the colonel smiled.

'There you are, nephew,' he said. 'My impatience was growing, and I was about to walk to your apartment to plead with your lady friend to wake you up. Did she pass on my message?'

'Of course I did,' said Reyn.

'I'll come with you to Igatz,' said Lahnos. 'Reyn is coming, too.'

'I have no objections to that,' said the colonel. 'Come; our boat has been ready to depart for over an hour.'

Lahnos pointed at Bauchlie. 'He shouldn't come. The Bullan will kill him on sight.'

'I have no intention of going to the Dragon Palace again,' said Bauchlie; 'but I will say this – do not sell this island to the Dominion. If the dragon child tries to assert his authority over Zamata, then I will resist. The struggle isn't over; it has just begun.'

'I know your feelings on the subject,' said Friel. 'Let us see what the new acting Governor has to say before we jump to any conclusions. And, needless to say, if we don't return alive, then carry on the cause in our name.'

Bauchlie nodded. 'I don't like this. They could arrest you as soon as you land. You are placing yourselves into the hands of the enemy.'

'Possibly,' said Friel, 'but this may be the only chance to negotiate that presents itself. What choice do we have? I led the rebellion, and only I can speak for the Zamatans.'

Bauchlie extended his hand, and Friel shook it.

'Remember my message,' said Bauchlie.

'I shall,' said Friel. 'Farewell.'

Bauchlie turned and walked back into the temple, then the others started to make their way down to the gates that led to the small stone jetty.

'Your scar is looking better, Reyn,' said Leona, as they walked.

'It's not,' said Reyn, 'but thank you for saying so. Will we really be arrested?'

'No,' said Lahnos.

'You seem awfully certain,' said Friel. 'I wish I shared your confidence.'

'The Demon Witch has probably told him what is going to happen,' said Leona. 'Isn't that right, Lahnos?'

'She hasn't spoken to me since I was in Handshore Naval Base,' said Lahnos, 'but I refuse to believe that the Bullan will do us any harm.'

'The Bullan will do whatever Lord Kheran orders them to do,' said Friel.

They passed through the ancient gate and walked down the jetty to the fishing vessel. The crew of rebel fighters saluted the colonel as they boarded, the ropes were untied, and the craft set off across the Cyasarta, its single sail fluttering in the strong breeze.

'Make for the northern ferry terminal on Igatz,' said Friel, and the crew got to work.

Lahnos sat by the portside railing, and Reyn joined him as the colonel and Leona stood by the bow.

Reyn took his hand. 'This will be my second time in Igatz,' she said. 'Do you remember the first?'

He smiled. 'Yes – our trip to the Temple of the Undying Serpent. That seems a long time ago.'

'It was less than a month ago, Lahnos. Is the temple still standing?'

'I don't think it was damaged in the fighting,' he said. 'The Gunstians would have burned it to the ground if they had won.'

'Perhaps it should be burned to the ground,' she said. 'The dragons aren't gods; why should they be worshipped?'

They passed the ferry terminal in Kaugatz that had been occupied by the Gunstians. The masts of the two sunken troop-carriers were poking up out of the water by the damaged quayside, and bodies were floating by the harbour walls.

'I wonder when the Gunstians will learn what happened here,' Reyn said.

'In a day or so,' said the colonel, striding over. 'Their agents will most likely be setting sail from the caves on the northern shores of Zamata, ready to carry their tale of woe to the Empire.'

'Will it be enough?' said Lahnos. 'Will this defeat teach the Gunstians to leave us in peace?'

'Who can say?' said Friel.

'Where did the Dominion fleet go?' said Reyn. 'I mean, after they left the island – where have they been all this time?'

'They probably visited the empty shores of northern Gunst,' said Friel. 'Very few people live in those regions, and there are several places where ships can take on water.'

'The Dominion fleet went to Gunst?' said Reyn, frowning. 'That seems an odd choice.'

'They would have been safe enough, what with the main Gunstian fleet still in the south chasing pirates. They could have plundered a few remote settlements before the local Gunstian patrols even knew they were there.'

Friel turned as the harbour of the ferry terminal on Igatz drew closer. Armed Bullan were guarding the quayside, and they watched as the small fishing vessel approached.

The colonel exhaled. 'Here goes,' he said. He raised his arm in greeting as the craft bumped against the quay. Bullan took the ropes of the vessel and secured them to the cleats, then several soldiers stepped down onto the deck as Lahnos and Reyn stood.

'The two Laimos traitors together?' said a Bullan officer. 'Have you come to surrender?'

'We have come to request an audience with acting Governor Lord Kheran,' said Friel. 'If his lordship orders our arrest, then we shall not resist.'

The officer nodded. 'Search them for weapons.'

The other Bullan stepped closer, and patted down the four rebels. A few glanced at the scar on Reyn's head, then at her horns and tail, but none commented.

'They're clear, sir,' said one.

'Very good. Escort them ashore, and put them into a carriage. We'll send a full company to guard them on the way to the palace – there are still plenty of Aucterians in Igatz who would like to lynch anyone bearing the name of Laimos.'

The colonel and Leona stepped up onto the quay, followed by Lahnos and Reyn.

'How many of the Klediomira Haga are still alive?' said Lahnos.

One of the Bullan soldiers eyed him. 'Where did you learn that, young Laimos?'

'One of your colleagues told me,' he said.

'Then I would ask you not to repeat it out loud for all to hear,' the soldier said. 'Our name is not to be shared by strangers.' He glanced away. 'Three and a half thousand of our kinsfolk still live, though barely two thousand are fit for active duty. The Gifted took a heavy toll on our numbers.'

'One and a half thousand Bullan were slain?' said Friel. 'You have my sincere condolences.'

'So says a rebel who was trying to kill us only a few short days ago.'

They left the quayside and approached a carriage flanked by twenty more Bullan soldiers. The side door was opened, and the four rebels climbed inside. The Bullan formed up into a flanking formation, and they set off, the wheels of the carriage trundling over the cobbled streets of Igatz, as the soldiers marched alongside. They passed through lines of ruined barricades, where Aucterian civilians were sweeping up the broken glass and debris. Armed sailors from the fleet were guarding some of the junctions, and they waved the carriage and its escort through. Lahnos gazed out of the window at the destruction. The closer they got to the palace, the worse the damage seemed, with burnt-out townhouses on either side of the road, and ripped up cobbles lying in heaps next to abandoned catapults. They skirted the main square of Igatz, where a huge pyre of Gunstian corpses was being built. It had yet to be lit, but sailors were pouring oil onto the mound, while a large crowd of Aucterians had gathered to watch.

The front gates leading into the palace gardens had been smashed and were lying on their sides, but a mass of Bullan was guarding the entrance. The carriage drew to a halt, and Lahnos listened to the sound of the Bullan conversing in their own language. His eyes went to the site of Lord Rufus's death as they waited. The body of the dragon had been removed, but the section of ruined wall where he had fallen was clear to see. Flowers had been placed on the ground, and Aucterian civilians were mourning, their tears and lamentations audible from where the carriage sat by the gates.

After a few minutes, the Bullan parted, and the carriage was allowed to enter the grounds of the palace. Reyn gasped at the sight. Most of the trees had been destroyed, and the ground was stained by the dead and churned up into mud. Another pyre was being constructed where a large patch of lawn had sat, and upon it lay the enormous body of Lord Rufus. Wood was being brought in by the cart-load, and sailors were stacking it around the body of the dragon.

'Lord Meer, and now Lord Rufus,' said Friel. 'So much for the undying serpents.'

Lahnos's temper surged. 'Don't say that. Lord Rufus sacrificed himself to defeat the Gunstians.'

A thin smile traced Friel's lips. 'Did he, indeed? That is the story we shall weave, of course, but all four of us in this carriage know the truth, my horned nephew. The only question is – will Lord Kheran believe it?'

'He needs to believe it,' said Lahnos. 'He needs to believe his father died a hero.'

The carriage slowed then halted by the main entrance to the palace. Its white façade was gleaming red in the last vestiges of light from the setting sun and the huge building seemed silent and empty. Bullan soldiers opened the carriage door and ordered its occupants out, and they climbed down to the gravel.

'Follow me,' said the officer, and they set off.

They entered the palace, and Lahnos glanced down at the rows of injured Bullan soldiers lining the walls. Dozens had wounds from blades or crossbow bolts, or had been burned in one of the many fires that had raged during the fighting. Lahnos stopped, and darted to the right before their Bullan escorts could stop him.

'Get back here, young Laimos!' one cried.

'In a moment,' he said. He hurried to the side of an injured Bullan soldier, and crouched down. The soldier was lying on the marble floor with grimy and stained bandages wrapped round his chest, and Lahnos shook his shoulder.

'You survived,' he said.

The Bullan soldier turned his head, and his eyes widened. 'Lucky Laimos? You recognised me?

Lahnos smiled. 'And you thought I wouldn't. How many others of the thirty made it out alive?'

The soldier stared at Lahnos for a long moment, then he lowered his gaze. 'I am the only one still breathing.'

Lahnos bowed his head. 'I'm sorry.'

'Don't be sorry, friend,' the soldier said. 'You allowed them to die with honour. Were it not for you, we would have been executed by the Gunstians in Kaugatz, and our shame would be indelible.' The soldier took his hand. 'We swear oaths and we serve. Sometimes, we die. That was the deal we made. I only wish I had died with them.'

'I'm glad you're alive,' said Lahnos.

The soldiers waiting for him coughed aloud.

Lahnos glanced at them. 'I'd better go.'

'My name is Efizel, horned boy,' the soldier said. 'Efizel of the Klediomira Haga.' He smiled. 'Tell no one.'

'You have my word, Efizel.'

Lahnos stood, and walked back to the others.

'Did I hear that right, young Laimos?' said one of the Bullan escorts. 'Did that soldier tell you his name?'

Lahnos said nothing. The Bullan guards glanced at each other, then they carried on, passing the last of the injured Bullan as they went deeper into the palace. They came to the great circular audience chamber. It was crowded with Aucterian officers and officials – some in Dragon Corps uniforms, while senior commanders from the Dominion Navy mingled with robed civilians. In the centre of the hall, surrounded by a thick line of armoured Bullan, sat Lord Kheran upon a great heap of cushions. The young dragon looked tired and ill, and the red weals and abrasions from the chains and shackles were like dark stains upon his silvery scales. Standing by his side was Lieutenant Cisca, and Lahnos watched as her eyes widened a little as she caught sight of the four rebels. He would probably be the only one she recognised, though she would no doubt have heard of his uncle.

The Bullan guards shoved their way through the Aucterians, and brought the four rebels to a position in front of Lord Kheran.

'My lord,' said the officer, 'you have visitors from Kaugatz.'

The crowd hushed into silence as the colonel stepped forward.

'My name is Colonel Friel Laimos,' he said, and the Aucterians began jeering and shouting, their faces contorted with rage.

'Silence!' cried the Bullan officer. 'Disrespect Lord Kheran again, and I will clear the hall!'

'Thank you, Captain,' said Friel. 'With me, Lord Kheran, is Leona of Kaugatz and Reyn of Chesson, along with...'

'I know who the other man is,' said the young dragon. 'Lahnos Laimos, yes?'

Lahnos nodded. 'Yes, my lord.'

The dragon child stared at Lahnos in silence for a long moment.

'My lord,' cried a Dominion naval officer, 'these... people are traitors. They should be arrested and hanged in the main square of Igatz. Every calamity that has befallen the Serpent Isle is because of their treacherous actions.'

'Not every calamity,' said Cisca. 'I notice that Bauchlie is not here.'

'I have spoken to Bauchlie, Lieutenant,' said Friel. 'He asked me to pass on his apologies. He is sorry for the pain he caused you and Lord Kheran. What he did was done in the name of freedom, but he is sorry nevertheless.'

Cisca stared at the colonel.

'Bauchlie is not forgiven,' said Lord Kheran. 'His crimes against the Dominion are not absolved simply because my father defeated the Gunstians. If he is caught, he will be hanged. Lahnos Laimos, on the other hand, I hereby pardon; while the two women standing before me I hold to be innocent of any crimes. That leaves you, Colonel Laimos. I am told that you were responsible for the death of Lord Meer. Is that correct?'

'Yes,' said Friel. 'Lord Meer intended to slaughter vast numbers of Zamatans, and it was my duty to stop him. I took no pleasure in his death, but I judged it better than the deaths of thousands of my people.'

'Traitor!' cried an Aucterian official. 'God-killer!'

Friel smiled. 'If Lord Meer was a god, then how could I have killed him?'

The crowd of Aucterians seethed, and the Bullan surrounding Lord Kheran tensed.

'We did not come here to discuss Bauchlie or Lord Meer,' Friel went on; 'instead, my lord, I wish to discuss the future of this island. Your forces are in control of Igatz, while the native Zamatans control the rest of the so-called Serpent Isle. What is to be done?'

Lord Kheran said nothing for a moment, then he glanced at Cisca.

'His lordship has reached a decision,' the young lieutenant said. She lowered her gaze as everyone in the hall waited for her words. She seemed reluctant to speak, as though her thoughts were conflicted.

'Yes?' said the colonel. 'What decision?'

'I have decided to evacuate the Serpent Isle,' said the young dragon.

The Aucterians in the hall gasped, and some cried out in protest.

'Silence!' the Bullan officer shouted again. 'This is your final warning. Let his lordship speak.'

'The Dominion shall withdraw the navy and the Bullan regiments from the island,' Lord Kheran went on. 'Any Aucterian civilian who wishes to leave can board one of the ships in the fleet, and then we shall sail for the East. We are going home. This island has brought me nothing but pain and misery, and I curse it with all my heart.' He turned to a naval commander. 'How soon can the fleet sail?'

'But my lord,' said the commander, 'we are under orders to remain here until your divine mother returns.'

'His lordship has made his decision,' said the Bullan officer, 'and he asked you a simple question. Answer him, or I shall have you arrested.'

The naval commander swallowed. 'The ships will be ready to sail two dawns from now, my lord; as soon as we have taken on enough food and water for the voyage.'

'Then it shall be so,' said the dragon child. He closed his eyes as if exhausted, and laid his head down onto his bed of cushions.

'Post instructions around Igatz,' said Lieutenant Cisca. 'Let every Aucterian know that they are welcome to accompany the fleet as it sails home.'

'Was this your doing, Lieutenant?' cried an officer, his face red with fury. 'Have you used your influence over his lordship to persuade him to abandon his post?'

Cisca said nothing.

Kheran raised his head again. 'Cisca counselled me to remain here,' he said, 'but I am the rightful authority upon this island, and I say that we evacuate. Does anyone here dare to disagree?'

The Aucterians stayed quiet, but their anger shone on their faces.

'Bullan,' said the dragon child, 'clear the hall. Let only the four Zamatans remain.'

The Bullan officer clicked his fingers, and the soldiers under his command began herding the Aucterians through the arched doorways, until only Lahnos, Friel, Leona, Reyn and the Bullan guards were left in the hall.

'It appears you have won, Colonel Laimos,' said the dragon child. 'The island is yours. I hope it sinks into the waves and is drowned by the ocean, along with every ungrateful Zamatan.'

The colonel bowed. 'Thank you, my noble lord.'

Lahnos narrowed his eyes. 'You are abandoning us?'

'Why would I stay where I am not wanted, Lahnos?' said the dragon. 'This rock, this tiny speck in the vast ocean is not worth the pain and suffering it has brought to my family. Did you not hear me curse it? You did something to my father – I am sure of it, though I would never repeat that fact in front of the Aucterians. Therefore, I curse you, too, Lahnos; I curse you all. Now go. You will see our ships leave two dawns from now, and perhaps then you will realise all that the Dominion has done for you.'

The Bullan officer gestured towards an arched entrance, and the four rebels turned and walked from the hall. Bullan soldiers escorted them through the crowds of furious Aucterians in the passageways, protecting them from harm, and they emerged out in the balmy evening air. The full moon was out, and was shining down on Igatz, making the buildings glow in its silver light.

'Back into the carriage,' said the officer. 'We shall escort you to your boat.'

'Thank you, Captain,' said Friel; 'and good luck.'

The Bullan officer shook his head. 'It is you who will be in need of luck, Colonel, not I. Enjoy your freedom. I estimate it will last as long as it takes for the Gunstians to discover that the Dominion has gone.'

They boarded the carriage. The door was closed, and they set off again, flanked by marching Bullan soldiers. Lahnos put his head in his hands. Where was the damned Demon Witch when he needed her? She would have fixed everything.

'I can't believe it,' said Friel. 'We are free. Truly free. As soon as the fleet leaves, we will be the masters of our own destiny for the first time in centuries.'

'Are you out of your mind?' Lahnos cried. 'We won't be free; we'll be defenceless.'

Friel smiled. 'Do you know where I will be when the fleet sails, nephew? Not here, and not in Kaugatz. No – I shall be several miles to the east of here, raising the great chains that bar the opening to the Cyasarta. We are not defenceless. This island is a fortress, and once the chains have been raised, and the Chain Castles manned, we shall be impregnable. Have faith, Lahnos – I have been planning for this my entire life.'

Reyn took Lahnos's hand and squeezed it.

'I thought the Demon Witch would have been there,' Lahnos said. 'How could she let this happen?'

Leona frowned. 'How do you know that she wasn't planning this outcome all along? Perhaps she was there, Lahnos – perhaps it was the Demon Witch who placed the idea to evacuate into Lord Kheran's mind.'

Lahnos stared at her. 'No.'

'I think Leona might be right,' said Friel; 'and with the Demon Witch on our side, how can we fail?'

At dawn two days later, Lahnos and Reyn were standing on the balcony of their apartment in Tsallon Anura, watching as the sun rose over the Cyasarta. The Dominion fleet had taken on thousands of Aucterian civilians, along with their possessions, and the ships were sailing in an orderly double line towards the ocean. In the centre of the fleet was the massive dragon carrier, and Lord Kheran was standing alone on its wide flight deck, the sunlight catching his silver scales and making them glitter.

'I'm glad they're going,' said Reyn. 'They didn't belong here. This is our island.'

He put his arm round her waist, not trusting himself to speak.

'Just think what we could do, Lahnos,' she said, 'with the Aucterians no longer lording it over us, and no Bullan patrolling the streets. We get to decide what happens next, not them, and not the Gunstians.' She glanced at him. 'Don't you want to be free?'

'I don't know what I want,' he said.

'We are Zamatan, and this is Zamata.'

'We are part-Bullan, too, Reyn, and I cannot forget that.'

'Why should we forget it, Lahnos? It is who we are.' She smiled at him. 'We are part-Bullan, we are Zamatan; and we are free.'

AUTHOR'S NOTES

JUNE 2023

Thanks for reading Serpent Dominion – I hope you enjoyed it.

In September 2022, my family and I moved to a new home, and I was without a place to write for a few months. A garden office was being planned for me, but would not be ready until Christmas, and I was faced with the prospect of doing no writing until then. As a solution, my wife suggested renting a tiny shepherd's hut in the midst of the Scottish Borders, and I ended up spending six weeks there, driving home every weekend, and heading back to the hut every Monday morning.

Serpent Dominion is the product of the work I did in the Shepherd's Hut – I planned the story, and wrote the entire draft there, while living the life of a hermit. There were no streetlights, and the nearest town was several miles away, and every night I would sit outside in complete darkness, gazing up at the stars as I pondered the fate of Lahnos and the Serpent Isle.

RECEIVE A FREE MAGELANDS DOMINION SHORT STORY

Building a relationship with my readers is very important to me.

Join my newsletter for information on new books and deals and you will also receive a Magelands Dominion short story that is currently EXCLUSIVE to my Readers' Group for FREE.

www.ChristopherMitchellBooks.com/dominion

ABOUT THE AUTHOR

Christopher Mitchell is the author of the Magelands epic fantasy series.

For more information:
www.christophermitchellbooks.com
info@christophermitchellbooks.com